THE VOWS OF RELIGIOUS LIFE IN A SECULAR SOCIETY

THE VOWS OF RELIGIOUS LIFE IN A SECULAR SOCIETY

Touching Wholeness

Judith A. Merkle SNDdeN

LONDON • NEW YORK • OXFORD • NEW DELHI • SYDNEY

T&T CLARK

Bloomsbury Publishing Plc, 50 Bedford Square, London, WC1B 3DP, UK
Bloomsbury Publishing Inc, 1385 Broadway, New York, NY 10018, USA
Bloomsbury Publishing Ireland, 29 Earlsfort Terrace, Dublin 2, D02 AY28, Ireland

BLOOMSBURY, T&T CLARK and the T&T Clark logo are trademarks of Bloomsbury Publishing Plc

First published in Great Britain 2025

Copyright © Judith A. Merkle SNDdeN, 2025

Judith A. Merkle SNDdeN has asserted her right under the Copyright, Designs and Patents Act, 1988, to be identified as Author of this work.

Cover design: Gita Kowlessur
Cover Image: Eugene Mymrin © GettyImages

All rights reserved. No part of this publication may be: i) reproduced or transmitted in any form, electronic or mechanical, including photocopying, recording or by means of any information storage or retrieval system without prior permission in writing from the publishers; or ii) used or reproduced in any way for the training, development or operation of artificial intelligence (AI) technologies, including generative AI technologies. The rights holders expressly reserve this publication from the text and data mining exception as per Article 4(3) of the Digital Single Market Directive (EU) 2019/790.

Bloomsbury Publishing Plc does not have any control over, or responsibility for, any third-party websites referred to or in this book. All internet addresses given in this book were correct at the time of going to press. The author and publisher regret any inconvenience caused if addresses have changed or sites have ceased to exist, but can accept no responsibility for any such changes.

A catalogue record for this book is available from the British Library.

Library of Congress Control Number: 2025935269

ISBN: HB: 978-0-5677-1588-3
PB: 978-0-5677-1587-6
ePDF: 978-0-5677-1590-6
eBook: 978-0-5677-1589-0

Typeset by Deanta Global Publishing Services, Chennai, India
Printed and bound in Great Britain

For product safety related questions contact productsafety@bloomsbury.com.

To find out more about our authors and books visit www.bloomsbury.com and sign up for our newsletters.

CONTENTS

Documents Cited and Abbreviations Used   vi

Introduction   1

Part I   Foundations

1   Touching Wholeness in an Age of Contingency   7

2   Touching Wholeness in a World of Interrelationships   29

3   Touching Wholeness in a Wounded World   49

4   Touching Wholeness: The Path of the Vows   69

Part II   The Vows of Religious Life in a Secular World

5   **Obedience: The Challenge of Autonomy and Plurality**   89

6   **Poverty: The Challenge of Agency and Finitude**   109

7   **Celibate Chastity: The Challenge of Singularity and the Other**   131

Bibliography   155
Index   163

DOCUMENTS CITED AND ABBREVIATIONS USED[1]

LG Lumen Gentium: Dogmatic Constitution on the Church (Vatican II, 1964)

GS Gaudium et Spes: Pastoral Constitution on the Church in the Modern World (Vatican II, 1965)

PC Perfectae Caritatis: The Adaptation and Renewal of Religious Life (Vatican II, 1965)

AA Apostolicam Actuousitatem: Decree on the Apostolate of the Laity (Vatican II, 1965)

JW Justice in the World (Synod of Bishops, 1971)

RH Redemptor Hominis: Christ the Redeemer (John Paul II, 1979)[2]

DM Dives in Misericordia: On the Mercy of God (John Paul II, 1980)

SRS Sollicitudo Rei Socialis: On Social Concern (John Paul II, 1987)[3]

RM Redemptoris Missio: On the Permanent Validity of the Church's Missionary Mandate (John Paul II, 1990)

CA Centesimus Annus: On the Hundredth Anniversary of Rerum Novarum (John Paul II, 1991)

CV Caritas in Veritate: Charity in Truth (Benedict XVI, 2006)[4]

EG Evangelii Gaudium: The Joy of the Gospel (Francis, 2013)[5]

LS Laudato Si: On Care for Our Common Home (Francis, 2015)[6]

FT Fratelli Tutti: On Fraternity and Social Friendship (Francis, 2020)[7]

DSC Document for the Continental Stage. General Secretariat of the Synod (27 October, 2022)[8]

---

[1] *The Documents of Vatican II*, ed. Walter M. Abbott, S.J. (New York: Herder and Herder, 1966).
[2] *The Encyclicals of John Paul II*, ed. and intro. J. Michael Miller (Huntington, IN: Our Sunday Vistor, 1996).
[3] All social encyclicals are cited from *Catholic Social Thought: The Documentary Heritage*, ed. David J. O'Brien and Thomas A. Shannon (Maryknoll, NY: Orbis, 2002).
[4] Benedict XVI, *Caritas in Veritate* (Vatican City: Liberia Editrice Vaticana, 2009).
[5] Francis, *Evangelii Gaudium* (Vatican City: Liberia Editrice Vaticana, 2013).
[6] Francis, *Laudato Si* (Vatican City: Liberia Editrice Vaticana, 2015).
[7] Francis, *Fratelli Tutti* (Vatican City: Liberia Editrice Vaticana, 2020).
[8] United States Conference of Catholic Bishops, https://www.usccb.org.

INTRODUCTION

Scientists say we are living in an age of unprecedented change, a time of "punctuated equilibrium." Massive shifts are occurring which can be compared to the geological plates that form the surface of the earth. Movement in these plates is driven by the molten core or "magma" of the earth. Today social, economic, and political plates ride on a fluid mixture of changed technology, ideology, and cultural redefinitions which provide a new state of the world.[1] One manifestation of this world is the secular society. Modern religious find themselves today challenged to take responsibility for the forces which shape this world and find their role in it.

This book is about the vows of religious life in secular society. In contrast to a time past, when religious life would be concerned mainly with personal conduct within a stable order of value, today is different. Now questions regarding the significance of religious life relate to issues of the life, death, and flourishing of humanity as such and the fate of the created order in which we live. For this reason, this book will use the image of "touching wholeness" to relate to the wider pursuit and purpose of religious life in church and society. *Gaudium et Spes*, the Vatican II document on the Church in the modern world, stated this issue many decades ago.

> Never has the human race enjoyed such an abundance of wealth, resources and economic power, and yet a huge proportion of the world's citizens are still tormented by hunger and poverty, while countless numbers suffer from total illiteracy . . . political, social, economic, racial and ideological disputes still continue bitterly, and with them the peril of a war which would reduce everything to ashes . . . Finally, man painstakingly searches for a better world, without working with equal zeal for the betterment of his own spirit. (*Gaudium et Spes*, no. 4)

This writing will assume that the significance of religious life is not just in the service it offers but in the quality of living to which it witnesses. The theme of "wholeness" serves to link religious life not only to the better world of the Kingdom of God but also to the holistic sense of humanity required for the peace and flourishing of global society.

This text will draw on the work of Charles Taylor and his analysis of secular society, not just as a development of past social arrangements, a former society minus religion, but as a distinct social pattern which flows from new sources. Taylor provides one approach to name the distinct and recognizable patterns of secular forces which envelop our lives.

---

[1] Lester C. Thurow, *The Future of Capitalism* (New York: William Morrow and Company, 1996), chapter 1.

We will call on theology, sociology, and psychology to weave together a picture of the inner and external dimensions of the wholeness which marks both the faith journey of religious and the aspirations shared with all humanity for a better world. In places there will be a commentary on the state of religious life, its' changed context, current challenges, and the task before it for the future. Periodically, we will offer questions for individuals and groups, and examine perspectives nationally and internationally, which express in their distinct contexts a desire to move religious life into the future.

This book is not a complete treatment of the vows of religious life, rather a commentary on their significance for a life of wholeness and service. While consecrated life in the church includes many forms of association, the reader will recognize that the focus of this writing is on religious institutes of women and men. However, people who follow other forms of consecrated life will find meaning in these reflections. The book will assume that religious life is on the same path of renewal as the whole church, represented by the Synod; therefore, its transition will be marked by the same values and attention to the guidance of the Holy Spirit. Each vow will be examined through a threefold lens: as a human challenge, a lived reality, and a spiritual capacity and way of life. Each will also be related to a human question confronted by all people in their life journey. It is hoped that this writing provides support for those living religious life currently and information for those considering it as a life choice. We welcome all those who have an interest in the well-being and future of religious life to consider these observations.

Part I addresses the foundations of this study. Chapter 1, "Touching Wholeness in an Age of Contingency," offers the thought of Charles Taylor on the meaning of the secular age and explain contingency as a chief characteristic of the current context of the world and religious life. It will introduce the image of wholeness as a heuristic device to indicate a life worth living, as well as a goal for a new civilization. It will locate religious life in an age marked by contingency, one that confronts people with situations which are new, which do not follow a pattern of life lived previously. Contingency characterizes the present age by underlining the increased options available for individual action which exist in the social imagination. Chapter 2, "Touching Wholeness in a World of Interrelationships," situates religious life within internal and external changes which impact its expression today. Theological shifts, a prevailing evolutionary view of the world, changed role of religion in the world, movement in understanding the relationships between the sacred and the secular, and evolution or *ecclesiogenesis* in the church affect the understanding of and living the vows. The chapter will unpack how a modern sense of interiority and the actual life history and current context of an individual shape the vowed life of a religious. It will point to how a primary relationship with Jesus Christ is the integrating factor in a life journey made through relationship with community, charism, church, and the earth. Chapter 3, "Touching Wholeness in a Wounded World," addresses the role of engagement with the wounds of the world and its relationship to the life of the vows. Dealing with a world where contradiction exists both in personal life and across the globe also forms a backdrop to religious life. This chapter examines the theological background which underscores the moral-spiritual endeavor involved in the mission of religious life. Topics include: an evolutionary understanding of Jesus

Christ, justification, salvation, community, and an introduction to the vows of poverty, obedience, and celibate chastity considering the human polarities shared by all that they address. Chapter 4, "Touching Wholeness: The Path of the Vows," concerns some of the more formal aspects of religious life as an adult lifestyle in the Church. Questions address: What is a counsel of the gospel? What is the origin of the vows? Why do people make vows? What does a vow express? This chapter is especially for those for whom the idea of a vow is unfamiliar.

Part II, "The Vows of Religious Life in the Secular World" addresses the three vows of obedience, poverty, and celibate chastity in subsequent chapters. Chapter 5, "Obedience: The Challenge of Autonomy and Plurality," begins inquiry into the vow of obedience with a discussion of autonomy in secular society. It treats some inner dynamics of the capacity to obey in developmental stages of life according to Erik Erikson. As a lived reality, obedience engages issues of authority and power in adult life, and requires collaboration and discernment throughout a lifetime. The chapter looks at the contours of transformational obedience and leadership that do more than maintain what already exists. As a way of life, a life of prayer is essential for a healthy living of obedience, with the paschal mystery as the grounding of its spiritual capacity. Chapter 6, "Poverty: The Challenge of Agency and Finitude," begins with linking the vow of poverty to human finitude, the human awareness of a void within that only God can fill. Sorting out the use of material things in an economy often of abundance and runaway consumerism challenges religious to live the vow of poverty at a deeper level than thriftiness. It calls them to embrace the finitude of being human and remaining whole. The human challenge of poverty begins at an early age when holding on and letting go mark the creation of a self. It continues into old age with its call for integrity as the human capacity for order and meaning amid diminishments. The chapter will draw out the challenge of the lived reality of the vow of poverty for congregations to advocate for the economically poor and to have a bottom line more than solvency. It calls for a transformational poverty that discerns how charism, faith, and mission call a congregation to rethink categories like impact, success, and what is essential for their life and mission. As a spiritual capacity and way of life, poverty leads to altruism and generativity. It is the willingness to let go of whatever in my life keeps me, or in the case of the congregation, keeps us, from fully responding to the call of God. Religious poverty in this sense assists in turning life inside out and directs it to God, neighbor, and bringing life to the world. Chapter 7, "Celibate Chastity: The Challenge of Singularity and the Other," approaches celibacy aware that questions of human sexuality in society and Church are undergoing evolution and debate. However, it asserts that religious have a role in these contemporary discussions, beyond being considered a "non-player" in the sexual realm. Celibacy shares with marriage a need for a more adequate language of human sexuality and its significance for wholeness. The chapter frames the choice of celibacy within the wider human dilemma of singularity and the Other—how am I, a unique individual, connected to those who are other than myself, also unique individuals? In celibacy as a human challenge, we address how sexual faculties serve the wider goal of becoming fully human, becoming increasingly capable of loving relations. The chapter addresses questions surrounding celibacy. What are the conditions which foster healthy psychosocial maturity? How does the human quest for identity, search for intimacy, and need to be generative function in a celibate lifestyle? Can a celibate live close to God and their deepest desires as well as develop broad and deep interpersonal relationships and communities of support? Is celibacy simply a giving up of love or does it also promise a self-fulfilling love? As a spiritual capacity and way of life, how can a transformational celibacy impact the world today? This book is a development of *Sensing the Spirit: Toward the Future of Religious Life* (2023) which relates its key ideas to the vows in secular culture.

I would like to thank my own religious community, Sisters of Notre Dame de Namur, for the many ways they have fed my life as a woman and a religious. I thank the many congregations who have helped me on my way and witnessed the living of the vows of religious life in changing times. The Institute of the Blessed Virgin Mary in Toronto, the Sisters of St. Joseph of Toronto, the Basilian Fathers, the Congregation of the Mission, the Sisters of Mercy of Buffalo, the Franciscan Sisters of Stella Niagara New York, the Franciscan Sisters of St. Joseph of Buffalo, the Sisters of Charity of Cincinnati, the Sisters of the Precious Blood of Dayton, Ohio, and the Jesuit teachers, directors, and colleagues who have companioned me. I am grateful to the library and religious studies faculty at Niagara University, New York, for their support in writing this book. I am indebted to Anna Turton at Bloomsbury/T&T Clark and her staff for their careful attention to this text. I am grateful to the Lay Centre in Rome, its directors and students, for their hospitality during my research period there. I am thankful to my colleagues at the Catholic Theological Society of America and to my family and friends for their care and friendship which have carried me over the years.

PART I
FOUNDATIONS

CHAPTER 1
TOUCHING WHOLENESS IN AN AGE OF CONTINGENCY

The meaning of religious life today is intertwined with the broader question of what it means to be human in an increasingly secular world. We live in a world marked by unfolding possibilities as well as limitations and threats. Religious engage in the same world as everyone else, yet with their own call. Far from the picture of religious life as a journey to perfection along a tried-and-true path of asceticism and self-renewal, today religious face the vulnerability and fragmentation shared by many across the world. Despite these challenges, congregations sense the open-ended possibility of new times and continue in hope.

Communities today seek answers to questions not posed to their immediate forebears. Those in past centuries faced the human, spiritual, and societal questions of the Industrial Revolution and major World Wars. Religious shaped their lives and ministry, especially those in active ministry, to engage the ministerial and ecclesial response to these challenges.[1] Where industrialization occurred, religious built institutions which educated and offered health care to receive those immigrants of the second Industrial Revolution. Then, gas as a new source of energy fueled industry and modernized households and medicine. Religious today live in societies where the issues of the third Industrial Revolution—the impact of computers, the internet, biotechnology, and nuclear energy—affect everyday life, yet remain unsolved. Some engage in situations where a fourth Industrial Revolution imposes new challenges for ministry and the interpretation of human existence. Here, they encounter a "Secular Age,"[2] where the ethical linkage of artificial intelligence and technology blurs the meaning of human life and tends to fuse the physical, digital, and biological dimensions of existence.

The encyclicals of Pope Francis address these changed conditions.[3] *Laudato Si* and *Fratelli Tutti* point to how the interconnections between human beings and nature go beyond scientific sectors to the restructuring of human relationships. The Pope relates consumerism to ecological decay and individualism to social inequalities. Despite

---

[1] Patricia Wittberg reminds us that when religious congregations operated mainly parallel institutions, even congregational governance was impacted by this organization of mission. See Patricia Wittberg, SC, *From Piety to Professionalism and Back: Transformation of Organized Religious Virtuosity* (Lanham, MD: Lexington Books, 2006).
[2] Charles Taylor, *A Secular Age* (Cambridge: The Belknap Press of Harvard University Press, 2007).
[3] See Thomas Massaro, SJ, *Pope Francis as a Moral Leader* (Mahwah, NJ: Paulist Press, 2023).

the world having advanced communications and transportation systems, the Covid epidemic surfaced areas of breakdown in global cooperation. Established democracies evidence a decline in civility and a carelessness around the disciplines of governance. Pope Francis cautions that a technocratic paradigm shapes the imagination and power structure of a world community where misuse of social media and rising autocratic governments threaten democracy. Daily, incivility and violence in populations challenge the meaning of human life.[4] Many observe that we live in a civilization which appears to be more nonreligious than most before it. At the same time, there are increasing signs of the instrumentalization of religion for the accomplishment of political rather than humanizing goals.

Religious join those across the world who desire a better quality of human life in these new conditions. They search to express the meaning of religious life for this new world. Pope Francis observes that humankind, as in every age, is looking for values that will serve as a foundation for individual and collective conduct and give people a reason for living (*FT* 6). Religious recognize that discerning their own place and contribution to meeting this challenge is key to their ministerial life as well as the transformation of religious congregations across the world. Michael Czerny SJ reminds religious that their lives witness to the truth of transcendence. Essential to their mission is to bring their openness to transcendence to contemporary societies' debates regarding the meaning of life.[5] The significance of faith, hope and love, grace in human agency, signatures of transcendence, lies at the heart of this witness today.[6] Religious life, in every culture in which it is embedded, witnesses to the path to human wholeness. It responds to the perennial human question, what is a life worth living? This means that the future of religious life in secular culture involves its service to the world, yet surpasses it. Amid great diversity, complexity, and fragmentation, people also search for the meaning of wholeness which undergirds life itself. "Wholeness," in this sense, points to deeper realities than evidenced in the technical resolution of our human dilemmas. It touches on a vision of a quality of life worth living and one which provides horizons for a new civilization.

The Search for Wholeness

Wholeness embraces many levels of meaning. As such, it is a "thick" concept. It suggests a vision of a whole person in these times, which addresses the integral dimensions of being human as well as the variations of a fully lived life. Wholeness can refer to the

---

[4]Michael Amaladoss, SJ, "Mission in Asia: Perspectives and Challenges," *SEDOS* 54, no. 7/8 (2022): 22–6 at 23.
[5]Michael Czerny, "*Fratelli Tutti's* Message for Contemporary Religious." *Concilium*, no. 2 (March, 2022): 126–30 at 127.
[6]John Paul II claims that failure to search for the truth of human dignity in its transcendent and permanent nature undermines the vision needed for essential political conditions in our world. See Judith A. Merkle, *From the Heart of the Church: The Catholic Social Tradition* (Collegeville, MN: The Liturgical Press, 2004), 231.

process of integration in every human life. Wholeness can also symbolize a harmony of communities, societies, nations, and care of the earth. Wholeness is experienced only partially on a life journey, yet remains an object of human striving and hope. Christians assume wholeness will only be known fully in the life to come, as wholeness is interpreted also as life with God now and in eternity. These images of wholeness do not exhaust its meaning, but its multidimensional nature offers a good lens for thinking about the vows in religious life.

Congregations and Wholeness

There are diverse opinions among religious as to what will restore or bring about a new wholeness in religious life. Some hold that wholeness will come from a retrieval of a discarded past in the church or congregations. Others envision wholeness as something totally other and unlived in the present time. Members claim religious need to abandon much of what we know of religious life in order to bring it in line with modern life patterns. There seem to be few benchmarks of what this new life might be. A third group sees wholeness as their past, the past they created through meeting the renewal challenges of Vatican II. These "successes" need simply to be adjusted and expressed in different ways, and the path to wholeness will be achieved. Others, perhaps unconsciously, assume wholeness will evolve from best management and business practices in congregations without too much attention to corporate spirituality or the core spirit of their congregations. As in the wider culture, spirituality can remain relatively privatized. While these are simplifications and characterizations of "talk" in religious life, they indicate a range of opinion as to a path forward.

This writing will not give an answer to the above positions; rather, it will ask how religious life creates a possibility for the wholeness that men and women seek today. It will do so by relating wholeness to the meaning of the vows in secular culture. The vows do not exhaust the meaning of religious life, anymore than marriage vows fully encompass all the dimensions of marriage. Wholeness, however, can take on a heuristic function in our inquiry through its capacity to shed insight into the meaning of the vows that other foci might not evidence. The vows, therefore, will not be examined as rules of life, a way of perfection, or a higher state of life.

Ultimately, wholeness in the Christian life is union with God and love of neighbor. In relationship to the vows, it has this same grounding. While wholeness touches many dimensions of the vows, theologically it remains a gift of grace. However, it is also an end goal, a process, and what is recognized partially in our lives and accomplishments. It is a project of our lives of which we play a part. It is a social reality we receive and seek to create through our ministry and community life. It is a concrete sign in a world, which is often not total and often fragmented. Wholeness is an invitation to faith, to which religious responds when they enter and continue in religious life. Jesus invites, "I come that you may have life, and have it to the full" (Jn 10:10). Jesus' invitation to human wholeness can be interpreted as God's response to the contingency and fragmentation of our times, a signature of God's offer of grace. St. Irenaeus in the second century said, "The glory of God is a human being fully alive." The desire for wholeness is an internal longing of our lives, which we share with all human beings. Then and now, it is an invitation and promise which grounds life in every age. Therefore, it is a fitting lens through which to view the vows.

Paradoxically, wholeness is more than what we create through our plans and activities. It is more than a life plan or program of perfection. Rather, we touch into wholeness and are moved by it. When we experience wholeness, we know in faith, it is God's promise and gift. Wholeness shows itself as something real, present in our encounter with life. In prayer, we grasp this. Even when we meet the wholeness of another, we know it is a reality that must be revealed and cannot be forced. An encounter with wholeness is sacred and not under our total control. It is something we encounter rather than create. In this sense, "Touching Wholeness" is referred to in this writing as a life encounter we do not fully control. Vows, in this sense, are doors to more than our actions to live them, yet their concreteness at times separates real fidelity from its counterfeits. The vows are not goals in themselves but lead us to a completion that wholeness symbolizes. Their practices witness to transcendence and its importance to the wholeness of life. We never fully grasp this wholeness; rather, we touch into it along the course of religious life, never fully possessing it, but knowing it is real. The vows faithfully lived over a lifecourse are one way in the Christian life which illumines the meaning of the scripture: "For now we see in a mirror dimly, but then face to face; now I know in part, but then I shall know fully, just as I have been fully known" (1 Cor. 13:12).

The Secular Age

Charles Taylor, a Canadian philosopher, in *The Secular Age* comments that we live at a time of galloping pluralism, creating a "nova effect" for believers and unbelievers alike. To live in secular times is to meet an ever-widening variety of moral and spiritual options—which offer to our imagination contours and structures for a life worth living—which previously were not imagined. As people search to carve out for themselves and their communities workable life contexts and articulations of meaning, this vast pluralism of options forms a central element of their lives. Both those who believe and those who do not are challenged to explain their patterns of activity and choices in a manner which makes sense in this world. In other words, people have quite different ideas of what wholeness means, the possibility of finding it, knowing it, or reaching it. This pluralism of vision forms the backdrop in which religious ask questions about their future. Often religious sense they live in a vastly different world than the past. Taylor explains broader parameters of this difference, which can assist in understanding new circumstances which impact the living of the vows in religious life.

What Is a Secular Age?

Charles Taylor argues that the secular is not a zone in society which people enter and leave. It is the common climate where our spiritual, ethical, and ordinary life pursuits take place. Believers and unbelievers share the same secular culture. Taylor claims that today this background is marked by the experience of the secular. In contrast to people who lived 500 years ago, we come to belief or assume a posture of unbelief using a new set of conditions marked by secularity.

There are three indicators of secularity in modern experience. One, we live in societies where public space is emptied of the mention of God. Two, we notice around us the falling off of religious belief. Most importantly, three, the conditions of coming to belief have drastically changed. In contrast to a former age when it was difficult not to believe in God, we come to belief in a climate where belief in God is one option among others to explain the integrity of life. While there have always been rival theories to the existence of God and the meaning of life, modern living brings us side by side with people who have quite different interpretations of the same life. For many, that which brings meaning to the life of a believer is absent in their lives.[7]

Secularization

In modern society people assume a separation of what is of public interest, such as the political activity of citizens, and the private sphere of personal interest. In this sphere religion is a private interest, and adherence to it is seen as one option among many. The decline and eventual elimination of religion is imagined as a type of subtraction theory in societal life, as modernization increases, religion decreases. The secular stands in contrast to the religious setting of earlier societies, where religion was everywhere, interwoven with everything else, and in no sense construed as a separate sphere of its own. The shift to secularity involves a move from a society in which belief in God is unchallenged and, in most cases, unproblematic to one in which it is considered as one option among others, and not the easiest option to follow. Both the believer and unbeliever live in this same context. Therefore, we have moved in our conditions of belief from a situation in which it was virtually impossible not to believe in God, to one in which faith, even for a strong believer, is one human possibility among others.

While Taylor's initial descriptions of the secular climate might not fit all people in all circumstances, he offers a language to identify trends in culture which were not predominant in times past. Previously, they may have represented some elements of a culture; however, today they are more pervasive. Together they form a type of social

---

[7]See Judith A. Merkle, *Discipleship, Secularity, and the Modern Self: Dancing to Silent Music* (London: T&T Clark, 2020), 29–30.

imaginary, or how people unconsciously view their lives and their future. It can be argued that they also impact the culture within religious life itself.

Exclusive Humanism

Exclusive humanism is a type of option not offered in the same way to people in past centuries. Since the eighteenth century it has become possible to imagine a fulfilled human life without religion, and a sense of completion or fullness within the boundaries of a type of human perfection which can be reached in the "natural" passage from birth to death. We need not go beyond the boundaries of this life to reach fulfillment, nor do we need the love of God which takes us beyond human perfection through its power. There is no higher good. Taylor argues that the various reasons given for moderns "falling away" from religion are inadequate. Rather, modern identity as secular arises from new inventions, newly constructed self-understandings and practices, and cannot be explained in terms of perennial features of human life.

Modern Identity and the Questioning of Religion

Modern identity, or what it means to be human in secular society, is marked by a sense of inwardness, freedom, individuality, and being embedded in nature.[8] Moderns are aware of a sense of "self" as their center. Their sense of freedom and individuality is focused on ordinary life and rejection of most hierarchies from earlier historical periods. Their sense of nature goes beyond an awareness of biological life; people also turn to nature as an inner moral source. Moderns are not without morals. Their aspirations for freedom, benevolence, and the affirmation of ordinary life evoke a demand for universal justice, equality, self-rule, and beneficence that carry a sense of moral obligation which is almost unprecedented in human history. They put a high priority on ending suffering in society. While most agree on these standards, there is less agreement on the moral sources which underpin them. The pluralism of thought, as well as contradictions within schools of thought, becomes a source of cross pressures in modern life where the standards demanded of the modern person lack a conceptual support which can bear their requirements. For instance, helping the poor is important, but what grounds its continued practice over the long term when other choices conflict with it? The modern person faces a dilemma as they encounter the tensions between the ideals of modern living on a principled level and its markers of success and fulfillment, which are often reduced to productivity, efficiency, and rationality amid a culture where consumerism

---

[8]Charles Taylor, *Sources of the Self: Making of Modern Identity* (Cambridge, MA: Harvard University Press, 1989), ix–x. See also Merkle, *Discipleship, Secularity and the Modern Self*, 35–7.

shapes almost every facet of life.[9] In contrast to a postwar culture which corresponded in broad outlines to values held by religion, secular society is silent if not unfamiliar with its meaning. This silence also impacts the "middle structure" of public culture, which experiences a fragmentation of once standard values. The affirmation of the goodness of life in the immanent frame only raises the question of whether anything more than a "well lived" life is needed for happiness.[10] When religion can seem like extra baggage on the journey, the notion of religious life can appear remote if not unthinkable.

Expressive Individualism

The questioning of religion and indirectly of religious life also stems from the experience of new resources within the human person, in nature, in the economy and political life that appear within reach of the human community. This experience gives rise to an age of authenticity and the social imaginary of expressive individualism. Expressive individualism holds that human beings are defined by their individual psychological core and that the purpose of life is allowing that core to find social expression in relationships and self-expression. Anything that challenges that core is deemed oppressive. While at first glance, this view might be shared by many religious, indirectly it offers a view of life which does not consider the role of mediation or the middle structures of human life: family, culture, customs, education, the state, media, and so on. It overlooks that some life goals require the ongoing shaping of one's life toward values which transcend self-expression. This way of thinking provides a lack of plausibility structures to interpret values of community life, the role of institutions in shaping a life, collaboration, shared economy, friendship in faith, sexual integrity, and lifelong commitment, which are integral to religious life and the vision it has of being human.

Theory of Progress

Most problematic is religion, and religious life do not concur with a key interpretative framework of modern life, a theory of progress. This explanation for the future of society claims that the modern economy, propelled by human greed, holds the secret to progress. The desires of one generation become the necessities of the next. For religious in the North American/European context, this paradigm of meaning poignantly contrasts with the experience of decline in membership, institutional power, and place in the church. Religion and religious life also threaten a vision of society based on progress alone

---

[9]Vincent Miller, *Consuming Religion: Christian Faith and Practice in a Consumer Culture* (New York: Continuum, 2005).
[10]The term "immanent frame" refers to a mentality that the reality of this life is earthly life from birth to death. This life is all there is. See Taylor, *A Secular Age*, 41–54.

through the promotion of self-restraint. It holds, as well, the conviction that material desires can be satiated; they are not limitless. Religion calls for the possibility of directing sensual pleasure and the erotic impulse toward other human goals of relationship and family. This challenges a rather unqualified trust in natural instinct. Religion holds it has the right to object to prevailing public sentiment and point to the significance of human dignity if it is being overlooked. In this sense, religious life reveals a different image of being human.

The Evolutionary Challenge

Charles Taylor provides a language which describes the secular climate which serves as a backdrop for the interpretation of religious life today. While there is great cultural diversity, a shift in cultural patterns and thinking impacts religious life in both the North and the South. Religious life, therefore, faces a challenge. Will it survive the evolutionary challenge of "survival of the fittest," or be shuffled to the dustbin of history? Might its counter-cultural lifestyle offer a key to the sustainability of the human community across the globe? While religious life is primarily a religious reality, it offers a powerful witness to common human questions of justice, liberty, solidarity, and equality for all. Its values stand opposed to vicious developments in the world such as fundamentalism, majoritarianism, autocratic populism and the like.[11] The vows at their core are religious responses, yet the vowed life expressed in a human community impacts secular frameworks. This added dimension makes the vowed life a creative and critical response to issues of our times and the search for a shared humanity, one which is sustainable both at the human and environmental levels. This capacity is not something "put onto" religious life but a retrieval of what religious life has always been in society. The structures of religious life have not only been a trajectory of grace for a human and spiritual journey but also a statement against the forces in each age which undermine the human spirit and destroy communal life.

Religious Life and the Renewal of Religion

The significance of religious vows for the journey to wholeness is interrelated with the kind of religion which can sustain the human community in secular times. Why is unbelief or no affiliation with an organized religion so easily embraced in society today? A closer examination of some accounts of unbelief suggests that often the religion a person

---

[11]Joseph Lobo, "Synodality in the Public Square: Synodality, Post Consciousness, Majoritarianism and Public Rationality," *Third Millenium: Indian Journal of Evangelization* XXV (2022): 1, 6–19.

has left behind has been an immature, Sunday-school faith which is easily dropped.[12] Religion, which is magical, superficial, illusionary, or based just on external practices to begin with, is a religion without the roots needed in a secular society.[13] It does not address a deep level of the human person, the true freedom of Spirit, and capacity for personal commitment. This type of response—an obedience in faith—is a mark of the mature Christian in a diverse and secular society.

We recognize that a childish version of religion can be projected onto religious life itself. It can be viewed as an escape from adult living and the common societal problems which confront humanity. Furthermore, churches can encourage a passive or mechanical approach to membership. Both "right and left" interpretations of Christianity can collapse membership into practices of nostalgia or reduce it to social activism of one type or another. Also, the church cannot ignore the weakening of faith brought on by its own scandals. But these misinterpretations of faithful practice do force a clarification of the continuing practice of religion, with the query, what kind of religion? If the kind of religion needed is one which addresses the real malaise of our times, then understanding the questions raised in the secular age is important not only for the future of the church but also for religious themselves as they seek to understand the vows they profess, and the expression of their vocations needed today.

It follows that the renewal of the church and of religious life are inseparable. The significance of the vowed life in secular culture has relevance to the degree it responds to the consequences for human dignity, authenticity, the search for wholeness, the credibility of the church, witness to the Kingdom of God, and service to neighbor addressing the whole church in our times.[14] Religious share with the church the same challenge of renewal as both seek to be faithful to the gospel in new circumstances.[15]

An Age of Contingency

An important image used to capture the atmosphere of secularity is the characteristic of contingency. An age marked by contingency confronts people with situations which are new, which do not follow a pattern of life lived previously when social conformity held sway. We call contingent that which is neither necessary nor impossible. Contingency characterizes the present age by underlining the increased options available for individual

---

[12]This does not minimize the reality that religion has been left behind because of scandal, sexism, racism, and failure to address impasses with modern culture.
[13]Hans Joas, *Do We Need Religion?* trans. Alex Skinner (London: Paradigm, 2008), 13. See also Merkle, *Discipleship, Secularity and the Modern Self*, 90–1.
[14]Rafael Luciani, *Synodality: A New Way of Proceeding in the Church*, trans. Joseph Owens, SJ (Mahwah, NJ: Paulist Press, 2022).
[15]For background on the call to the whole church to participate in the reform called for by the Synod, see John Burkhard, *The Sense of the Faith in History: Its Sources, Reception and Theology* (Collegeville, MN: The Liturgical Press, 2022).

action. Behaviors which were necessary through custom or lack of options in the past are optional today, as no "counterforce" or necessity requires them.[16] A culture characterized by expressive individualism feeds a climate of contingency through its belief that one must create his or her own life. Today, more than ever, people must find out what they wish to do, should do, and are able to do on a daily basis. They not only have to recognize what values are important but also must create a framework in which to live. This gives rise to a great plurality of approaches to life as well as an increased attention to the here and now. Less attention is paid to perennial questions such as the existence of the next life and its meaning.

It is challenging to search for wholeness and avoid the impact of societal fragmentation in this context. To some degree, religious since Vatican II have engaged with this new situation. Unreflective openness to society and the world, however, can lead to the impression that the vows in religious life have been defined for an age which no longer exists. While the core of their meaning still stands, their interpretation is diverse. Broader society interprets religion more easily with cultural values—such as the therapeutic, its role in overcoming personal suffering or assuring happiness and prosperity. It is difficult to offer a language of religious identity beyond these benchmarks. However, when religion is reduced to these values, it can easily be interpreted simply as humanly created, filling a social need, but with little meaning or appeal beyond these instrumental values. In this light, it is difficult to express the meaning of the vows as a Christian lifestyle as well as culturally relevant.

A common assumption in an age of contingency is it is possible to live in an elective universe where humans can fill all needs without a deity. Religion, therefore, is presented as either clearly distinguished from society or almost identical to it. The result is a presentation of religion and religious life can be so other-worldly that someone who loves this world and its gifts would not recognize it as a call to wholeness or flourishing in this life. Or a religious vocation is explained in a manner that only appears religious. Its ideals are set low enough that the necessity of an internal spiritual journey is absent, and the role of religion is instrumentalized. This offers a practice of religion which is simply a desire to spiritualize values which can be found elsewhere and more realistically achieved, such as through a career itself. Religious today must reinterpret the significance of the vows, avoiding the limitation of these approaches, yet realizing they represent core life issues for discipleship in modern society.

The experience of contingency can be an enemy or a promoter of the Christian life, as well as the vowed life. Renewal of religious life has certainly freed religious from a time where practices were made sacred which no longer were culturally appropriate, religiously significant, or humanly constructive. Yet modern secular culture can emphasize the importance of choice and autonomy in life, and the pressure such freedom imposes, that there is the temptation to live just in the now and be deaf to a call for continued

---

[16]Joas, *Do We Need Religion?*, 30.

conversion. People simply give up believing it is possible to do anything together and question whether the lifestyle itself has a future. Yet the climate of contingency in the wider culture can draw from religious new skills, which open life to undiscovered satisfactions and results.

A New Spiritual Path

The age of contingency sets the stage for a type of spirituality different from that of the past. It was common to use the image of a journey or pilgrimage, to measure forward progress by the shrinking distance to the goal, with the idea of a clear goal in sight. Professionally, we might draw up a five-year strategic plan to set achievable goals for an organization. Sociologist Zygmunt Bauman suggests today we need new images to capture how to proceed in the face of the obstacles which can block our progress. Two ways of being in the world, the postures of vagabonds and tourists, seem to "catch" the chances our times offer as well as the ambushes they hold. They offer a narrative of two patterns of behavior which slip into our lives of personal and congregational renewal.

A vagabond does not know how long he will stay where he is now. He will read the signs and make a stop over here and there. What he does know is the stopover will just be temporary. What keeps him on the move? He is propelled by a tension between disillusionment with the last place and hope that the next place he has not yet visited will be free of the faults which drove him from what he has already come to know.[17] In a free space, the vagabond structures the space he passes through, as well as dismantles it as he leaves. He is propelled forward by hope untested and pushed from behind by hope frustrated. Each structuring is episodic, temporary, and untethered to any broader vision.

The tourist shares with the vagabond the knowledge that she will not stay for long at the place where she has arrived. Nothing structures the importance of the places she visits. Nothing beyond "her time" links together the order or pattern of her journey. Her curiosity, sense of artistic interest, desire for novelty, amusement, or pleasure "structures" the tourist's world. She does not live with the uncertainties of the vagabond or his need to survive. According to Bauman, the tourist pays for her freedom. She can pass through a country, observe yet also disregard its native concerns or needs. Instead of taking in the meanings of the people, she can construct her own understandings of the situation, be independent of it, and quit a world which does not fit into her wishes.[18] She can sample exotic food, observe someone else's daily routines, and take pictures. Bauman finds the reusable videotape a good symbol for this lifestyle, as it can be used and erased for the next adventure. While not all travel fits into Bauman's image of a tourist, nor does the life

---

[17] Zygmunt Bauman, "Morality in an Age of Contingency," in *Detraditionalization: Critical Reflections on Authority and Identity* (Cambridge, MA: Blackwell Publishers, 1996), 53.
[18] Pope Francis counters this cultural mentality when he encourages ministers to have on them "the smell of the sheep."

of a vagabond equate with the need to move from place to place, his "ideal type" of both captures an element of modern life posed to some religious and their congregations, as they wrestle with the reality they have lost their "niche" in the church and society which previously gave them structure.[19]

Real Presence

Real presence conveys life beyond that of the vagabond or tourist. Real presence is based on the premise that human life involves traveling with other human beings; it involves community. Real presence is in tension with the image of the journey of modern life as one of expressive individualism. Stephen Carter illustrates that when people ride together on a train, they must behave differently than driving independently in their cars. Civility on the train are the sacrifices we make to travel together.[20] Physical proximity involves moral proximity, or responsibility. For the vagabond or the tourist, there is freedom from moral duty or responsibility. One can sink into a wave of people who simply "pass through" life. These travelers face few imposing expectations, one does what others do, one does not deal with the future, as an exit ramp for the vagabond and tourist is nearby. One's uniqueness as a person hides behind the anonymity of travel. There are no ties; one has a free pass to enjoy oneself. Bauman argues that vagabonds and tourists are not just inventions of modern times or the postmodern era. Every age has had its drifters. What is new is they are no longer marginal conditions. They slip into our imaginations and become ideals of daily life, standards of happiness, and a successful life in general. The "feel good" society suggests that instead of a holiday being a break in routine and the immersion of commitment to make routine livable, entertainment is now the norm and the routine, becoming the measure of what is worthwhile and a commodity to which one is entitled.[21]

The life of the vows, as a search for wholeness, is distinct from life based on the cultural assumptions of contingency. Religious life is a life centered in the gospel, expressed in a gestalt of life. It is embedded in a community and a culture and is circumscribed by the interrelationship of all three vows, which shape a distinct life course. As a religiously formed lifestyle, religious life is a public witness to the transcendent in secular society. It is relational, develops lifelong friendships in faith, engages in the ongoing search for authenticity, is based on a desire for union with God, and seeks to serve real needs over a lifetime. Religious life as a real presence counters an identification of religious life solely with "works," or dismissal of the spiritual journey of membership within the spiritual tradition of a congregation and the church. The focus on real presence

---

[19]See Judith A. Merkle, *Sensing the Spirit: Toward the Future of Religious Life* (London: T&T Clark, 2024), Chapter 2 "The Niche of Religious Life," 35–58. See also Wittberg, *From Piety to Professionalism and Back*, cited in note 1.
[20]Stephen Carter, *Civility: Manners, Morals and the Etiquette of Democracy* (New York: Harper and Row, 1999).
[21]Ibid., 56.

encourages investment in measured commitments and questions a drift by individuals and groups from project to project without making any connections to a group's charism or its contemporary interpretation.[22] A culture marked by a "nova effect," that of many options, can create a strong temptation for religious to leave the hard questions of the future to another generation or another geographical location to work out.[23] The call to a "real presence" is a challenge to move toward responding realistically in some manner to current needs in specific circumstances. The call to engage laypeople more in congregational structures and mission may be a consequence of assessment of needs and a desire to be something rather than nothing ministerially. These steps forward may also foster the synodal movement of engaging all members of the church in their baptismal call and unfold the role of religious in this process.

The Nova Effect and Seekers and Dwellers

The path of renewal has opened pathways or trajectories of a life journey for religious with more options than in previous generations. This is the "nova effect" of living in a secular age, which evokes different responses among members. Some are seekers on this journey and are alert and ready to see themselves in motion, prepared to face the unfamiliar and to live with lack of clarity.[24] Others, dwellers, find in religious life a place of stability, familiarity, and meaning which provides an orientation to the world. Amid the nova effect of secular society, the religious practice of dwellers provides a place of bearings in a world of varied experiences. Both responses to modern religious life are present in every religious congregation.

Both seekers and dwellers witness the work of grace and renewal called for by Vatican II.[25] Vatican II encouraged the church not only to *aggiormento*, to renewal, but also to *ressourcement*, to retrieve elements of the faith of church life to express them meaningfully in new times. To bring to light the meaning of the vows in secular times, religious need to call on both postures of renewal. If one shifts through attitudes toward the future of religious life across the world, one finds both seeker and dweller sentiments expressed

---

[22] Sociologist Patricia Wittberg comments on the vacuum left by the dissolution of institutionally based religious life, which gets resolved by borrowing identities from other groups in society. See Wittberg, *From Piety to Professionalism and Back?*, 265.

[23] It is not uncommon to hear religious in the North say their congregations are growing in countries in the Southern hemisphere, without asking what are the signs of the times in the church and society in the North calling them to do? The challenge facing religious is how to blend freedom of choice with a shift from a Catholic Action model of ministry and make a corporate response. See Wittberg, *From Piety to Professionalism and Back?*, 259–81.

[24] See Roger Haight, SJ, *Christian Spirituality for Seekers: Reflections on the Spiritual Exercises of Ignatius Loyola* (New York: Orbis Books, 2012).

[25] Philip Rossi, SJ, "Seekers, Dwellers, and the Plural Contingencies of Grace: Hospitality, Otherness and the Enactment of Human Wholeness," in *Seekers and Dwellers, Plurality and Wholeness in a Time of Secularity*, ed. Philip J. Rossi (Washington, DC: Council for Research in Values and Philosophy, 2016), 285–300.

in diverse conditions and contexts.[26] Also, seekers and dwellers need each other. Both are called to risk the hard conversations about their concerns. The challenge is to find a common ground in which each contributes to and shapes the substance of the human, moral, and spiritual elements of religious life as it moves into the future. Most adults, over a lifespan, are both seekers and dwellers. Amid the nova effect of modern culture, God's presence is often recognized in life passages of arrival and departure. Where a seeker might see a plurality of attractive life-shaping possibilities, a dweller could find instead a disorderly field of distractions drawing attention away from a settled center that offers true, reliable, and lasting life-orientation.[27] It is only through compassionate listening to the other in community and trust in the God who loves both in their moment of faith that a religious congregation can build a common future.

The Search for Wholeness

The search for wholeness amid the fragmentation of public meaning impacts the lives of all adults, including religious. While secular culture reflects the various ways of living of the nova effect, public meaning does share some similarities. Common outlooks such as "this life is all there is" and "life is to be lived solely in the here and now"—life in an immanent frame—are widely held in modern societies. Combined, they support a plurality of lifestyles and expressions of the meaning of life. These represent not just superficial differences but rather conflicting and alternative core life visions. Even practical solutions to everyday problems are questioned by an alternative of what might be, or has been, other and otherwise. Even shared events can be registered as unexpected in our collective experience.[28] Events like the Covid epidemic, devastating hurricanes, and crushing earthquakes are experienced as interruptions rather than occurrences. These seem different than war, the threat of nuclear weapons, and the reoccurring erosion of public trust experienced in the past. While the latter are remembered as difficult, the former seem unexpected. They carry a new sense of fissures in what was once "common sense" and the ordinary.

---

[26]"Seekers" and "dwellers" might best be understood as types of responses that represent stances toward faith, the church, and/or the future of religious life within congregations, acknowledging that there are a range of combinations in relationships to both. Pope Francis' image of the church as a polyhedron captures this pluralism in both church and congregations. The synodal process recognizes these are not exhaustive categories. For instance, people estranged from the church, feel excluded, indifferent to religion, unconcerned are "dwellers" but in a nonreligious posture. It is hard for them to even imagine a world of meaningful religious identity. While these postures may not be as visible in religious congregations, underlying sentiments of alienation do exist in various forms with different expressions across the globe.

[27]Rossi, "Seekers and Dwellers: Plurality and Wholeness in a Time of Secularity," 286. The "nova effect" with its plural options overshadows the meaning system once meted out in renewal. It adds an "encompassing ambient" dynamic of expanding and irreducible plurality both for religious congregations and those who interact with them who live in these times of secularity.

[28]Lieven Boeve, *God Interrupts History: Theology in a Time of Upheaval* (London: Bloomsbury, 2007).

Public shootings are met not only with outrage but with incomprehension—as their motivation transcends common patterns of understanding. While life options seem expansive, on a lived level they evoke a new sense of finitude. No person's life is long enough, nor their bank account full enough, to completely ward off the evil and suffering that threaten. No one's sense of control is pervasive enough to protect themselves and their loved ones from the unexpected. A culture of metaphysical naturalism, the belief that reality is only a matter of natural forces, removes an aura of protection in the public imagination. Believers and unbelievers share a common dilemma which surfaces in nagging questions. How does one find a wholeness worthy of one's life journey which has sufficient reliability before the undeniable fragility and limits of life? How does one live in this abiding condition of humanity and the created cosmos it inhabits?[29] How does one respond to the nihilism of those who deny there is an answer? Even the image of the lone cowboy, the image of self-sufficiency held at the turn of the millennium, is questioned. Is this the only way to proceed in life? Are humans more than people with needs, but people of human life who desire and tend toward something more? Are the churches up to offering people an existence that goes beyond the give and take of the market?

Toward the Meaning of Wholeness

The meaning of wholeness, the purpose of our human lives, is interpreted today in a climate of historical immanentism. This is the cultural tendency to exile not just the church but the supernatural altogether from intellectual and cultural life. The question of whether a mystery underlies this life or if a life beyond this one exists is met with ambiguity or outright denial, thus making the substance of life's meaning left up to personal opinion. Questions such as the meaning of our time together on this earth and where the world is headed are answered with extreme solutions. Some see the "end" of life on earth as a total Armageddon, the disappearance of all into a black hole. Others assume the end of history will result as a type of reconciliation in which it and in the means to achieve it, all will arise simply from within the human spirit, with no connection to anything supernatural. These bookends of response are often depicted in feature films which draw public interest. However, they do not convince everyone. Both believers and unbelievers find such answers unconvincing. At some point, superficial explanations do not stand up to the fragility of meaning contained in life experiences today, even though moderns reach for answers.

Some search for the success of the economy, both shared and personal. Yet consumer culture can leave people caught in the emptiness of the repeated, accelerating cycle of desire and fulfillment. Others try to find, in the simple rituals of daily living, a sense of peace and fulfillment. Yet the routines of daily living are interrupted by the stresses of a

---

[29]Laurie Brink, OP, *The Heavens Are Telling the Glory of God: An Emerging Chapter for Religious Life. Science, Theology and Mission* (Collegeville, MN: Liturgical Press, 2022).

fast-paced society. Overwork and overcommitment, poor health, joblessness, or a sense of exile from what was once a hub of belonging may stir a restlessness for "more." What is paradoxical is the attempt to find fullness through immanence alone generates the nova effect. Looking only in the here and now, within the immanent frame, inevitably leads to limits and ignites the question of what it means to be whole.

Those on this life journey who are open to God, as the ground of wholeness, understand Augustine's reflection, "our hearts are restless until they rest in you."[30] Yet for believers and all who search, this awareness is only experienced "dimly" (1 Cor. 13:12). Amid the cross pressures of a world interpreted as "all there is," the awareness of God is also experienced as an "absence." A vague or unarticulated sense of transcendence may stir involvement in existing religions, limited practice in some, or be the source of an "unaffiliated" stance in occasional spiritual customs.

This ambiguity also impacts the lives of religious women and men. While most stand within the church, mixed attitudes toward the need for prayer, retreat, spiritual direction, liturgy, and participation in the wider life of the church exist for various reasons. God is the very ground of religious life. Yet the nova effect of contrary options touches the religious search for the "more" of faith in secular times. Religious as well as all believers share the same pursuit of wholeness. Faith impacts this search through its trusting surrender to God, and the realization that wholeness cannot be grasped totally or mastered through willpower alone, nor through any system of thought, political party, or stance in the church that promises itself as the answer. All must discover continually in secular times how their lives exist in an intrinsic relationship to God, as its transcendent source. It is their relationship with God which is both the origin and the destination of their search for wholeness and the ultimate meaning and witness to the world. For this reason, we will consider the life of the vows first from this perspective.

What Can We Learn from Spiders?

> Using fragments of varying lengths, spiders can create webs that span almost any shape, connecting multiple dimensions of space. Their weaving entails continual reweaving, stitching together old and new fragments, to create a web that persists across time. The spider's web is a visual representation of the interconnectedness—the myriad, embedded layers of mutual influence—explored in analytical frameworks from systems theory and ecology to social psychology and global politics. The spider's capacity to creatively participate in environments that it cannot control makes it a suitable image for thinking broadly about what it means to be human in finite conditions.[31]

---

[30] Augustine of Hippo, *Confessions*, trans. Henry Chadwick (Oxford: University of Oxford Press, 2009).

[31] J. P. Lederach, *The Moral Imagination: The Art and Soul of Building Peace* (New York: Oxford University Press, 2005), 81. As quoted in Heather M. Dubois, "An Ever-Stitched Wholeness: Multidimensional Relationality in Trauma Theory and Schillebeeckx's Theology of Salvation," in *Salvation in the World: The Crossroads of Public*

The activity of spiders speaks to the experience of both fragmentation and possibility, which challenges Christians in an age of contingency. Amid those who sense all is not right with this world, it is common for people to think that goodwill is enough. Religion is not needed, as it really does not make any difference. The good to be done is done, with or without religion. However, for Christians, what is possible in life is marked by the gift of salvation from Jesus Christ. This puts their life in a fundamental relationship, to which they can respond or not. Their posture toward their neighbor is more than a coincidence between their sense of altruism and their neighbor's need. It is informed by a posture toward God and one toward people in general and to creation itself before a situation of need is encountered. This web of interconnections frames the agency of the Christian, as well as that of the spider. It identifies the web in which God touches our lives. The call to wholeness, therefore, is not done within the individualized framework of exclusive humanism, which focuses only on my choices as positive or negative. But a Christian framework of life is a matrix of becoming. The grace of baptism calls me, like the spider, to keep weaving, knowing my wholeness is both assured through the gift of Jesus Christ and in process through my response. The spider realizes it must rely on many factors beyond itself to survive; it is contingent. The web of the life of the gospel impacts my ideas. It is my role to combine this knowledge with the best available in my culture to sort out the truth and act on it. We are supported by this web as well as make our contribution to it. For many believers, this awareness of the interconnected reality of life comes slowly. Awareness of the gift of salvation engages us uniquely in the changing cycles of life. What difference does the gift of salvation in Jesus Christ make? It gives us hope. Beyond the activity of what we do, the web of our lives has already been made firm, in a way which we cannot do for ourselves, by God in Christ Jesus. While we only see the piece of the web in which we are engaged, God engages us daily in the call to more—more life, a deeper version of ourselves, a fuller community, and a future which is ours to plan and fashion. Our salvation comes to us in all the dimensions of our lives, and growth shows itself in the glimpses we get from time to time of the pattern God is creating through us. The call to renewal in religious life, and in the life of every religious, is only understood within this web. It is a call to wholeness.

Edward Schillebeeckx and the Christian Life

According to Edward Schillebeeckx people come to realize salvation in their lives often in a fragmentary manner, through a "contrast experience." This awakening is evoked through negative experiences, contradictions, and setbacks, not just positive experiences of success and loving relationships. It is common for people to experience something amiss in the world. Continuing war and famine, shifting markets, and forced migration change the lives of millions. A visit to the doctor's office brings a challenging diagnosis,

---

Theology, ed. Stephen van Erp, Christopher Cimorelli, and Christiane Alpers (London: Bloomsbury, 2017), 229–41 at 229.

families can have estrangements, and violence marks the streets of modern cities. Third World poverty, disaster, and political unrest make it difficult for people to find a home in this world.

When good people have this awareness, something inside them says, no, this should not be! Behind that no, is a yes, a hope for something better. Often this does not remain an empty hope; rather, it spurs action and collaboration with others. A plan is launched. It is not a perfect plan, but it is an attempt to address needless suffering and confront evil. People choose to make things better, believing love is worth their effort, and act from a vision of a better life which fuels their energies.[32]

This desire to reach out to the world to improve it reflects the human experience of transcendence. In the face of evil, in life or in the world, we reach for more. But what is the basis of our hope? Often the effort to move beyond ourselves, improve our world, and shape our lives opens the door to the need to do it again. Continually we find that people seek to make sense out of the world, even in the face of the fact "that things go intolerably wrong."[33] Belief that the world makes sense, in the face of the experience of its complexity, is the basis of every responsible action for change. This belief frames not only our lives but also the meaning of all of life. For Christians, the ground of this hope is the existence of God. Faith, therefore, is not attention to a set of beliefs alone but that which gives reason for a hope that expresses itself in love.

Karl Rahner claims that faith in the Spirit of God is the positive and unconditional acceptance of one's own existence as meaningful and open to a final fulfillment, "which we call God."[34] Faith concerns not only a way to live in this world but also the human search for meaning in it. Salvation, therefore, is not generated by history alone, an easy life, or things going our way. Rather, faith responds to God as the ground of our lives despite all evidence to the contrary. Salvation is not something we do; it is what God does. Our response and efforts are first grounded in this gift. This is the experience of salvation to which the gospel testifies, and it is the ground of the practice of the Christian life.

Contrast Experience and Wholeness

Modern men and women can encounter wholeness through their experience of suffering and evil, as well as success and fulfillment. Schillebeeckx contributes to the inclusion of suffering and evil as doors to wholeness, in contrast to modern sensibilities, which shun these human experiences as meaningless. He affirms that as moderns grapple with suffering in the world, they can be opened to the meaning of transcendence as they respond to life beyond themselves. Instead of denying or avoiding situations which

---

[32] Edward Schillebeeckx, *Church and the Human Story of God* (New York: Crossroads 1990), 22.
[33] Susan Neiman, *Evil in the Modern World: An Alternative History of Philosophy* (Princeton: Oxford University Press, 2002), 322.
[34] Karl Rahner, "The Certainty of Faith," in *The Practice of Faith* (New York: Crossroad, 1983), 3.

express injustice and suffering, by listening to their inner sense there can be more, they can experience anew their connection to God.

In this sense, a recognition of what should not be is also awareness of the goodness which should be there. Transcendence is experienced not as wishful or magical thinking, rather as an awakening or sense of longing for a fullness or wholeness not yet grasped. Recognition of what is not right with this world then becomes a "critical epistemological force" which leads to new action and anticipates a better future. Schillebeeckx holds that an understanding of the experience of salvation from God in Christ must always relate to some sense of human flourishing, which involves the naming, confronting, and overcoming of evil and suffering.[35]

Schillebeeckx acknowledges the contingency of the world and the search for wholeness within it. The world today is often experienced as fragmented, without a readymade script of directions to live by. Instead, life presents itself as a cacophony of meaning. Even if family life and social circumstances offer stability, today's world of contingency can break through with interruption. The path of discovering life's meaning is encountered in a fragmentary fashion, in moments of meaning and awareness, and darkness and confusion. Yet the wholeness of time itself, eschatological fullness, is mediated in and through history, the very history in which we live.[36] Like the spider, through trial and error, we construct meaning in life, amid situations of both light and darkness, sin and opposition, grace, and possibility. Schillebeeckx clarifies that because of the paschal mystery of Jesus Christ, evil and suffering do not cancel out the possibility of meaning, as modern ethos suggests. Meaning can be found even in one of the most desperate situations of the modern age.[37] Acknowledging there remain situations of human suffering, which leave human beings speechless, and devoid of any explanation— the absurd—yet amid the goodness and suffering of life, experiences of meaning are possible. The total meaning of our lives and of history itself cannot be known except through another. The gifts of faith, hope, and love lead us there. The totality of wholeness cannot be fully discerned because history is still in process. Glimpses of the whole can be only seen or "touched," not possessed or held.

For Schillebeeckx experiences of wholeness—ultimately encounters with God—are only possible in this life through practical reason and liberating praxis that seek to reduce meaningless suffering. We do not find salvation primarily by means of a correct interpretation of reality, but by acting in accordance with the demands of reality.[38] Wholeness can be found in an encounter with reality, and the meaningfulness which

---

[35]Edward Schillebeeckx, *Christ: The Experience of Jesus as Lord* (New York: Herder and Herder, 1984), 818. For an overview of the Christology of Edward Schillebeeckx, see Robin Ryan, *Jesus and Salvation: Soundings in the Christian Tradition and Contemporary Theology* (Collegeville, MN: The Liturgical Press, 2015), chapter 5.
[36]Edward Schillebeeckx, *The Schillebeeckx Reader*, ed. Robert J. Schreiter (New York: Crossroad: 1984) 47, 66–7.
[37]Victor Frankl, *Man's Search for Meaning* (Boston: Beacon Press, 2006).
[38]Edward Schillebeeckx, *Christ: The Christian Experience in the Modern World*, trans. John Bowden, CW, vol. 7 (London: T&T Clark, 2014), 47 (61).

grounds, if we do not cling to a program, an ideology, or a system of thought as the meaning of the whole and substitute it for a totality it cannot produce. We need plans, models, programs, and interpretations of reality to capture our narratives of hope, to approximate a "meaningful whole." Yet, openness to their incomplete character increases our capacity to make sense out of finitude, impermanence, and the problems of suffering, fiasco, failure, and death.[39]

The Contrast Experience of Jesus

Jesus himself experienced a contrasting experience in his relationship with God as "Abba." This was the secret of Jesus' own sense of purpose, being, message, and way of life.[40] Jesus' Abba experience entailed an awareness of God's love for him and his love for the Father, but as a power which not only embraced all people but made them truly free (Jn 8:36). In Jesus' confrontation with evil and suffering, Jesus knew the pain of the world. God, "Abba," was known to Jesus as Goodness, as the opponent to suffering and evil. The Kingdom of God, to which Jesus witnessed, proclaimed a God engaged with the concerns of people and whose coming rule promised wholeness for all, especially the most vulnerable. The Kingdom of God involves new relationships which heal, support, affirm, strengthen, and enable the People of God. The God of the Kingdom of God is the God of life whose presence is expressed in visible and concrete ways. The God whom Jesus discloses in word and deed is purely the source and ground of life, of the good. Neither death nor any other form of negativity finds its source in God.[41] This conviction marks the way Schillebeeckx interprets the meaning of Jesus' death on the cross.

The Paschal Mystery and Wholeness

Rahner and Schillebeeckx approach the mystery of Jesus' incarnation and paschal mystery in a manner which speaks to the search for wholeness in an age of contingency. This approach provides a horizon for the vows in a secular age through the interpretation of the Christian life in tune with the modern search for meaning. Rahner's understanding of grace leads him to stand with Dun Scotus in his assertion that God would have become incarnate in Jesus Christ even without sin coming into the experience of human existence. Redemption precedes sinfulness. God intended from the beginning of creation for men and women to share in God's life.[42] The incarnation of Jesus Christ was an expression of this love. Even though sin entered the God-human relationship, sin

---

[39]Ibid., 734–6, 740–1.
[40]Edward Schillebeeckx, *Jesus: An Experiment in Christology* (New York: Crossroads, 1981), 256. Robin Ryan, *God and the Mystery of Human Suffering: A Theological Conversation across the Ages* (Mahwah, NJ: Paulist Press, 2011), 225.
[41]Schillebeeckx, *Church: The Human Story of God*, 124.
[42]Karl Rahner, "The Christian Understanding of Redemption," in *Theological Investigations*, vol. 21, *Science and Christian Faith*, trans. Hugh M. Riley (New York: Crossroad, 1988), 244–7.

was not the intention behind the incarnation. Rather, God's desire for union with all God created is God's intention for creation and the incarnation.

Neither Rahner nor Schillebeeckx ignores the importance of redemption nor denies human sinfulness and its role in human life. However, neither depicts the reason for the incarnation as primarily a means to remedy sin. God's becoming human, God's gift of Self in our human history, is intended from the beginning. The incarnation is the summit and height of the divine plan of creation.[43] It is not the case that God's presence and grace are not needed in our lifelong effort to move out of ourselves in love rather than into ourselves in egotism. Ultimately, it is communion with God that saves us from all that blocks us from loving others and touching wholeness. This is the meaning of salvation. Rahner emphasizes that the only ultimate salvation for humanity is God in God's very Self. He says, "Salvation here is to be understood as the strictly supernatural and direct presence of God in himself afforded by grace."[44] It is only through God's gift of Self that sin is forgiven and evil overcome.

Schillebeeckx highlights Jesus' solidarity with humanity in his living and dying. He writes, "On the cross Jesus shared in the brokenness of our world. This means that God determines in absolute freedom, down the ages, who and how he wills to be in his deepest being, namely a God of men and women, an ally in our suffering and absurdity."[45] Jesus was not abandoned by the Father on the cross; rather, he was in unbroken communion with God, through the response of his freedom and the unrelenting presence of the Father to him.[46] Rahner understands human freedom to be, at its roots, the capacity for definitive self-disposal before God. This was the freedom and love Jesus exemplified on the cross, as well as throughout his life. Jesus could be open to the Father even in the face of the cross. Also, freedom is the capacity to make something of oneself before God, to become the kind of person God calls one to be. Neither theologian interprets Jesus, as Aquinas, as always having the beatific vision of God. Jesus was conscious of his unique immediacy to the God whom he addressed as "Abba," and was aware of his unique redemptive mission. But this unique consciousness did not provide detailed, objective knowledge about the future. Jesus, like all of us, had to face his reality as a full human being and reach out to touch wholeness with his life.

Wholeness, Contingency, and Religious Life

In the theology of Rahner and Schillebeeckx, salvation is wholeness experienced in fragmentary or momentary fashion, while eschatological fullness is mediated in and

---

[43] Karl Rahner, "Christology in an Evolutionary View," in *Theological Investigations*, vol. 5, *Later Writings*, trans. Karl-H. Kruger (London: Darton, Longman & Todd; New York: Seabury Press, 1966), 185.
[44] Karl Rahner, "The One Christ and the Universality of Salvation," in *Theological Investigations*, vol. 16, trans. David Moorland OSB (New York: Seabury Press, 1983), 200.
[45] Schillebeeckx, *Church: The Human Story of God*, 126.
[46] Kathleen Anne McManus, OP, *Unbroken Communion: The Place and Meaning of Suffering in the Theology of Edward Schillebeeckx* (Washington, DC: Rowman and Littlefield, 2003).

through history. Their theologies integrate the Christian understanding of mystical or contemplative glimpses of the whole of reality with a more philosophical understanding of the integrity of the fragment, in light of the failures of grand narratives to meet the search for meaning today.[47]

Religious life is not simply an ascetic journey to rid oneself of sin. It is an encounter with God's grace, a reach for wholeness on a personal journey of authenticity, a communal journey of faithfulness, an ecclesial journey of mission, a societal journey of diversity and equity, an environmental journey of sustainability, and a global journey of peace. Sin and grace impact every step of the way, but the wholeness which sustains hope is the salvation to which the gospel witnesses and the promise of the Kingdom of God. It is the life of the spider, a weaving of webs in interconnections; some hold our personal lives, others provide a way for wholeness to be experienced by others. As we explore the life of the vows, we will call upon this image of wholeness to enlighten our path.

---

[47]Dubois, "An Ever-Stitched Wholeness: Multidimensional Relationality in Trauma Theory and Schillebeeckx's Theology of Salvation," 230. How do the fragments of our life's efforts fit into the Whole that only God can bring to fulfillment?

CHAPTER 2
TOUCHING WHOLENESS IN A WORLD OF INTERRELATIONSHIPS

Religious life is not a stand-alone reality; it exists in a web of relationships. We will take a closer look at selected aspects of those relationships and ask how they might impact our understanding of the vows of religious life and their capacity to "touch wholeness." Several key assumptions will be employed to interpret the vows. First, a response to a perceived call from God is a decision, but not a self-creation. The power to respond to a religious vocation is beyond a simple act of the will, like a decision to work out in the gym. Rather, its signature is the experience of being moved by an energy beyond the self. One touches into this reality, yet never fully grasps it. While a response to a call requires focus and effort, a person is not always conscious of the gift or givenness of a vocation. Overtime, in prayer, this dimension of a vocation comes to light. Prayer leads to a fuller awareness of the presence of God as well as fosters the personal relationship with God without whom religious life does not make sense. Prayer expresses the willingness to encounter God on this personal level. Practice of prayer is an essential aspect of the web of interrelationships in a religious vocation. Prayer itself can be an experience of touching wholeness.

A second assumption is that the life or power which grounds wholeness is an energy which cannot be forced but must be allowed to gradually reveal itself. In theological language, this is an experience of grace. Grace shares with all that is sacred the fact that it cannot be controlled. Attention to and encounter with God, essential to the vowed life, sets it apart from the noble becoming of exclusive humanism, which is based on self-reliance alone. The vows in this sense link together a web of interrelationships of key aspects of a whole life: knowing oneself, relationships with others, life in society, and one's unfolding understanding of God. The vows are both "doors" to and a means by which religious are immersed in the web of life. It is a life shared with others yet entered into through a unique approach. Understanding the vows requires faith.

Third, vows form a unity necessary for a lifestyle—a type of web—rather than exist as moral practices in isolation from one another. Their mutual impact on one another signifies religious life as a distinct way of living.[1] The choices represented by the vows over time are not just isolated decisions but become reflexive standards by which a religious evaluates his or her preferences and shapes communities. At one level, the vows have

---

[1] See Maryanne Confoy, RSC, *Religious Life and Priesthood: Rediscovering Vatican II* (New York: Paulist, 2008).

canonical boundaries: at another, they are preferences of value based on experiences of self-formation and self-transcendence. In scripture, they are "counsels" of discipleship.[2] At a broader level, they express a vital aspect of a communal charism.[3] It is possible that the vows are a way to touch wholeness because they are embedded in a wider web of relationships within the church as the People of God. In this, they flow from a baptismal commitment.[4] They are not a private spiritual pursuit but an adult stance within a wider community of believers and disciples of Jesus Christ.

Fourth, the vows of religious life are understood today in an evolutionary rather than static web of relationships. The "within" of energy in contrast to the "without" of energy impacts their unfolding in modern experience. Past interpretations pictured the vowed life as an ascetical journey of purification, the call to "be perfect." The web created through the choice of religious life in modern sensibilities emphasizes the use of freedom in the one and only life of the religious, and less on an abstract vision of a uniform way of being human. One does not become a religious because of social pressure, their place in the order of the family (as was true in some periods of history), or because it is a higher path to perfection. A person becomes a religious because they want to become one. Societal values today do not confirm this choice. It must come from within.

The "within" of the energy which propels religious life, however, is expressed in a web of relationships. The path of a religious is formed through the web they create from their own choices: relationship with Jesus Christ in the gospel, the uniqueness of their own life journey, response to a particular context, and desire to be embedded within a chosen community and charism. This web distinguishes the vowed life from the image of human flourishing implied in exclusive humanism.

The Web of Theological Shifts

Religious today stand in a different theological web of understanding. The theological setting which serves to ground the vows is different than in the past. This web is unfolding and impacted by the fact that theology today is done internationally. Different sectors of the church interpret the Christian life from diverse locations and perspectives: globally, socially, economically, and politically. Religious life has a unity in the gospel and the church, yet also a diversity in its expression. Along with this diversity of expression, within theology itself, there have been important shifts in the last sixty years which offer direction to how religious life is lived today.

---

[2] Sandra M. Schneiders, *Selling All: Commitment, Consecrated Celibacy, and Community in Catholic Religious Life* (Mahwah, NJ: Paulist Press, 2001).
[3] It is recognized that various lifestyles can express a communal charism in the church.
[4] This image of the church of Vatican II is not an exclusive image; its other realities, such as its communal and institutional dimension, remain. However, it is a primary image of Vatican II and certainly a central starting point of the Synodal movement in the church. See Rafael Luciani, *Synodality: A New Way of Proceeding in the Church*, trans. Joseph Owens, SJ (Mahwah, NJ: Paulist Press, 2022), 15–22, 139–44.

There have been new understandings of relationships between the church and the world, as well as the sacred and the secular. The call of Vatican II was for religious to get involved in the world. Since Vatican II, religious have sought a language to express its meaning in line with Vatican II understandings of theology. They were careful to avoid identification of religious life with societal views of life alone. This can be seen in the renaming of the Christian life and religious life as a flight from the world to one of healing and creating in history. Approaching the world with an evolutionary perspective, done by many today, also impacts this change of perspective.[5] Care for creation and encounter others of good will outside the church are seen to be core to the Christian life in a way they were not emphasized in other historical periods.

Modern culture is also part of the web of religious life. In this sense, the "world" is not an enemy of religious life. To express the meaning of religious life in any culture means to embrace what is "correct and valuable" in the culture and name what it omits. It is important to recognize that what is significant for human wholeness and holiness is found not just in Western cultures, but in the many diverse cultures in which religious live today.[6] Probing these webs of interrelationships assists religious to offset an over-identification with one's culture and discern what is essential in each cultural context.

A key shift in the web of relationships in which religious life stands is the change in the situation of religion in modern culture. As stated earlier, this shift is no longer just the tension between belief and unbelief or the marginalization of religion in society as secularization outlooks hold. The scientific, social, and technological structures of today are based on only a "this worldly" order, which can be understood on its own terms apart from anything transcendent of supernatural.[7] This order leaves open the question of whether ultimate meaning, spiritual transformation, or just making sense even needs a vision of transcendence.[8] It also leaves legitimate goals of modern life, to relieve suffering and bring about universal benevolence without a sustaining foundation for the long struggle required to accomplish them.[9] Religious may find that the significance and witness of their lives may increasingly lie in this nexus.

---

[5] See Karl Rahner, SJ, "Christian Living Formerly and Today," in *Theological Investigations VII*, trans. David Bourke (New York: The Seabury Press, 1971).
[6] This writing will be limited in its capacity to address diversity adequately but hopes to provide a framework for others to do so. See Mary Johnson, SNDdeN, Mary Gautier, Patricia Wittberg, SC, and Thu Do, LHC, *Migration for Mission: International Catholic Sisters in the United States* (New York: Oxford University Press, 2019). Maria Cimperman, RSCJ and Roger Schroeder, SVD, eds., *Engaging Our Diversity: Interculturality and Consecrated Life Today* (Maryknoll, NY: Orbis Books, 2020). Patricia Wittberg, SC, Mary Gautier, Gemma Simmons, CJ, and Natalie Becquart, XMCJ, *God's Call is Everywhere: A Global Analysis of Contemporary Religious Vocations for Women* (Collegeville, MN: Liturgical Press, 2023).
[7] The sciences are independent areas of knowledge. This position assumes they can explain all of reality. See Charles Taylor, *A Secular Age* (Cambridge: The Belknap Press of Harvard University, 2007), 594–5.
[8] For an exploration of the sources and repercussions of the lack of awareness of an ultimate end of human life in modern society, see Jeffrey P. Bishop, M. Therese Lysaught, and Andrew Michel, *Biopolitics After Neuroscience: Morality and the Economy of Virtue* (London: Bloomsbury, 2022), 196–214.
[9] Judith A. Merkle, *Discipleship, Secularity and the Modern Self: Dancing to Silent Music* (London: T&T Clark, 2020), 198–206.

For the spider, the creation of identity is a rather straightforward project. Instinct directs the spider not only toward its place in the world but also to know who it is, what it does, and how to survive. Religious identity, and more specifically that of vowed religious, goes beyond instinct, as human identity is not just biological but rooted in the symbolic and the ultimate. Religious life has been created throughout centuries of the church, in different societies, in various forms, and through cycles of fragmentation, suppression, and vitalization. For religious today to touch wholeness in the secular age, they will be called to make choices to move toward this integration in a new time in history. The search for wholeness in a world of interrelationships requires a map for this journey. While a full map is not possible, key markers of secular and religious "signs of the times" may indicate a way ahead.

The Web of Interrelationships: Marking the Territory

The Frame

The classical language of the vows was formed in a world which had a different mental organization than the evolutionary view most common today. Any worldview is an attempt to name the interrelationships in it. Most importantly, it depicts who the human person is in respect to wider relationships. The world of premodern times is seen as a Great Chain of Being. It depicted being itself as existing on several levels. The cosmos manifests hierarchy and order. This hierarchy provides a key to understanding what is real. The same superiority, for example, of the soul over the body, the king over subjects, and the lion over the animal kingdom "correspond" to order in other realms. The whole is bound together by realms of hierarchical complementarity. In the religious realm, this worldview upheld that there are objects in this world, like the Host or blessed candles, which deserve respect, not because I think so but because they do. They are sacred.[10] The cosmos draws attention beyond itself and functions as a sign of what is more than nature. It testifies to the divine purpose and action. Its order and design point to the creator, and an order and purpose for all created.[11] What things mean are independent of human perception or attribution. Individual actions have meaning considering the order which unites human action, community, and the cosmos, the web of relationships as then understood. This framework offers a vision of what is higher and lower, more important and less important, distinguishing the honorable from the less worthy.[12] Religious life in this worldview was named as a higher state of perfection in the Christian life since its focus was on the spiritual life.

---

[10]Taylor, *The Secular Age*, 161.
[11]Ibid., 25.
[12]Judith A. Merkle, *Sensing the Spirit: Toward the Future of Religious Life*, (London: T&T Clark, 2023), 17–18.

Later Developments

In the fifteenth and sixteenth centuries, René Descartes and Isaac Newton added to this synthesis insights which shifted understandings of the human person, nature, and the source of energy. The fundamental Newtonian assumption was that reality functioned like a machine, that matter can be broken down into small particles and that everything that happens is caused by a physical force exerted upon an object, like a foot kicking a ball. Isaac Newton conceived the physical world in terms of matter and force in a void of space. This made the world composed of interchangeable parts that can be repaired or replaced from the outside. The energy or force in this world came from without. Descartes, in contrast, is known for his "turn to the subject," in his famous dictum, "I think therefore I am." Material reality was completely distinct from the human mind and will. He divided the world into *rescognitans* and *res extensa*. Nature was seen as inert and passive matter and as completely different from the human being. This set the stage for human intelligence to manipulate the material world and use it anyway it desired.[13] Often humans themselves were the force "from without." These ideas fueled the world we know as the Industrial Revolution and brought many benefits to people, as well as some of the environmental and social crises we experience today.[14]

Religious life in this view of the world was reinterpreted to meet the needs of the times. Its leaning toward a mechanical view of the world is mirrored in a spiritual and moral life which relies on measurement and detail for clarity. Priests could "sin" while offering Mass, through multiple infractions and details in celebration. A catechesis of atonement was pastorally offered, influenced by Jansenism and Puritanism.[15] The prevailing cultural view of reality impacted a catechesis which depicted Christ paid for original sin, paying a debt for us, in a transactional manner.[16] Emphasis in moral life on questions of how much and how far likely were easily understood when the rest of the world was viewed in a manner of measurable almost mathematical law.

What has changed since the era of the Great Chain of Being is that the whole is indexed to a personal vision.[17] There is an interweaving of the subjective and the transcendent in the human imagination. Energy and power remain an external force. We commercially harness it, fight wars over it, and seek new sources of it.

---

[13]Hyun Chul-Cho, SJ, "Interconnectedness and Intrinsic Value as Ecological Principles: An Appropriation of Karl Rahner's Evolutionary Christology," *Theological Studies* 70 (2009): 622–33.
[14]Charles Taylor, *Cosmic Connections: Poetry in the Age of Disenchantment* (Cambridge: The Belknap Press of Harvard University Press, 2024), 181–90.
[15]Merkle, *Discipleship, Secularity and the Modern Self*, 144–6.
[16]This transactional image of soteriology does not reject the complex description of salvation found in the New Testament. It simply indicates how a prevailing mechanical view of the world entered theological imagination. For the deeper truth, which exists in the New Testament, that Jesus accomplished for us through his cross and resurrection something which we cannot do for ourselves, see Robin Ryan, CP, *Jesus and Salvation: Soundings in the Christian Tradition and Contemporary Theology* (Collegeville, MN: Liturgical Press, 2015). See also, Merkle, *Discipleship, Secularity and the Modern Self*, 101–25.
[17]Charles Taylor, *Sources of the Self* (Cambridge, MA: Harvard University Press, 1989), 510.

Energy as influence is also experienced as social power "without," as people debate over the impact of social media, the state, marketing, and the role of these forces in what appears as our most personal opinions. Yet emotionally, moderns sense their personal power comes from within. In contrast to the ancients who found what is deep and timeless in a world of external forms, moderns find this is an inwardness of experience. If one goes deep enough, one will encounter the mythic, the archetypical, and the luminous.

While it would be naïve to assume that external forces do not impact modern life, this shift in consciousness suggests that the power of external reality, even as authority, has less power in human imagination today. The resistance, for example, of people across the world submitting to an external order to wear face masks during the Covid pandemic suggests an attitude toward decision-making that relies heavily on personal choice and autonomy. In religious life, there also has been a shift from the "external" to internal power. While often this is an awareness of maturity in decision-making, it is also reflected in one's approach to life and personal identity. In this changed context, the traditional adage "keep the rule and the rule will keep you" likely does not inspire as it once did. Its value requires reinterpretation for a modern sensibility. These passing reflections simply illustrate that we cannot rely only on classical understandings of the vows to carry their meaning in modern life.

The Turf: The Sacred and the Secular

In the 1960s, John XXIII and Vatican II shifted the church's understanding of the relationship between the church and the world. The world was no longer considered a distraction from spiritual life. One did not have to "leave the world" to find God. Rather John XXIII turned the face of the Church toward the world.[18] John was positive not just about the world in general. He was hopeful that the world before him, the modern world, would be a new era for the human family.[19] He hoped that the benefits that had already reached many in modern society would soon touch those not yet released from their poverty by the improvements accomplished in industrialized society. This shift in the relationship between church and world had a great impact on religious life. In retrospect, we find the relationship between the secular and the sacred remains a perennial question in the church.

---

[18] This did not remove a type of "withdrawal" needed for a contemplative outlook but replaced a spirituality of enclosure, which was no longer suitable for ministry for apostolic religious in the expression of their charism in the modern church and society.

[19] Peter and Margaret Hebblethwaite, *John XXIII, Pope of the Century* (New York: Continuum, 2001). E. E. E. Hales, *Pope John and His Revolution* (New York: Image Books, 1966).

St. Augustine

The struggle to understand the relationship between the secular and the sacred has gone on for centuries in the Church. St. Augustine, at the time of the Roman Empire, reflected on how the sacred and the secular intertwine through his depiction of the two kingdoms. He envisioned the cosmos itself as divided into two realities, the city of God and the city of the earth. The *saeculum* is the realm in which the carriers of the two cities are intertwined.[20] The earthly city has two dimensions and is not limited only to sinful humanity. On the one hand, it is the world, which is profane, and rejects God. It is the realm of the impious and the reprobate. On the other hand, the earthly city is simply the material world. It is the actual space of life, the empirical city where good and bad mix. The earthly city and its institutions have a moral dimension; they can be better or worse in their service of human life. The care of the *saeculum* or the realm in which the two cities intertwine, has importance for believers and nonbelievers alike. It is the real world in which all must live.

Religious life, once described as "leaving the world," in the web of relationships in which it stood, is impacted by the understanding of the sacred and the secular today. As religious engaged society in new ways after Vatican II, they also encountered issues of *sacralization*, or the process of making sacred elements of culture. While Jesus said simply to render to Caesar what is Caesar's and to God what is God's, the institutionalization of Christianity into society brought new challenges. When Constantine ended Christian persecution and began a new relationship between Church and state that developed into the Holy Roman Empire, a this-worldly reality called Christendom became sacralized. It became a humanly organized arrangement of life, which included religion, that morphed into being identified with the sacred itself. To some extent, when religious life adapted to greater involvement in "the world" after Vatican II, it too developed an institutionally formed interpretation of religious life. This new form of living did correct limitations in pre-Vatican approaches to religious life. Yet, in some cases, this renewed form became identified with religious life itself. We find this evidenced in the reluctance of some religious to continue to renew after the initial post-Vatican changes in their congregations. Another reaction is an apparent turn to corporate or managerial language alone to address congregational life. Both suggest the absence of a deeper vision of meaning that has the power to draw religious life into the future. The decline of entrants to religious life, together with the deinstitutionalization of its ministries, has challenged the maintenance of this model as synonymous with religious life itself.[21]

---

[20] Robert A. Markus, *Christianity and the Secular* (Notre Dame, IN: University of Notre Dame Press, 2006), 48.
[21] See Patricia Wittberg, SC, Pathways *to Re-Creating Religious Communities* (Mahwah, NJ: Paulist Press, 1996), 58, 61–76.

Christendom

When new views of the web of the universe and humanity were raised by Descartes, Copernicus, Newton, Darwin, and Freud, they confronted the sacralized view of the world and the human held by Christendom.[22] The church historically rejected the new thought offered by these thinkers to the point that some argue that the rise of secularism in Western society was fed by the church's non-dialogical tone. Because of the growing disjunction between the Church and cultural imagination, people automatically dismissed the church from having any contribution to make. The historical ambiguities of the crusades, the Inquisition and the Conquest, moved many to turn from the church, either by its suppression in revolution or banishment through law. While in many instances the church needed to question ideas of modern culture, and still does, these conflicts raised the question: To what degree was the church defending a world it had created, and to what degree was it defending the Word of God? Since religion and the church today face new transitions, the same question can be asked of their response. If religious argue that the renewal of religious congregations was completed after Vatican II and today all we need to do is to resuscitate it, they likely will not be convincing to those who also recognize the good and potential in postmodern society. For those who view religious life as identical with modern culture, believing its future will just organically emerge, their posture also may be questioned. It overlooks that religious, in their post-Vatican II renewal have not successfully substituted a new definition of their role within the church which carries the visibility and impact of their previous institutional model. In Patricia Wittberg's words, "Until we can articulate who we are and why we are, and until we can do so in a way that is attractive to twenty-first century Christians . . . we will not be able to refound our communities."[23] To do so involves the capacity to distinguish the form of religious life which has already been created from the religious life to which religious are called by the gospel in a new context.

The Role of Religion

The role of religion in a culture has a significant part in the web of interrelationships of religious life. Broadly, the relationship of religion to culture sets a context for its comprehension as a viable life option. However, the web of this relationship goes beyond the compatibility of the ethos of the culture with the idea of religious life. It goes much deeper. Every culture has elements which harmonize with the ideals of the church and those which contradict and oppose it. The church, alternately, has a role and significance in every culture. The challenge in each generation is to express the meaning

---

[22]See Nicholas Olkowich, "Complicating the Reception of Lonergan on Sacralization and Secularization," *Irish Theological Quarterly* 86, no. 2 (2021): 164–83.
[23]Ibid., 58.

of the Christian life in an evolving cultural matrix, as neither the church nor culture are static realities. People tend to think of cultures as unities, yet within cultures there exists diversity. Kathryn Tanner states, "it seems less and less plausible to presume that cultures are self-contained and clearly bounded units, internally consistent and unified wholes of beliefs and values simply transmitted to every member of the representative groups as principles of social order."[24] This is true of church and society. Nor is this an ideal to be sought. Tanner notes, even if members of a group declare the same beliefs and values, it is unlikely they will all mean the same things by them.[25] A consensus on values is important in a group, as well as the attempt to form one, even if there are differences regarding interpretation of how to apply them. This consensus gives shape to how a community adopts, founds, validates, and communicates a way of life, either social, ecclesial, or congregational. Social forms of life, at all levels, therefore, have norms. An effective outcome of inculturation, or positively constructing the web of interrelationship with culture, involves the dual process of distinguishing inauthentic or ineffective representations of a meaningful human life. The life of a congregation or ecclesial group has the power to shape a life only by the way people struggle over their meaning and the importance of the values they profess to share.[26] The idea of religious congregation as a lockstep unity is a false ideal. Also mistaken is the belief that a group is sustainable if it is full of individual prophets but stands for nothing visible as a unity.

Misconceptions of the web of relationships within and between the church and culture can cripple it. The model of a monolithic church not only contradicts the world church image of Vatican II but also misguides a church culture built on who you are against rather than the core of the gospel that you are for.[27] In both instances, ideology, or ideas how the world works, is framed in Absolutes constructed as liberal or conservative—with little wisdom attributed to the other. Today these postures are seen more accurately as identity politics, as their connection to power through ideology is unveiled. Both positions, if non-dialogical, represent the choice to find one's place in a pluralistic world defined by who you are against. This stance forms a web of relationships closed to new ideas and exclusive. It fails to mediate the real power of the truth of the gospel to a wider world because of a failure to relate them to the common ground of humanity and its real needs. The challenge of relating religion to culture for religious involves the creation of a life among themselves that speaks to the discontinuities and spiritual hunger in the society at large. Religious life should offer a meaningful alternative lifestyle for members. This establishes it in a wider web of relationships as a witness which attempts to meet the spiritual hunger in its society and its social, economic, and cultural discontinuities. Response to this call is one signpost of direction both for the renewal of a congregation

---

[24]Kathryn Tanner, *Theories of Culture: A New Agenda for Theology* (Minneapolis, MN. Fortress Press, 1997), 38.
[25]Ibid., 46.
[26]Ibid., 50.
[27]Judith A. Merkle, *Being Faithful: Christian Commitment in Modern Society* (London: T&T Clark, 2016), 149–67.

and its contribution to the synodal church. It is a call to be communities that witness to the transcendent in the world of today through their offer of a path of healing and creating in history. The Church is not just "in the mind" it exists in a web of relationships, as does religious life. By grappling with the above issues which concern the relationship between the sacred and the secular, congregations can continue to grasp the significance of these interrelationships for the renewal of religious life as well as for the renewal of the church.

Following the Trajectory of Vatican II

At Vatican II, the church adopted a renewed posture toward the secular world.[28] It owned its right to resist a secularization which was secularism, the attitude that the secular is the only reality. It acknowledged that there is a rightful autonomy of the secular necessary to build the *saeculum* in which all share. Inspired by Aquinas' efforts to affirm "the reality of human nature and the legitimacy of its proper sphere of activity," theologian Marie-Dominique Chenu called for the Church to dismantle the "mental and institutional complex of Christendom."[29] He called for a desacralization of the image of Christendom as a model of the mission of the Church.

Desacralization is the process which questions the place of something as an expression of authentic religious consciousness. It seeks to abandon illusions and move toward a better harmony between religion, the church, and culture. It involves respect for the legitimate autonomy of the sciences, with their own methods and procedures. It affirms the progress of natural and secular forces to free both the world and the Word of God to be themselves. While sacralization is a necessary process, it becomes a problem when the sacralization of the past prevents what should be rightly sacralized or fostered in the present. The ambiguity, lack of time to "test" long-range effects of practices, and so on make this a challenging task.

Likely the culture wars which pervade in many political and ecclesial contexts across the world represent inauthentic ways people maintain a sense of identity in this dynamic. Religious congregations should not mirror them. Religious are called to witness that there are values and constructive forms of human life in society which they also affirm. These are cultural forms which are part of the *saeculum*, which all people need and desire. They promote human growth and global well-being and reflect a shared human search for better knowledge and sustainable values. Vatican II called these the "signs of the times." Since they are key indicators in the history of the movement of the Spirit among all the peoples of the earth, they provide meaning and direction for

---

[28]See Catherine Clifford with Stephen Lampe, eds., *Vatican II at 60: Re-energizing the Renewal* (Maryknoll, NY: Orbis Books, 2024).
[29]See Claude Geffre, OP, "The Tension between Desacralization and Spirituality," *Concilium* 9, no. 2 (1966): 57–66.

congregations. Among them are all processes which affirm human rights, peace among nations, the rights of women, equality among races, environmental sustainability, the meaning of human sexuality and the importance of family, literacy, health care, peace-making and the rise of conscience among people's world. The church's identity as the People of God and its openness to the role of all the faithful in decision-making through the synodal process also is a sign of the time and an expression of its forward movement as "ecclesiogenesis," an evolving church.[30] It is not the case that the church or a congregation has all the answers; rather, both need to read the signs of the times to discern the direction of the Spirit.

In the web of interrelationships in which religious life exists, therefore, lies the mystery of grace. If grace comes to us in our history, grace builds on nature, then the coming of the Kingdom to which religious witness happens on this "turf," the relationship between the sacred and the secular. For this to happen, religious must distinguish between what is sound and what is not in the choices and visions of fulfillment offered in secular society. To intentionally make this conversation and collaboration a priority is to foster a vision of the church and religious life for the future and for the next generation.

The Search: Authenticity and Wholeness

Action in the web of interrelationships of religious life happens primarily in the *saeculum*, the life in which all people share. It is the same realm where the mystery of God's healing and creating in history is expressed. Religious participate in this mystery in a particular context with its own understanding of human fulfillment. In contrast to the world of Aquinas, who envisions the fulfillment of a human life as knowing, willing, and loving the Absolute, the modern person expresses this purpose of life with a different nuance. They imagine becoming a "self" in relation to the Absolute. They seek to relate the unique "I" that is one's identity to the Absolute, as a marker of human fulfillment.[31] For this reason, the consideration of the vows of religious life, through the lens of "touching wholeness," is to envision this wholeness and how one gains access to it. It implies that the vows of religious life involve authenticity of life, and a commitment to growth as a healthy man or woman. Since religious life is lived in a web of relationships, and not one of leaving the world, the intentions involved in the vowed life necessitate ongoing discernment of what elements are beneficial or detrimental to human and spiritual development and a committed life in each context.

For instance, we find that expressive individualism impacts the meaning of modern life. It holds that human beings are defined by their individual psychological core, and that the purpose of life is allowing that core to find social expression in relationships and self-expression. However, this sole focus on life's meaning leaves unanswered the goal

---

[30]Lucinai, *Synodality: A New Way of Proceeding in the Church*, chapter on ecclesiogenesis.
[31]Christopher Steck, SJ, *The Ethical Thought of Hans Urs Von Balthasar* (New York: Crossroad, 2001), 76.

or the path to unfolding which the journey to fullness or authenticity involves, beyond that of personal aspiration.[32] Thus, both the gospel and the social sciences are needed to distinguish healthy becoming from narcissistic withdrawal.

A language of authenticity and inauthenticity involves a judgment that not all paths lead to growth or fullness of life. Christians living in the secular age must distinguish between the authentic and inauthentic not only in general in terms of visions of the human handed on from one generation to the next but also in terms of the times in which they live. The path to authenticity must, on the one hand, be integrated with the cultural matrix of becoming in their context and, on the other hand, have boundaries of Christian identity distinct at times from the cultural matrix. As religious live in their culture, they will find matters which diverge from this matrix of identity and are questioned and tested; those in accord with it and are embraced; and that which is incompatible which must be rejected. Wholeness, as it relates to authenticity, is experienced in the interrelationship or dialectic among these elements. What should be sought or rejected; welcomed or tested and judged, is discerned along the way.

Interiority and the Vows in a Web of Interrelationships

Interiority is a signature quality of the modern person in the secular age. Interiority is a capacity of self-appropriation, becoming familiar with the dynamics of one's own consciousness. It involves awareness of one's own way of sensing, imagining, questioning, weighing evidence, coming to a decision, speaking, loving, and the like. Unlike the character Topsy in Huckleberry Finn who responded to the question, "How did you come into the world?"—with-Ah "spect ah just grow'd"; human interiority is the capacity to come to one's own sense of meaning.[33] The vows today are sustained by the capacity of interiority and the development of interiority to which they lead. Interiority is one path of the knowledge required to become an authentic person.

Theologian Bernard Lonergan sees the process of becoming authentic not in a vacuum or as the result of a long sit in one's easy chair with a candle lit and a cup of coffee. Rather, it occurs through two fundamental and complementary kinds of relationships: those of achievement and of heritage. In his words:

> For human development is of two different kinds. There is development from below upwards, from experience to understanding, from growing understanding to balanced judgment, from balanced judgment to fruitful courses or action, and from fruitful courses of action to new situations that call for further understanding, profounder judgment, richer courses of action. But there also is development from

---

[32]See Taylor, *A Secular Age*, 309.
[33]Bernard J. Lonergan, "The Mediation of Christ in Prayer," *Philosophical and Theological Papers, 1958–1964*, Vol. 6, ed. Robert C. Croken, Frederick E. Crowe, and Robert M. Doran (Toronto: University of Toronto Press, 1996), 160–82 at 179.

above downwards. There is the transformation of falling in love: the domestic love of the family; the human love of one's tribe, one's country, mankind; the divine love that orientates man in his cosmos and expresses itself in worship.[34]

Human interiority is not just a capacity for self-reflection. It is a process by which we are faithful to the deepest and best inclinations of our mind and heart, by continual attention to how we respond. We do make mistakes, and we can reflect on them. We also experience being "in tune" with the world or another and find ourselves personally moved.[35] We can discover the basis of our misunderstandings and false judgments. Did we ignore important data? Did we jump to conclusions? We can learn to recognize our biases, prejudices, fears, and anxieties, and become aware of not just what we know but how we know. We can also become aware of the "common sense" we have received through living, and ask, is this really true? Interiority is developed through the complex relationships and opportunities which form us, and our response. Through interiority, we are constantly learning and unlearning about life, relationships, ourselves, and God. We not only experience life and learn from it, but interiority also engages us in a personal search for meaning within it. The life of the vows is not sequestered from our life as a whole, its history, and the people in it. Interaction with the world which formed us, as well as the world before us, forms the web of interrelationships in which the vows are lived.

Two Ways of Development

Lonergan's understanding of two ways of human development is based on his theory of knowing. While in places Lonergan's language can seem formal and abstract, its gift is that it describes internal processes we often perform automatically and without reflection. The web of interrelationships in which religious live the vows, however, is both internal and external. We will draw on his analysis, therefore, to help understand these dynamics.

Lonergan sees all human knowing as composed of four levels of conscious and intentional operations. Development from below upwards begins with an attentive experience of data, then moves from an understanding of the data to critical reflection on this understanding, and from critical reflection to responsible decision. Development from above downwards, on the other hand, begins with awareness of the meaning of responsible decision, critical reflection, intelligent understanding, and attentive

---

[34]Bernard Lonergan, "Healing and Creating in History," in *The Lonergan Reader*, ed. Mark D. Morelli and Elizabeth A. Morelli (Murray) (Toronto: University of Toronto Press, 1997), 106.
[35]Hartmut Rosa, *Resonance: A Sociology of Our Relationship to the World*, trans. James C. Wagner (Cambridge: Polity Press, 2019), 164–74.

experience through relationships and frameworks which shape one's life. This second way has its source in gift, but the first is the way of achievement.[36]

Lonergan speaks of this second way, practically and spiritually. At first look, it may seem that the second way is simply a consciousness of the spiritual, like being grateful. However, gifts "from above," as provided, include major dimensions of life like socialization and education. In his words, "By that process there is formed our initial mindset, a worldview or horizon. On that basis and with its limitation we slowly begin to become our own masters, think for ourselves, make our own decisions, exercise our own freedom and responsibility".[37]

Our interiority is the capacity to examine our own thinking and affirm or correct it. If we decide to move beyond what is considered common sense around us, we do so by calling on other levels of meaning in our life experience. Lonergan cites six realms of meaning as realities which correspond to the demands and desires of the human spirit to know what is real. They are the realms of common sense, theory, interiority, transcendence, scholarship, and art. No one of them is sufficient to provide all the meaning needed for human life.

The tradition and values which we receive from education and socialization impacts and shapes us in the Christian life, and therefore are to be welcomed. We learn settled patterns of cooperation, how to reach common agreements, and techniques to accomplish routine tasks. We receive such frameworks through our family and the manners they convey, society and education, the state and the law, the economy and technology, and the church. Each constitutes the commonly understood and already accepted basis and ways of cooperation. These aspects of life tend to change only slowly.

Change, as distinct from breakdown, involves a new common understanding and a new common consent.[38] At times, we sacralize these processes while also recognize they are inadequate in ways that fail to serve the human good. Frameworks such as family, church, and society throughout our lives appear as givens. Our response to adapt them to new circumstances engages us fundamentally in our own becoming. Our interiority helps us to integrate what we have already learned and continue to search for meaning, rather than just leave life unexamined. The role of the transcendent realm of meaning is key here, especially in religious life. In this realm, religious love comes to the fore. This is the realm where God is known and the deepest needs of the human spirit are fulfilled. Our task becomes to integrate what is ultimate in life with the givenness of life thus far, along with our achievements and mistakes, and then to respond.

The role of interiority, as a path to meaning, is critical in the life of a religious living in secular society, not only for the integrity of the individual but for the future of religious life. In a community, it is a lifelong task to grow in sensitivity to the various

---

[36] F. E. Crowe, *The Lonergan Enterprise* (Cambridge, MA: Cowley Publications, 1980), 72–3.
[37] Bernard J. Lonergan, SJ, "The Ongoing Genesis of Methods," in *A Third Collection: Papers by Bernard J.F. Lonergan*, SJ, ed. Frederick F. Crowe (New York: Paulist Press, 1985), 156.
[38] Bernard Lonergan, SJ, *Method in Theology* (Toronto: University of Toronto Press, 1990), 48.

experiences which have shaped those with whom we live and work. As religious, deepening understanding of the vows involves this same pattern of weighing received patterns, engaging with their core values in new circumstances, and believing in the guidance of the Spirit in new times. We make these adaptations not just alone; we engage with others beyond the boundaries of our communities. This requires attention to the gospel, charism, and church, the human sciences, and ultimately to the various ways God engages us in the interrelationships of life. We will continue to see how the web of interrelationships in which we live the vows are both external and internal.

The Idea of Mediation: Interrelationships and Responsibility

Again, Lonergan uses the more formal term "mediation" to describe what comes between a vision, such as "I desire a life well lived," and its manifestation in real life. Mediation is how such a goal is reached. The word "mediation" distinguishes a source, origin, or basis of something, like a life goal, from whatever results from it.[39] In Lonergan's framework, neither development from above nor from below is seamless. Positive development is a result of the desire to be authentic. Authenticity is the consistent struggle to be attentive, intelligent, reasonable, and responsible. However, the desire to be authentic can be overshadowed by conflicting desires not set on these aims. Authenticity is thwarted by inattentiveness, obtuseness, unreasonableness, and irresponsibility.[40]

The ongoing effort and capacity to reinvest one's life, to live out the desire to be authentic, to grow in knowledge and values, is self-mediation or responsibility. Some would include this as "inner work." It has tangible results in human development.[41] Attentiveness alerts the person to the practical information learned through the senses and then extends to the deeper information gleaned through awareness and consciousness. The first plunges the person into the real world of sense experience, learning how to do things. The second directs the person to notice the world of interiority, to notice what is happening as he or she acts. Such consciousness is expressed in our intentions. Intelligence opens the person to ask questions, and if not thwarted by bias, allows their questioning to continue unrestricted. Reasonableness calls the person to move beyond drifting and reach a conclusion. This requires the courage to ask questions like; Is the truth as I understand it, or is it not? We then raise the question of worth or value, which leads to the need to prioritize, to decide, and to act. We conclude, "If this is worth my effort, how do I begin?"

---

[39] Lonergan, "The Mediation of Christ in Prayer," 163.
[40] Lonergan, "Healing and Creating in History."
[41] *The Dynamism of Desire: Bernard J.F. Lonergan, S.J. on the Spiritual Exercises of Saint Ignatius of Loyola*, James J. Connor, SJ, and the fellows of the Woodstock Theological Center (Saint Louis: The Institute of Jesuit Sources, 2006). The aim of the Spiritual Exercises, according to Ignatius, is to order one's life toward achieving its end. See Chapter 2 "Authenticity and Self-Transcendence," 25–35. This involves the intention to follow "inbuilt laws by which humans can, with God's grace, transcend self-centered desire and reach out toward human authenticity and genuine Christian holiness." at 35.

This capacity of self-mediation, or doing our inner work, can also be crippled by our choices. Through bias, our own and that of others, we limit personal flourishing and authenticity, as well as that of others. Bias is the distortion or blockage of intellectual development, which affects individuals and groups. Bias can be dramatic, such as the unconscious motivation brought to light by depth psychology, which can block the individual from an insight that he or she needs. There is the bias of individual egoism, which will limit an individual's questioning to only those things which contribute to one's own point of view. Every new situation is limited to the exploitation of his or her need. Group egoism is the corporate blindness used by a group to ignore a situation, fail to deal with the problem, or dismiss a remedy simply because it could limit its power. Finally, there is general bias or the insistence on an immediate result, which leads us to forsake working toward values and goals which are long in coming. The interrelationships of a vowed life include the relationship of self-mediation, or doing one's inner work, as well as a congregation doing the same. Lonergan's insight counters the popular but false view of religious life as handing over personal responsibility to another, or a group's assumption that if everyone seems to agree on a decision, it must be right.

Mutual Self-Mediation: The Web of Community, Charism, Church, and the Earth

The path to wholeness as human authenticity involves more than personal desire and individual integrity, or self-mediation. For Christians, the core of individual integrity occurs in the web of relationships with God, community, neighbor, and the earth.[42] This is "mutual self-mediation"— the self alone is not a sufficient arbitrator of the task. To live religious life within a wider cultural matrix requires that discernment is done by communities. To test what is novel and dubious, to drop that which has been made sacred and should not be, to reject what is destructive and to give hospitality to what is welcomed requires that every generation of religious life examine its internal and external life. Often, chapters and assemblies are the ordinary means by which this is done formally. The charism of a religious community gives direction to this process. These public dimensions of the vowed life are expressed within a web of interrelationships.

Religious move from individual action to communal action through the influence of their charism. Every religious needs to clarify what is to be welcomed, rejected, given hospitality, and desacralized in their culture through their daily choices. This personal attentiveness brings depth to communal decisions. What does it mean to be a good Dominican, Franciscan, or Jesuit? Charism helps a religious consider not only the works

---

[42]See Daniel Castillo, "'To Praise, Reverence, and Serve': The Theological Anthropology of Pope Francis," in *The Theological and Ecological Vision of Laudato Si*, ed. Vincent J. Miller (London: T&T Clark, 2017), 95–108. Margaret Scott, "Greening the Vows: *Laudato Si* and Religious Life," *The Way* 54, no. 4 (October 2015), 83–93.

of their mission but also what it stands for as a contribution to human becoming. Often charism serves to distinguish not between good and bad but between goods and priorities. Theologian John Haughey remarks that while "charisms are notoriously elusive," we can reflect on some patterns they share with other creativity in history.[43] Charisms are God's way of building up families, communities, parishes, schools, hospitals, agencies, the Church, but also businesses, neighborhoods, cities, and even international relations. Charisms function where there are human needs.

The charisms in the church today, including those of religious congregations, go beyond Paul's mention of them solely in an ecclesial framework (1 Cor. 12:7). Vatican II clarified that charisms are to be expressed not only in the church but also in the wider society (*AA* 3). A special role for congregations arising from the Synod is their place in facilitating the incorporation of the charisms of laypeople in new ways in the church

Charism in History

Charism offers communities direction on how to proceed. Religious life, as a historical legacy of monasticism, belongs to the charismatic structure of the church. Its beginnings in Christian life gave the Church a language to speak of charism not simply as a possession of individuals, a dimension of the Church, but as a structure in the church. Early monastic communities were seen as charismatic communitarian expressions within the church and as something new. By the Middle Ages, the word "charism," translated into Latin in the Vulgate, was often referred to as *gratia* or "grace" or "gift." Theology in the Middle Ages stressed the work of the Holy Spirit to inhabit us, to dwell within, to innovate us, to make us new. In modern terms, the Holy Spirit leads not only individuals to authenticity but communities as well. In his study on grace, Thomas Aquinas distinguishes what we know today as charism from other graces or gifts from God mentioned throughout the New Testament. In the *Summa Theologica* he wrote:

> According, grace is of two kinds. Firstly, there is the grace by which man himself is united to God and this is called sanctifying grace (*gratia gratium faciens*). Secondly there is the grace by which one man cooperates with another so that he might be brought back to God. Now this kind of grace is called freely bestowed grace (*gratia gratis data*).[44]

Theologians today agree on the identification of *gratia gratis data* with charism.[45]

---

[43]John Haughey, "Charisms: An Ecclesiological Exploration," in *Retrieving Charisms for the 21st Century*, ed. Doris Donnelly (Collegeville, MN: The Liturgical Press, 1999), 1–2.
[44]See *Summa Theologica*, I, II, 3,4, and II qq. 171–8.
[45]Albert Vanhoye, SJ, "The Biblical Question of 'Charisms' after Vatican II," in *Vatican II: Assessments and Perspectives: Twenty-Five Years After (1962-1987)*, Vol. I, ed. Rene Latourelle (Mahwah, NJ: Paulist Press, 1988), 439–88 at 441.

The distinction between grace given to sanctify the individual and grace given to foster the common good points to how religious life in the church is both a charismatic structure in the church and involves a personal path to wholeness beyond self-improvement alone. Religious life as a lifestyle is a bridge between the sacred and the secular. Religious provide this bridge, or witness, through their collaboration in community as both a path to God and service to neighbor. In addition, their mission is to foster the common good of the church, community, the earth, and society. Ultimately, they are to serve as a sign or witness to God's creative love in history and society through the Holy Spirit.

The relationship between religious congregations and the *saeculum* is addressed by John Paul II. He identified the bond between church and culture as marked by transcendence and compenetration.[46] The living out of the charism of a religious congregation is marked by transcendence since it is an unfolding of the gift of God's presence in our lives. Yet its expression in ministry is characterized by compenetration. While essentially religious, it takes on real forms in the everyday life of the church and society; it forms the *saeculum* in which both the believer and unbeliever lives. It mediates a religious identity, mainly through its affirmation of human dignity. It does so within the web of interrelationships between culture, religion, and the affirmation of transcendence to which they witness. Charism functions in the various ministries of the church in its offices, in the services it provides as church to its members and beyond; as well as in the broader mission of the church to the world. The charism of a religious congregation is expressed not just individually but communally. It is one expression of the charismatic life of the church, one means by which the church is involved in the daily life of every socio-political reality.[47] Religious life is more than the search for personal wholeness; it also witnesses that it is possible to "touch wholeness" through service to others. It is a public witness to the divine in secular society.

The vows of religious life form a gestalt or path of being in the world, lived in a web of internal and external interrelationships which include self-mediation or interiority and the work of mutual self-mediation in community. The vows clarify one's place in the world, an adult lifestyle, and shape choices regarding material goods, relationships, and power within the network of relationships. Fidelity to the values of the vows has personal, communal, and public dimensions. Openness to the questions which arise from within each century makes possible the integration of gospel values into each dimension of living and feeds the initiative to respond. At its core, religious life is not fully understood without the lens of faith, which grounds the Christian life, religious life, and the life of the vows, and is deeply linked to the identity of Jesus Christ.

---

[46]"Compenetration" is a term used by John Courtney Murray, SJ, stating that as the church is engaged in its religious ministry, it should be engaged in the daily life of every socio-political entity. See Judith A. Merkle, *From the Heart of the Church: The Catholic Social Tradition* (Collegeville, MN: The Liturgical Press, 2004), 236ff.
[47]Judith A. Merkle, *Beyond Our Lights and Shadows: Charism and Institution in the Church* (London: T&T Clark, 2016), 126.

Mutual Self-Mediation through Another: Jesus Christ

Religious life engages one in life in community. Because we are human, there are limits to our understanding of one another in community life. Living many years in a community with someone does not necessarily mean you know them at a deeper level. Members often rely on the public aspects of a person's story: their place of origin, their education, their accomplishments, the personality they have encountered in public events. Positive and negative perceptions of each other are inseparable from belonging to a group.

Living and ministry opportunities often provide more associations with some members of the community. Shared history, sometimes decades in the making, also creates lifelong relationships and familiarity, which form a true blessing of religious life.

At another level, the community provides one framework for the development of friendship. The journey of self-discovery and self-communication is personal, its own story. This knowledge is not the property of everyone; it is known only if the person shares it. Living together provides a framework to learn aspects of another's personal story; others are communicated in friendship. With those few, a person shares an intimacy and a mutual confidence not experienced with the many.[48] In a variety of relationships between the few and the many, a religious grows and develops in the community and finds a home. A religious also forms friendships through ministry, family, and broader associations.

The human experience of finding oneself incomplete and needing others raises the question of belonging in the Christian life. For a woman religious, entering a religious order is more than belonging to the girl scouts as a child. For a male religious, membership in a congregation is more than a professional move, where one joins an association with others for a common purpose. As important as our horizontal relationships are in the web of relationships in religious life, community life also forms part of the theological unfolding of life itself.

In the Christian life, we hold that deep in the process of becoming myself is Christ mediating to us the Father (1 Tim. 2:5) and the Holy Spirit mediating to us Jesus Christ (1 Cor. 12:3). Christ's presence in the Christian life is as real as the perimeters of one's birth certificate or career path. My human experience is more than a narrative of a passage from birth to death; grace is mediated through it. Personal experiences of grace engage a person in the deepest meaning of being human, yet can remain unconscious unless brought to awareness.[49] St Paul remarks, "Or do you not know that your body is a temple of the Holy Spirit within you, which you have from God, and that you are not your own? For you were bought with a great price, therefore glorify God in your body" (1 Cor. 6:19-20). Over the course of a lifetime, the challenge to a religious is both to

---

[48] See Lonergan, "The Mediation of Christ in Prayer, 177–81.

[49] This is the core meaning of Karl Rahner's supernatural existential, the fact that God has graced human beings through creation with the potential to act in a supernatural way. Karl Rahner, *Foundations of the Christian Faith: An Introduction to the Idea of Christianity* (New York: Herder and Herder, 1978).

become themselves and to know, love, and serve God within the very concreteness of their history and becoming. They take responsibility for their lives and its direction in self-mediation. Yet this also occurs in relationship to another reality. Lonergan explains this as "supernatural realities that do not pertain to our nature, that result from the communication to us of Christ's life."[50] This is a path of personal development in relation to another person, but different from a relationship between equals, as with a husband and wife or in friendship. It is to follow Jesus Christ, who as human also developed and acquired human perfection, but also in relationship to his Father, whom he named as Abba. Lonergan summarizes:

> One becomes oneself not just by experiences, insights, and judgments but by choices, decisions, conversion, not just freely and deliberately. not just deeply and strongly, but as one who is carried along. One is doing so not in isolation, but in reference to Christ. The Father predestined us to be conformed to Christ, through the example of Christ. Consequently, there is an element not merely of personal development, but of personal development in relation to another person.[51]

This development of the person in relation to another person is not only a self-mediation through another but also a mutual self-mediation. When Christ made his choices through his life, He did so in relationship to the Father, but also in his relationship to the concrete others in his own life, the others who are also us and all men and women. In a world where science often dictates what is real, the concreteness and the mystery of this relationship take us into mystery. We are not just impersonal souls trapped in matter as once held; rather, our human transcendence participates in the web of our interrelationships and carries matter into the Absolute mystery—into God's personal love. In the next chapter we will explore this reality and its relationship to the vows.

---

[50]Lonergan, "The Mediation of Christ in Prayer," 178.
[51]Ibid., 180.

CHAPTER 3
TOUCHING WHOLENESS IN A WOUNDED WORLD

After the resurrection, the apostle Thomas struggled with his relationship with Jesus as well as with the direction of his life. In some ways, the struggle of Thomas reflects the search for many religious today. The Jesus that Thomas knew and followed was dead. The life that he had hoped to find with him seemed to be over. While Thomas still valued the life he found with Jesus, he knew it more by absence and longing than through certainty. The good that he wanted to accomplish appeared out of reach. The testimony of others, the apostles, that they had seen Jesus, and he was alive, was not convincing. Thomas made this clear: "Unless I see the mark of the nails in his hands and put my finger in the mark of the nails and my hand in his side, I will not believe" (Jn 20:24). Thomas needed a mediation—a connection—a new pathway—to continue his following of Jesus.[1]

Religious today find their lives at a similar crossroad. The cultural change, especially in its posture toward religion, the decline in the impact and size of the congregations, and uncertainty regarding the future, creates a perplexity as to the way ahead and the meaning of religious life today. For Thomas, the intimacy of touching Jesus' wounds overcame the impasse which negated the possibility of new life. Jesus transformed Thomas' unbelief to belief through his invitation to touch.

Religious today are invited also to touch the wounds of the resurrected Christ through their touch of the wounds of the world and of their own humanity. This mediation or pathway of encounter with suffering and contradiction is paradoxically not a confrontation of what leads away from belief in God, as culture might suggest. Rather, it is essential to the ongoing integration and fulfillment to which a life of the vows embraces.[2] In the following, we will unpack how such an encounter fosters an understanding of the vows of religious life.

---

[1] Bernard J. Lonergan, "The Mediation of Christ in Prayer," in *Philosophical and Theological Papers, 1958–1964*, Vol. 6, ed. Robert C. Croken, Frederick E. Crowe, and Robert M. Doran (Toronto: University of Toronto Press, 1996), 160–82 at 163.
[2] Hartmut Rosa, *Resonance: A Sociology of Our Relationship to the World*, trans. James C. Wagner (Cambridge: Polity Press, 2019), 134. Rosa argues that having a strong evaluation of something, the sense that a reality places a demand on you, and can move you, is necessary to respond to a contradiction of that value and act in a transformative way. Strong evaluations are senses of what is good which are beyond personal desires or preferences. The vowed life is centered in strong evaluations as gospel values which form the possibility of its transformation.

Rahner: Jesus Christ in an Evolutionary Framework

The Great Chain of Being of the ancient and medieval world is considered by many as naïve and uncritical. Yet moderns long for its certainty in their search for wholeness and meaning today. Before a world that appears fragmented, people search for a worldview that is coherent and in tune with modern sensibilities. Science alone has not provided it, yet its wisdom cannot be left out of any synthesis. Neo-Darwinian biology certainly offered insights into physical reality, which was once relegated to the mysterious. Evolution has shown that created reality from its very beginning has undergone a continual process of change. Today scientists claim that what we know as living species is only 1 percent of what has already existed on this earth.[3] These facts lead us to understand reality differently than it was viewed in classical times. Instead of being passive observers in a fixed world of natures which revealed the intentions of God, we live in a world for which we are responsible and interconnected with all its parts. Pope Francis reminds us in *Laudato Si* of our "ecological citizenship." This awareness in the Christian life impacts our relationship with self, one another, God, and the world itself. It translates into a call for ecological conversion by which, for Christians, their encounter with Jesus Christ should "become evident in their relationship with the world around them" (*LS* 217). The world in this sense is not something out there but a reality intimate to our lives. The world is that which is already given prior to our consciousness of it. Men and women find themselves always embedded in and related to the world as a whole. They are objects in the world and yet are those for whom the world can become an issue. Our being in the world therefore seeks a relationship with the world in which we desire that it makes sense to us, and speaks to us, as well as we aspire to engage the world and influence it. We do not find God by leaving the world but through it.

With Kant, most theologians would agree that it is not possible to experience God as an object in the world like other sensible objects, like a flower or the human body. Rather, an implication of the inwardness of the modern person is the presence of self-consciousness that allows one to become aware of the wider horizon of everything we know. At the same time, I know about a period of English literature, I am aware there is so much more to learn. In other words, a broader horizon of knowing remains in the face of everything I learn.

Karl Rahner based his theology on this awareness of human consciousness and knowing. He claimed that human inwardness or subjectivity has a primary attribute: it is oriented to a universal, dynamic orientation toward Reality/Being itself. He called this, theologically, the supernatural existential—a universal attribute of human nature.[4] All human beings are "hot-wired" to the infinite, God, simply because they exist. If

---

[3]Terrence P. Ehrman, CSC, "Ecology: The Science of Interconnections," in *The Theological and Ecological Vision of Laudato Si*, ed. Vincent J. Miller (London: T&T Clark, 2017), 51–73 at 52.
[4]See Karl Rahner, "Relationship between Nature and Grace: The Supernatural Existential," in *A Rahner Reader*, ed. Gerald A. McCool (New York: Crossroad, 1975), 185–90 at 185.

scripture testifies that God created human beings in God's own image and likeness, then God's offer of grace, relationship, must impact human nature itself with the capacity to respond—to accept or reject this offer. This orientation toward the infinite flows from our experience of inwardness/self-consciousness, as it seeks to know the world around it. It extends beyond any empirical experience of sensing an object. Transcendental consciousness, the sense of the more behind every learning and choice, is not something I can grasp; rather, it is a field of unbounded awareness within which all that can be encountered is manifest. Humans cannot know God as the Absolute, directly, but they can become aware of a Reality which is nonempirical, which is present and mediated within this horizon of consciousness itself. This awareness is confirmed in what we call religious experience, and its sense of conviction and commitment.[5] Christian revelation, community, rituals, and the church confirm that an Absolute being exists who can provide total fulfillment in response to the holy longing of the human spirit. God's revelation always comes through a means grounded in sensible experience. Rahner calls experience categorical, or sensible, in time, concrete when it comes through the world, or in the inwardness of one's own consciousness. While he refers to the wider horizon of knowing, the Absolute, as transcendental.

Karl Rahner understood the problems that someone with an evolutionary outlook would have with traditional understandings of Jesus Christ. Modern people understand Jesus of the gospels through his humanity, as it is closer to their experience of daily life and the path they know to become familiar with him. In every era, Christians face the problem of how to connect Jesus of Nazareth to the Christ of faith. How does one connect Jesus to the world-centering Logos, the meaning of all we know as created and testified to in the first chapter of John's gospel? For a person with an evolutionary mindset, they ask how can someone who had to be part of an evolutionary process have genes, be made up of atoms also be called God (Col. 1:15-17)? To understand how Jesus is both divine and human has something to do with how men and women today can be in touch with the Absolute while being enmeshed in the material world. Rahner responded to this challenge.

He held that God's main intention is to communicate and be in relationship with human beings. The reason for creation and the incarnation is the desire for this self-communication in grace. Matter and spirit are not opposed; they are one. They come from the same source. Both created by God and inseparable in the human person.[6] In evolutionary thought, human nature is precisely the place in the evolutionary chain where the tendency of nature to come to self-consciousness takes place. Christian faith testifies that human wholeness or fruition is deeply and thoroughly a matter of grace. In an evolutionary mindset this means that God's own loving engagement both in human affairs and in evolutionary natural history are key to their meaning. Evolutionary

---

[5]Stephen Duffy, *The Graced Horizon* (Collegeville: The Liturgical Press, 1992), 209.
[6]For this explanation, I rely in part on a very helpful exposition of Rahner's thought by Denise Carmody, "Christology in Karl Rahner's Evolutionary View," *Religion in Life* 49, no. 2 (January 1980): 185–210 at 195.

development has gone on for numberless years as a matter of interaction with a divinity that has loved the world and communicated with it. Human self-understanding and direction epitomize the strivings of prehuman evolutionary history. The potential for inwardness that we can glimpse even in the lower levels of life is finally actualized and takes place in human nature.

The incarnation is where God's self-communication fully discloses itself. Logos joins itself to Jesus' human nature, in the hypostatic union. In this, the process of material evolution toward self-consciousness, the tendency of matter to discover itself in spirit reaches a climax. Rahner claims there is nothing more qualitative for evolution, matter, or human spirit to accomplish than total self-transcendence and fulfillment in substantial identification with the divine nature. In other words, the incarnation of God is the unique and supreme actualization of human reality. Men and women enter the wholeness which grounds all of creation, in so far as they give themselves up in love.[7] Since God's own loving engagement marks human affairs, it is only in contact, connection, and cooperation with such engagement that human self-transcendence takes place. In Rahner's terms, the God-Man is the initial beginning and the definitive triumph of the world's self-transcendence into the Absolute closeness to the mystery of God.[8] The theological goal of evolution is divinization, radical closeness to the creative, mysterious energy and goodness called God. Revelation does not take away the Absolute mystery in which this is shrouded. Rather, there is a unity of creation, all things are created by the same God, the same originating power. Matter and spirit equally stem from the one God. Their unity, which is the basis of matter's tendency to discover itself in Spirit, has its basis in their common source. In this sense, the unity of Jesus' humanity leans toward showing the unity of spirit and matter in humanity.[9] Matter is not the enemy of the spirit. We become who we are, inseparably linked with matter, by our orientation to the Absolute mystery of God. We become who we are by being moved, contacted, taken up by Absolute mystery. In other words, we are not impersonal souls trapped in matter. Our human transcendence carries matter into the Absolute mystery—God's personal love.

Spirit bears matter to its destiny, while matter serves the spirit by anchoring it in the world with a certain givenness. Since we live in time and space, we cannot summarize ourselves in one complete act or grasp who we are totally. In this sense we experience a type of alienation, an inability to completely communicate ourselves, to know others, and be known. As Francis of Assisi said, "Who are you my God, and who am I?" Yet on the other hand, matter is the basis of our communication, a way we participate in human meaning and warmth. Alienation, though, is also a possibility. It extends to the human capacity to say no to God's summons to participate in love and goodness and embrace God's call to transcendence and wholeness. The very essence of our relationship

---

[7] See "On the Theology of the Incarnation," in *A Rahner Reader*, ed. Gerald A. McCool (New York: Crossroad, 1975), 145–53 at 146.
[8] Karl Rahner, *Foundations of Christian Faith*, trans. William V. Dych (New York: Crossroad, 1982), 161.
[9] Carmody, "Christology in Karl Rahner's Evolutionary View," 198.

to God is freedom, the free offer of God's love to us, the offer of God's very person and our free response. The horizon (God), which makes freedom of choice possible, becomes itself the object of a decision.[10] God becomes the object of this choice—not directly but indirectly. The decision about God takes place in decisions about finite things, since God is ultimately present in every act of choice as its ground and goal. God is the ground of the world, of other persons and our own essential nature. Insofar as we say no to this finite reality and its truth, we say no to God. Freedom is always mediated by our materiality, time, and space, and our moment of history.[11] This understanding of the human person makes each man and woman both justified and a sinner. The Christian is a sinner because of the ingrained self-love which leads to sin and its habitual imperfection. Yet the Christian is also justified because Christ's grace within contends against this sinfulness. Human dependence on the grace of Christ thus is essential for any progress in the spiritual life. In Rahner's words, "On the one hand, we are in fact sinners who hope always to be allowed to escape again out of their sinfulness into the mercy of God. On the other hand, there is justice, and if it is really in us through God's grace, it is always also threatened and tempered and hidden from us."[12] To grasp what it means to touch wholeness through the wounds of the world involves finding a center in the world, where we experience brokenness as well as transformation. In religious life, Jesus Christ is central to this search. Touching wholeness entails the capacity to see goodness along with evil and alienation—not just "out there" in structures but within—as we acknowledge the impasse in our lives and relationships. Finally, to touch wholeness through engaging the wounds of our world requires us, as it did the early Christians, to give a reason for our hope.

Justification

There is an ambiguity, common in modern society, regarding the place of sin in human life. Awareness that all is not right with the world is a universal experience. Yet modernity's belief in human perfectibility makes it difficult to identify the disarray which confronts humanity and the earth. Many drift away from any serious consideration of the validity of sin and evil or its impact on their lives. Some struggle with the effects of a pedagogy of sinfulness, which blinded them to their own goodness. Others are so aware of sinful structures that they lose touch with their links to the destructive impulses of humans themselves. Medical, psychological, and sociological learning has given us a broader

---

[10] Karl Rahner, "The Dignity and Freedom of Man," in *Theological Investigations* II, trans. Karl-H. Kruger (New York: Crossroad, 1990), 235–63 at 247.
[11] Ron Highfield, "Freedom to Say No? Karl Rahner's Doctrine of Sin," *Theological Studies* 56 (1985): 485–505 at 487.
[12] Karl Rahner, "Justified and Sinner at the Same Time," in *Theological Investigations* VI, trans. Karl-H. Kruger (New York: Crossroad, 1982), 218–30 at 228.

context for understanding human behavior, yet moderns struggle with a language for malice and its impact on human responsibility.[13]

Theologically, at the time of the Reformation, the doctrine humans are both justified and sinners received two interpretations from different sectors of Christianity. Reformed Christianity emphasized the radical turn from sin toward God necessary for the Christian life. The human person cannot save herself or himself by their own power. Grace, justification, and salvation arise from God's mercy alone. Human beings are always and everywhere dependent on this justifying mercy of God. "The man of the Reformation always stands and continues to stand as a sinner vis-à-vis God."[14] Through faith and hope, despite awareness of sinfulness, the Christian places an unlimited trust in God. Through this trust, men and women know they are saved.

The Catholic response is justification causes something new to happen which cannot exist "simultaneously" with the old state. Salvation-history is true history and an individual history of salvation. This means something happens and takes place which is now and was not before. The human person is a new creation. The emphasis in Catholic theology is not on our experience of justification but on God's action and deed. "God's own power alone is the really effective and decisive factor in the justification of man."[15] The emphasis here is on God's action and God's assurance to men and women which grasps them and interiorly changes them. Rather than being suspended in a dialectic between sinfulness and holiness, through the grace of justification, the Christian has crossed the boundary of sin and death and can draw on this grace to allow God's action to become effective in them, despite the pull of sin.

Pope Francis draws on this consciousness of sin and the ability to respond in *Laudato Si*. His message challenges religious in their process of renewal. While our awareness of care of creation is dimmed by spiritual, cultural, political, and economic habits and sensibilities that prevent us from seriously engaging with the challenges. This is not the whole picture. Before us, the challenge to do better is based on our awareness of the capacity to do so. We can become aware of our unwillingness to pay attention to the deeper values needed to shape our lives and the world today. We note in the North the fragmentation and alienation which flows from superficial living and over-dependence on social media and the digital world. We can move away from superficiality, which is a distraction from the real tasks before us, and a comfort zone which keeps us from the true dialogue needed in our communities and attention to the concerns of the poor. *Laudato Si* "makes the case for a moral-spiritual web of concerns, borne of our willingness and capacity to pay attention to one another and the world we share . . . Our capacity to see and cherish the world for what it is, whole and unbroken and holy,

---

[13]Two popular books which explore this dilemma are classics: Karl Menninger, *Whatever Became of Sin?* (New York: Bantam Books, 1978). Scott Peck, *People of the Lie: The Hope for Healing Human Evil* (Greenwich, CT: Touchstone Books, 1998).
[14]Rahner, "Justified and Sinner at the Same Time," 220.
[15]Ibid., 222.

enables us to respond to it more thoughtfully and carefully."[16] This capacity is a gift, an outgrowth of our baptism as Christians. Religious can touch wholeness in a world of broken and transformed relationships because of this grounding.

Evolutionary Christology and Interconnections

Christian faith holds that since God has entered into the constitution of cosmic and human history, it now has a divine pledge of definitive achievement through the gift of salvation and peace. The cosmic importance of grace is that the world has in a measure already received its fulfillment through the immediate self-gift of God as its ground.[17] This is the eschatological dimension of the Christian life. Whenever a person investigates the abyss of mystery of the world as we find it, which apart from grace could be horrid and void, and surrenders trustingly, the spirit of love is actively present. Rahner sees humanity coming into the evolutionary process where transcendent nature comes to the threshold of taking over more of its own development, trying consciously to increase its growth into a fuller being. We are called to move beyond survival, as Benedict XVI reminds us. We as a church have a mission to contribute shared visions and institutional expressions for which we have few precedents to a new civilization (*CV* 24, 25, 26).

An evolutionary understanding of Jesus Christ impacts an approach to the vows in religious life as it reflects a spirituality of religious life in a new era. Religious are more than agents of exclusive humanism, people who seek to make the world a better place through their own efforts alone. Theologically, the shaping of the matter of our institutions and culture is part of the broader mystery of matter joined with spirit, going beyond itself. This self-transcendence, aimed at the good of others and creation itself, expresses itself along the line between our autonomy and our dependence on God, our action and our passive endurance, our doing and receiving. It testifies to our collaboration with God's own action in the world. In face of all the complexities that divide every person's and communities' life, we seek to develop and tap into that power from within, which is confirmed by God's own promise. This struggle for the more is intrinsic to one's time and history, and to the embedded presence and context of each congregation. Since God's love and presence penetrate to the core all the becoming in life, newness and history are not autonomous but theonomous—not indicated solely by its own will but shaped by God's presence and care.[18]

---

[16]Douglas E. Christie, "Becoming Painfully Aware: Spirituality and Solidarity in *Laudato Si*," in *The Theological and Ecological Vision of Laudato Si*, ed. Vincent J. Miller (London: T&T Clark, 2017), 109–26 at 116.
[17]Carmody, "Christology in Karl Rahner's Evolutionary View," 201.
[18]Ibid., 199.

The Vows of Religious Life in a Secular Society

Touching Wholeness in a Wounded World

A sense of salvation as wholeness sheds light on how wholeness can be encountered through engagement in a wounded world. This adds an important insight into the understanding of the vows.[19] Salvation is the restoration of God's creation to wholeness. The life of the vows can be understood as a mediation or pathway of openness and participation in this ongoing act of salvation in the world of today. Salvation in human life includes the restoration of the whole human person—materially, spiritually, interpersonally, socially, and politically, and the social conditions which make this possible. The life of vows engages in all these dimensions of life. The encounters in these facets of human living invite religious throughout life to know and love Jesus Christ. We do this as we foster human dignity for others and experience the healing of our own woundedness and limitations. Religious life is counter-cultural today in its witness that union with God is core, not counter, to the development of human freedom and fulfillment, as well as healing and creating in history.

Salvation and its meaning are eschatological; it speaks to the ultimate goal and end of human life. We experience the fingerprints of salvation wherever human beings experience freedom and fullness of life. However, we only "touch" it; we never encounter the experience of salvation fully. Theologian Edward Schillebeeckx claims this is not because it is impossible on earth but because salvation is so far incomplete in terms of our experience. Human salvation continues to be brought about through the cooperation of God and human beings acting for the good of humanity. As people struggle for authenticity and integrity to become men and women of service in ministry, people of faith recognize God-given salvation in their effort. Human action alone is not enough to bring about the fullness of salvation. Salvation is more than human beings can imagine or accomplish. We are always partial in our attempts to bring about the Kingdom and often can only perceive its possibility in hope.[20]

Jesus announced and referred to the restored world, the fullness of healing and creating in history, as the Kingdom of God. Our own belief in the integrity of creation can set us free for our intended tasks in the world: to love creation as creation and to love God as creator. This means we love ourselves and other human beings as created, finite, and contingent creatures who are always "on the way," invited to growth and capable of making mistakes. A life of the vows is one embedded in the human condition. We are not freed from our finitude, as finitude is part of the condition of being created. Our finitude is the condition of possibility of our capacity to relate to God and others. God's creative work is incomplete and will culminate with the full restoration of the world through love; not perfect love but love as embodied in the real world. The path to the

---

[19] Julie Feder, "Salvation," in *T and T Clark Reader in Edward Schillebeeckx*, ed. Stephen Van Erp and Daniel Minch (London: T&T Clark, 2023), 155–6.
[20] Judith A. Merkle, *From the Heart of the Church: The Catholic Social Tradition* (Collegeville, MN: The Liturgical Press, 2004), 55–9.

Kingdom is not pre-ordained. It is up to us to create paths of healing and creating in history, in union and cooperation with God. Religious unite with imperfect others, in an imperfect world, as we pray with all Christians, Thy Kingdom Come. We can be sure that the Kingdom is on the way because evil and oppression can have no transcendent future. Goodness and evil are not equal forces. Only goodness can have a future beyond death.[21] Religious witness to this eschatological promise that all things will be restored through their investment in what can be brought about in the present. The mission of apostolic religious congregations for the future is to find their role to restore the communion with God, others, and with creation itself, which is needed to foster the Kingdom in their circumstances.

Touching Wholeness in a Wounded World in the Web of Community

When Thomas encountered Jesus he did so in community. It is interesting to note that Jesus could have met Thomas in many ways, in a dream, in a prayer, alone on a solitary walk. But the gospel story shows Thomas meeting Jesus among the apostles as they gathered, yet through an individual encounter which was his alone. The gospel here provides an icon of community life. The communal dimension of the vowed life counters the postmodern theories of the self, which claim that pluralism and fragmentation in modern life overwhelms the possibility of community. The mediation of the other in religious life cannot be compared to the partnership of a lifelong other in marriage. Yet the mediation of community in religious life is a concrete factor in becoming. The vows are not simply personal practices in the spiritual life of an individual. Even though some forms of consecrated life may interpret the vows as lived in other contexts,[22] we will treat them as part of the gestalt of community life, as one finds in religious institutes. Community as found in religious life is not the only type of community, but for those called to it, it is an essential element of their life path.

The experience of a healthy community in both life and ministry helps the religious decenter from the self-structures developed in early life and move toward a more integral version of the self.[23] Life in community should foster a growth in maturity. The self-transcendence of vowed commitment can lead to enhanced moral sensibilities, a sense of personal identity, greater internal freedom, greater self-control, deeper insight into self and others, empathy, compassion, and generativity. These prosocial behaviors become dimensions also of greater freedom in one's relationship with God. The bridge between the sacred and the secular is fostered through the ministry of religious—often

---

[21] Feder, "Salvation," 156.
[22] See *Consecratio et Consecratio per Evangelica Consilia*, Proceedings of the International Seminar. Pontifical University Antonianum. Rome, 1-March 3, 2018. Congregation for the Institutes of Consecrated Life and the Societies of Apostolic Life. (Vatican City: Libreria Editrice Vaticana, 2019).
[23] See Mary Frohlich, *Breathed into Wholeness: Catholicity and Life in the Spirit* (Maryknoll, NY: Orbis Books, 2019), 75–98 at 90.

not by a group but by the presence of an individual or a few. Additionally, religious do not minister solely in the context of their own institutions. In this sense, the capacity of a religious to be free as a human being, free from their own compulsions and preoccupations, is often the measure by which they can be effective in fostering and cooperating to create a greater wholeness of life with others.

Religious can learn how to be effective in building community wherever they are. Community in religious life is a broader experience which includes but transcends the parochial community of past decades. Ministry involves unifying relationships with diverse human groupings, as well as prophetic action to name and act against what is dehumanizing. Neither of which can be accomplished by a self in community that is closed to personal transformation. This growth is fostered by both a spiritual life and life with others. The type of social, political, and ecological world called for today requires decentered people who can act with a balance of surrender and control in community. The life of the vows should foster this type of person.

When Thomas encountered Jesus, Jesus prepared him for the days when he would not be seeing him face to face. "Jesus said to him, 'Have you believed because you have seen me? Blessed are those who have not seen and yet have come to believe'" (Jn 20:29). We find the apostles next by the Sea of Tiberias, and Thomas the Twin was with them. He is not apart, nor is he the doubtful dissenter; he is among. It is often beyond the patterns of our personal lives amid the ebb and flow of community life that we are challenged to recognize the presence of Christ. In the context of the societal and ecclesial times in which we live, however, religious face new challenges regarding community life. Ministerial life requires more independence and autonomy than in previous generations, so how do we strengthen the bonds among us? We search today for the skills which support a sustainable communal life across the globe. What new patterns are required for life both embedded in a culture as well as global in its concerns? What is our role in sustaining, healing, and transforming the church at this juncture in secular society? Do we imagine ourselves living in a triumphant church or a marginal one, seeking its place in secular society? Are we called to help the church resolve its dysfunctions with society, or will we join the various forms of organized religion which hijack Christianity in the name of exclusion and power? How do we adopt the mission of dialogue and accompaniment in a wounded world? It seems today that the challenge to religious is a task for all in the church. Members are called to make sense out of this world and work to pass to the next generation a better world than they found. In embracing this task, they seek a wholeness in their lives which keeps in balance dimensions of human life which are contested and in tension in the lives of all as they respond to their world. We will explore how the vows touch on these areas.

The Challenge of Autonomy and Plurality (Obedience)

Rahner understands human freedom, or autonomy, to be, at its roots, the capacity for definitive self-disposal before God. However, modern culture approaches freedom differently. Cultural ideals both confirm and contradict ideas of human freedom in the Christian life. Positively, freedom is our capacity to bring about change. Freedom is the power to plan and invent, to harness the powers of the universe or market and create a better life. In modern culture, this view of freedom is linear and developmental. A free person progresses in a successive straight line of forward movement, usually one of upward mobility. A Hallmark graduation card will offer a congratulatory message for one achievement and an anticipation of a future one.

How does this view of freedom measure up to the gospel? We find a developmental view of life confirmed in the gospel: "And Jesus increased in wisdom and in years, and in divine and human favor" (Lk. 2:52). Yet a difference between a gospel worldview and that of modern culture is that freedom is set only in an immanent frame; this world is all there is. In addition, a backdrop to the modern view is a theory of progress. It envisions the course of history resting on the dynamism that the wants of one generation will be the needs of the next. Belief in the inevitability of progress and the insatiability of material wants is an invisible dimension of modern society (*LS* 11,82).[24] This "certainty" is primarily an economic one, which outshadows any transcendent view of life and its purposes.[25]

Freedom in the cultural view of life is also individualistic. It assumes individuals have the "right" to do what they want, when they want, and if they want. Freedom means the right to impose one's will to meet goals within the law, without interference from the church, the state, or the needs of others. Money and power raise the likelihood a person can execute this right. Autonomy in American culture is described by sociologist Robert Bellah as the capacity to be free from the influence of others.[26] The source of life values is simply that of personal choice.

Criticism of these views of freedom has been around for decades; however, today we are facing a deeper dimension of the fissures in civilization which they have caused. These are not just personal beliefs espoused by a few; they are images of how the world works, what counts, what our obligations are to each other, and what we can expect from life. Theologian Dorothee Soelle states it clearly:

> We live in a fragmented world which has a center and a periphery. In the center, where we live, life is productive and worth living. In the periphery, a place far from us, life is economically useless. We have rights, they are losers. Living in the center

---

[24] See Christopher Lasch, *The True and Only Heaven: Progress and Its Critics* (New York: Norton, 1991). Anthony Annett, "The Economic Vision of Pope Francis," in *The Theological and Ecological Vision of Laudato Si*, ed. Vincent J. Miller (London: T&T Clark, 2017), 160–74.
[25] See Vincent Miller, *Consuming Religion: Christian Faith and Practice in a Consumer Culture* (New York: Continuum, 2004).
[26] Robert Bellah, *Habits of the Heart: Individualism and Commitment in American Life* (Berkeley: University of California Press, 1985), 8.

of the fragmented world means most things can be produced and bought, accessed and possessed.[27]

If what unifies culture is simply a single economic system and its values, rather than some agreement on a transcendent vision of life, then contending with the vast pluralism in society is difficult and increasingly violent. Positively, the plural viewpoint in the world today offers a multiplication of possibilities for giving shape, substance, and direction to shared problems regarding life together and the possibilities for the earth as our common future. Negatively, a pluralism with no center offers contradictory frameworks of value or non-value, which are rationalized as an appropriate response. In addition, it is not uncommon today to observe behavior which appears to have no "why." Pope Francis reminds us that a certain societal consensus, which existed a few decades ago, seems waning in the public imagination (*FT* 13, 14).

We understand social problems such as the free market economy, security, war on terror, militarism, immigration, and so on considering our understanding of the world and essential relationships in it. This cultural context impacts our ethical framework, telling us in subtle ways what the problem means, what are its causes, and what constitutes its solution. Is this acceptable or unacceptable behavior? Is this abuse? Are we responsible for these situations? However, it can also limit our understanding of our world and ourselves. We can be led to feel our freedom is simply arbitrary, we can do what we want in response, or not respond at all. Pope Francis refers to this as a climate of indifference which paralyzes our societies today (*FT* 47).

We find in today's world that new technologies, global interdependence, and various dimensions of secularity impact "master narratives," which offer universal horizons of meaning. This "common meaning," however, is created through fear and is contested by many since it only affirm the lives of some. In this climate, efforts toward a more unified world are replaced by political activity which appeals not to people's horizons of hope but to "the basest and most selfish inclination of certain sectors of the population," which can eventually "lead to the usurpation of institutions and laws" (*FT* 159). Pluralism is met by a climate of polarization, which prevents any constructive dialogue toward problem-solving. It becomes impossible to express a viewpoint "without being categorized one way or the other, either to be unfairly discredited or to be praised to the sky" (*FT* 156). Deeply entrenched patterns of injustice, inequality, and exclusion are reinforced by a persistence of violence to maintain the status quo or countered by violence which has its source in the abuse of how institutions have functioned.

The development of true freedom which Rahner defined involves the effort to make sense out of this world and tie life together by building community. This is a conceptual enterprise, standing for values which matter, and a practical moral enterprise, making a difference. Religious touch into and create wholeness in this world as well as lead others

---

[27]Dorothee Soelle, *The Silent Cry: Mysticism and Resistance*, trans. Barbara and Martin Rumscheidt, (Minneapolis, MN: Fortress Press, 2001), 179.

to the next through accompaniment of others and forging interconnections that stabilize true freedom and flourishing in a changing world. The lens which lights up the meaning of the vow of obedience in our times is the call for religious to attend and witness to the transcendence which links the sacred and the secular. They do so by connecting freedom to the truth and relating the gospel to culture. Religious contribute to this effort not necessarily by creating a new master narrative but by lifting up in secular society those values which frame human wholeness beyond the limits of modern culture. In these times, the vow of obedience is a posture to address the radical contingency of the world and give an answer of hope and investment. It is to foster witness to God's presence in a world and the values to which it points—to attest that human good, wholeness, and flourishing are possible.[28] Dietrich Bonhoeffer once said, responsibility is measured in wholeness and hope. Responsibility is "the totality and the unity of response to reality given to us in Christ, as opposed to the partial responses we might give on the basis, for example of considerations of expediency or certain principles." Moreover, "for the responsible person the ultimate question is not: how heroically am I performing in this matter? but rather: how will the coming generation be able to continue to live?"[29]

The Challenge of Agency and Finitude (Poverty)

Moderns run up against a fragility of meaning when they try to attribute significance to their lives. The relentless accelerating cycle of desire and fulfillment in consumer culture drives them to ask, what is enough? The passing of time is often spent juggling flights from boredom, trying to "get things done," or scrambling to attend the next must-see event. They find themselves asking more than they would like, is this all there is? Charles Taylor cites these as symptoms of seeking fullness through immanence, which gives rise to the nova effect in modern life. In his words,

> We all see our lives, and/or the space wherein we live our lives, as having a certain moral/spiritual shape. Somewhere, in some activity, or condition, lies a fullness, a richness, that is, in that place (activity or condition), life is fuller, richer, deeper, more worthwhile, more admirable, more that it should be.[30]

This situation gives rise to a condition of doubt and uncertainty which impacts modern life. Humans look for love, meaning, and significance, a quasi-transcendence, within the

---

[28] Philip J. Rossi, "Contingencies of Grace, Hospitality, Otherness and the Enactment of Human Wholeness," in *Seekers and Dwellers, Plurality and Wholeness in a Time of Secularity*, ed. Philip J. Rossi (Washington, DC: Council for Research in Values and Philosophy, 2016), 285–300 at 298.
[29] As quoted in Sera Nocetti, *Reforming the Church: A Synodal Way of Proceeding* (Mahwah, NJ: Paulist Press, 2023), 86–7.
[30] Charles Taylor, *A Secular Age* (Cambridge, MA: The Belknap Press of Harvard University Press, 2007), 5–19 at 5.

immanent order. The universality of this experience is part of the human condition in modern times. Yet, when the immanent frame—the belief that this world is all there is—is the only source for questions surrounding personal significance, there are limitations. Even in assessing the course of one's life, a closed world offers little meaning for the passing of time beyond the hope that one will be remembered in the future. Investment in health, family, education, career, and the like are important. Satisfaction is attached to any greater realization of these goals. Yet we find that fulfillment is often challenged by other experiences. Life throws a curve, and what results is the emergence of exile. Whatever interpretation we have placed on life, or of its fullness, or the power of its source, is contradicted. These contradictions create a situation of tension. Some lives exhibit fullness on another basis, or an alternative model of fullness draws one away from a previous path. Taylor claims that moderns live their lives in a condition of doubt and uncertainty as they live in a cross-pressure of transcendence and immanence. What results is an explosion of ethical, religious, and atheistic options that surround us with explanations of a meaningful life. This is the nova effect. It offers a multiplicity of ways of becoming, yet at the same time withholds confirmation or support of a path apart from the testimony of those who adopt it.

A strong cultural belief in the power of human agency does not protect a person from the ambiguity and sense of limits inherent in the human condition. Even the best of our efforts confront the radical fracturing of plans, which render well-considered strategies susceptible to the complexity of our times. Besides those factors internal to the human condition, such as sickness, loss, misunderstanding, betrayal, and the like, and societal ones, including environmental disasters, untimely death, war, pandemic, and mass shootings, men and women today experience a loss of markers of identity.

The collapse of familiar boundaries of identity, ethnic, linguistic, religious and cultural, place actions before new terrain and unfamiliar challenges. We find that older solutions to dilemmas lose their meaning. Even though some simply repeat the former solutions, they prove inadequate. Others look only to money, and political, scientific, and technological power to ensure a buffer against contingency. All these attempts at problem-solving are not wrong, but when used as the only lens of action, grace is eclipsed. Over-reliance on the above solutions can hide a lack of hope as well as a disbelief that new grace can be given to enable change. Because there is no vision, one holds on when one should let go. In the secular realm, there is the assumption that any theistic or transcendent perspective, and the values it represents, is illusionary and useless.[31] In the ecclesial and congregational realm, there is no firm belief the Spirit can lead to more.

In the absence of a transcendent perspective or shared vision of human dignity, technical knowledge becomes the broker of truth. This champions the world's vision of the super-development of wealthy nations, to the detriment of the world's poor and the care of the earth. Attention to any ultimate questions is not needed. One not only holds

---

[31]Judith A. Merkle, *Discipleship, Secularity and the Modern Self: Dancing to Silent Music* (London: T&T Clark Bloomsbury, 2020), 181–8.

on to the status quo but backs up claims with "common sense" knowledge of how the world really works. Pope Francis cites the technocratic paradigm as a reliance on science and technology beyond their proper domain. He calls attention to the abandonment of deeper cultural and religious beliefs which have built civilizations and have enabled people to "let go" so something more can happen. Humankind is under the delusion that we have now become powerful enough and wise enough to apply our power to all things (*LS* 109). The deeper meaning of human autonomy is thus distorted. A modern concept of autonomy frees each of us to decree what is right and what is good with a moral authority once the prerogative of God.[32] The poverty of spirit, which fosters the capacity to hold on and to let go, the heart of the vow of poverty, stands in contrast to this mentality.

The vow of poverty attests that an embrace of finitude, or the limits of the human condition, is a door to the initiative of love, one capable of attending to the wholeness and the healing and creating in history which is needed in the modern world. The spirit of poverty highlights the purpose of a religiously focused lifestyle. At its heart, poverty is an expression of the desire for God which is at the heart of religious life. Poverty witnesses that human life can be fulfilled with simplicity in material things, and the appropriate dependence in human affairs which leads to quality of life for all. Creation is a gift to be received and shared, not just to be exploited for gain. The alternative mindset of gospel poverty recognizes the need for a more just distribution of goods and the creation of a sustainable environment and human community essential to a new civilization.[33] The lens which lights up the meaning of the vow of poverty today is its witness to the transcendence which fosters an alternative vision of the role and purpose of the economy in human life.

In First World Societies, it is evident that many are aware of the vast imbalance which exists between rich and poor nations. They concur with the insight; all is not right with the world as they witness the impoverishment of people and the destruction of the planet.[34] Many also face the obvious failures of the human community to create the universal benevolence it sets out to accomplish in the modern era. However, not everyone interprets these experiences in the same way. In one instance, people can say no to what is and invest in alternatives, feeling urged by the "more" in their own hearts. Others can respond with false realism. Well, what can we do? There will always be poor. Instead of seeking solutions, even if partial, they scale down hopes and limit vision. The strategy is to lower the bar of possibility and be satisfied with things as they are. If the immanent frame is all there is, it is likely all there should be.[35] The blindness caused by a lack of a transcendent lens only sees a world without injustice and does not feel any

---

[32]Philip Rossi, "Faith, Autonomy, and the Limits of Agency in a Secular Age," in *At the Limits of the Secular: Catholic Reflections on Faith and Public Life*, ed. William Barbieri (Grand Rapids, MI: Wm B. Eerdmann, 2014), 226–49 at 229.
[33]Here we have an example of what Pope Francis means by "integral ecology" (*LS* 141).
[34]Edward Schillebeeckx, *Church: The Human Story of God* (New York: Crossroad, 1990), 22.
[35]Rossi, "Contingencies of Grace, Hospitality, Otherness and the Enactment of Human Wholeness," 296.

obligation to work against the real problems which exist. Both believers and unbelievers can fall into this blindness. The practice of the gospel counsel of poverty, upon which the vow is based, is a lifelong practice to see and act in an alternative manner.

The vow of poverty acknowledges that the Kingdom of God belongs to the poor in Spirit. The spirit of poverty gives people the eyes to see the possible, and the hope to move to action. It motivates the asceticism to live with less, to be alert to what really matters in life. The vision developed from the practice of poverty helps us to meet the Kingdom already active in the world, and recognize and cooperate with it. We let the Spirit work through our initiative and creativity to express its signature hope in creating new possibilities for and with others.

Poverty also offers us a transcendent frame of reference when we consider ourselves and our world. The wholeness we seek personally has already been given to us in God's loving glance, which maintains our wholeness, especially when we feel its absence. Grace resides in the person we carry in our heart as a friend, as well as the one with whom we struggle to extend hospitality. Reliance on the presence of grace in this world impacts how we imagine a possibility for enacting wholeness in it and recognizing it when we meet it in ourselves and in others. Poverty alerts us to the vulnerability we share with all in the face of contingency and fosters community around collaboration rather than competition. As the spiders who know they do not control everything, we are free then to create webs of connection that can serve as we travel in the company of each other.

The contours of poverty are not predefined; they are a response to the call from God. They acknowledge there is more than meets the eye in every circumstance of our lives. They attest to the presence of transcendence and our relationship to it. What is permanent is the form of life set by the vow of poverty in congregations as an incorporation into community in forms upon which we depend. These are usually outlined in congregational documents. We do not ground our agency elsewhere. Renouncing a project and taking up one we did not plan, accepting what is given us in new circumstances, being moved by the poverty of the body of Christ, embracing a poverty of health or life we did not choose—all form the gestalt of poverty over a lifetime. It is the poverty we embrace when we are called which gives us the perspective to see grace at work in our lives. The vow of poverty responds to the dilemma of agency and finitude of our times with hope. It speaks to both what is good in our society and supports it, and offers an alternative witness to wholeness in face of the contradictions all around us.

The Challenge of Singularity and the Other (Celibacy)

A signature of modern identity is autonomy, the capacity to govern freely one's own action. Self-governance of one's own actions is seen as the heart of what it means to have responsibility for one's own life and to be a singular individual. Yet, wholeness does not mean sufficiency unto self. Humans become in and through a web of interrelationships with others, the world, and themselves. In other words, we need one another. Human sexuality is the way humans express their relatedness to others. Sexuality plays a crucial role in the ability to answer the call to love, for it is sexuality which reveals both our incompleteness and our relatedness. Sexuality is the biological, emotional, and psychological grounding of our capacity to love.[36] Despite our individuality, our singularity, we also need to reach out and touch, and embrace the other emotionally, intellectually and physically. The "other" is not us, yet without the capacity to connect with all that is not us, we cannot become. We need to be connected, and we do this through our sexuality. Sexuality is essential both to our human existence and to our becoming whole.

As men and women, we are always called to love, yet acts of love are not restricted to explicit physical sexual relationships. In many cases, these are not appropriate. The importance of the physical love expression of human sexuality, though, necessitates that its distinctiveness in the Christian life must be preserved and nourished. It is common to think of sex simply reduced to genital engagement with another; however, genitality is only one dimension of human sexuality. Failure to realize this reduces sexuality to genitality and sexual wholeness or fulfillment is equated with genital orgasm. The truth is our genitality has a quasi-sacramental function in our lives. The processes of genitality, that is being excited by another, point to the basic direction of human growth, that of going out of ourselves.[37] However, genital contact does not create sound relationships alone but can be an expression in ones developed at other levels.

This calls for the acknowledgment of another whole dimension to sexuality, its social or affective dimensions. Here, sexuality shows itself in the capacity to relate to others with emotional warmth, tenderness, and compassion. The opposite is engaging all that is not me with fear, opposition, and a need to control. Sexual maturity involves a primary capacity to come to an identity as a man or woman, to express it, and the capacity to relate healthfully with those of another gender. Human sexuality is the energy which moves us from within our experience of singularity, "I am an individual and unique," to our connections with what is other, other people, and the world. Our capacity to care, to be warm, to be intimate, and to make ourselves emotionally available to know others and to be known impacts our higher needs for sexual fulfillment, self-acceptance, and a sense of belonging. All these human needs can be reached without genital intimacy because genitality, as a physical need, is real but is not the highest need of the human spirit. The need for affirmation and for real intimacy is more fundamental and powerful than the need for genital expression itself. Our deepest relational needs are also more difficult to fulfill. It is possible to live fully and happily without the goodness of genital intimacy, but it is not possible to do so without developed affective relationships.[38]

---

[36] Vincent J. Genovesi, SJ, "Sexuality," in *The New Dictionary of Theology*, ed. Joseph Komonchak et al. (Wilmington, DE: Michael Glazier, 1989), 947–54 at 948.

[37] A post-Vatican treatment of human sexuality incorporating these various dimensions: Vincent Genovesi, *In Pursuit of Love: Catholic Morality and Human Sexuality* (Wilmington, DE: Michael Glazier, 1987).

[38] Genovesi, "Sexuality," 952.

Debates about norms in sexual ethics reflect the pluralism of modern society. They extend to the questions whether there should be any norms at all. The acknowledgment of the need for clarification and sensitivity in the church to the complexity of sexual issues in the lives of people stands side by side with the fact that many assume the church has no role in their sexual lives. We hear, "the church has no right to talk about what is going on in my bedroom!" This echo of the "subtraction" theory of modern faith, which suggests that as modernity and secularity unfold, the impact of the church should wane, is a familiar response even among people who take seriously moral limits. It simply points to one manifestation of the tension around how the freedom of individuality meshes with the connectedness necessary to give all aspects of life, meaning, and intelligibility.

A growing awareness in the church is sexual ethics engages a range of human issues beyond the traditional ones of sex outside of marriage, contraception, and abortion. Today, issues such as the relationship of sex and gender, the mutuality of the sexes, and the role of medicine in infertility and reproduction require a response. Because areas of sexuality are impacted by civil law, sexual ethics involves clarification of social rights, attention to sexism and violence, response to sex trafficking, and monitoring the role of the state in family life. To address the variety of sexualities encountered in society, the church searches for a response which addresses the virtue/vice grounding of all sexual practice: freedom, desire, vulnerability, interdependence, mutuality, love, justice, fidelity, and self-care.[39] For religious congregations, these questions also impact how a life of celibate chastity fosters the wholeness of a member and the community.

Our sense of singularity, being a distinct person, is linked to our autonomy in our imagination. Our capacity to set the direction of our own lives is a quality of freedom. Yet in the modern mind, autonomy is often associated with the "isms" of life today—individualism, relativism, subjectivism.[40] The ideal of being a singular human being leans toward the image of the "lone ranger," the individual not influenced by the group. The lone ranger type, even in the "grid" relationships of professional or associational groups, will not form lasting relationships but keep them fluid.[41] When these cultural models become the frame by which the vow of celibacy is interpreted, it is misunderstood. In the first case, it is mistaken as isolation or finding an emotional niche with a few people. In the latter, celibacy is expressed by a person who lives among others, but who no one ever knows. Celibacy is equated with continence alone but experienced as an incapacity for intimacy. How our autonomy links to our connectedness to others is a challenge of every age, but especially of modern life. It certainly forms a backdrop to the witness and living of a vow of celibacy on a personal level.

---

[39] See *Catholic Perspectives on Sex, Love and Families*, ed. Jason King and Julie Hanlon Rubio (Collegeville, MN: The Liturgical Press, 2020).
[40] Rossi, "Faith, Autonomy, and the Limits of Agency in a Secular Age," 227.
[41] These relationships are likely marked by competition unless taken beyond to friendship. For a description of grid relationships, see Judith A. Merkle, "Groups of Particularity and Profession: Speaking and Hearing the Truth," in *Being Faithful: Christian Commitment in Modern Society* (London: T&T Clark, 2010), 103–23 at 103.

Pope Francis comments in *Laudato Si* that our loss of a sense of how we are connected to one another and to creation itself breeds a climate of indifference and blindness not only to the condition of the world but also to the poor of the world (*LS* 208). Here celibacy is reflected in its social consequences. Our consumer society blinds us with a false sense of the freedom we have as individuals. We feel we are free as long as we can consume. A genuine sense of the common good disappears and "social norms are respected only to the extent they do not clash with personal needs" (*LS* 204). The deeper life issues involved in celibacy—belonging, recognition, friendship, and capacity to serve others with care and warmth—are inseparable from the gestalt of the response to poverty and of obedience.[42] Celibate chastity witnesses that the letting go of sexual and marital intimacy, in response to a perceived call, can channel human individuality into a connectedness to God and the People of God. Religious life testifies that in casting one's lot with others in community, ministry, and friendship, a woman or man can touch wholeness in a fulfilled life. This wholeness over a lifetime testifies to the Wholeness only given by God and promised in the life to come.[43]

The Law of the Cross: Touching Wholeness in a Wounded World

Jesus' relationship with his Father set the pattern for all human relationship with the mystery he lived himself. This is the paschal mystery of death and resurrection. The Christian life holds that everyone must engage in death and resurrection if they seek to touch a wounded world and find wholeness. Life will involve confrontation with contradiction and the mystery of evil, as well as the presence of God and love. We remember the thought of Lonergan on the meaning of life. We become ourselves not just by experiences and insights, judgments and choices, decisions and conversion; not just freely and deliberatively, not just deeply and strongly but also as one who is carried along. We respond not in isolation but through faith, hope, and love in Jesus Christ and in relationships with others. He reflects, "The Father predestined us to be conformed to the image of his Son, through the merits of Christ, through the grace of Christ, through the example of Christ. Consequently, there is an element not merely of personal development, but of personal development in relation to another person."[44]

Lonergan finds this development to be one of mutuality and participation in mystery. Christ himself, as a human person, developed and acquired human perfection. However, the human perfection he acquired was not the Enlightenment ideal of the self-made

---

[42] See Margaret Farley, "Celibacy Under the Sign of the Cross," in *Changing Questions: Explorations in Christian Ethics*, ed. and intro. Jamie L. Manson (New York: Orbis Books, 2015).

[43] These three tensions in modern life, autonomy/plurality, agency/finitude, singularity/connectedness to the Other are simply heuristic devices to view some life challenges reflected in the three vows and shared across the spectrum of adult lifestyles in the church in these times. They are not exhaustive and are interrelated in their scope and impact on each other.

[44] Lonergan, "The Mediation of Christ in Prayer," 180.

man. He lived with poverty and suffering, died unjustly and cruelly, abandoned by others. He did this, however, in relation to us, as human among us, for love of us, as the cost of being among us and united to the Father. The path of finding wholeness by touching the wounds of the world follows this path of Jesus Christ. We touch the cross that belongs to all of humanity to the degree we are able and choose it out of love because Jesus chose it on account of us. The Law of the Cross, therefore, is the way God confronts evil in the world. Evil is confronted by transforming evil into good. We transform evil in the world by absorbing it when appropriate, not perpetuating it as retaliation would dictate, transforming it when possible, and restoring goodness by creating situations in which the good can again flourish. We touch wholeness through the life of the vows when we do so as Jesus did, with Jesus, and in growing consciousness of how we are carried along in grace.

The second part of this text will address each vow individually and how each forms a path in religious life to touch wholeness, happiness, and fulfillment in life. All vows form a gestalt of a life of love of God and neighbor in a community of faith. It will not be an exhaustive treatment, but hopefully one which will aid the reader to consider the significance of the vows in their lives today, considering religious life as a life path or better understanding religious life in the church. We will first look at vows in general and their place on a life journey.

CHAPTER 4
TOUCHING WHOLENESS
THE PATH OF THE VOWS

All experience of God is mediated historically. God reveals Godself in ways humans can know in their daily lives. The vows of religious life are one such mediation. We are addressed by God through experience, and the vows are a response to this experience. To distinguish religious life from other adult stances in the church people in the past used the adage: religious keep the gospel counsels and the laity the precepts, or laws. This distinction might not serve well in the modern church. *Lumen Gentium* 39 explores the meaning of the counsels and their pastoral implications for all the faithful.

> For this is the will of God, your sanctification. However, this holiness of the Church is unceasingly manifested, and must be manifested, in the fruits of grace which the Spirit produces in the faithful; it is expressed in many ways in individuals who in their walk of life, tend toward the perfection of charity, thus causing the edification of others;

Vatican II goes on to say how this call to holiness through the counsels, given to all the baptized, applies to religious life.

> in a very special way this (holiness) appears in the practice of the counsels customarily called "evangelical". This practice of the counsels, under the impulse of the Holy Spirit, undertaken by many Christians, either privately or in a Church-approved condition or state of life, gives and must give in the world an outstanding witness and example of this same holiness. (*LG* 39)

At the heart of the term "counsel" is the ideal of a wholehearted and free response to God's invitation of grace through the Holy Spirit, revealed in its fullness in Jesus. The "good life" offered in the scriptures is one of generosity which goes beyond the exact observance of a code of regulations.[1] Often the exhortations we read in the gospel surpass a legalistic formula. Advice such as "Be perfect as your heavenly Father is perfect," Mt. 5:48, is an encouragement to be wholehearted in one's following of Jesus. A calling to religious life

---

[1] Rene Carpentier, "Evangelical Counsels," in *Sacramentum Mundi*, Vol. 2, ed. Karl Rahner (New York: Herder and Herder, 1968), 276–9 at 277.

is understood as something more than what is necessary, in the face of a God who is beyond a requirement in one's life. It seems fair to say that the logic of superabundance and a sense of gift touches the vows of both the religious and those married in the Christian life. The Spirit, who grounds the religious experience of being loved by God in both commitments, evokes joy—even when such awareness fluctuates between knowing and unknowing, lacks words, or is anxious in the face of the unknown.[2] Joy flows from an experience of givenness, rather than what one has earned. It is a perception of infinite mystery wrapped in a personal appeal, a sense of being addressed, which creates a personal relationship that begins to fulfill us as persons.[3] Those responding with marriage vows have this experience through their mutual relationship—those making religious vows experience this in their singularity before God.[4]

The good life in the New Testament presupposes the presence of God and the implicit movement of God's love, which unites us into the life of the Trinity (1 Cor. 13; Jn 14:15-23, Eph. 5:2, Rom. 13:10). The new obligations taken on in marriage and religious life carry both the spirit and expression of the inner meaning of a counsel, love in a manner beyond the letter of the law, as a response to being loved. Love God with your whole mind, heart, and soul and your neighbor as yourself has this same horizon of invitation. While the duties of different states of life have both similarities and distinctions, they are united in that they each convey how the presence of God is in one's life and the ultimate value of every faithful effort and action.[5] The objective requirements of each state of life, through the lens of a counsel, are not just an impetus to be better or impact our lives as serious obligations, but they invite us to the "more," the superabundance which goes beyond simple calculations of effort and safety. We move from the "freedom from" the lifestyle we once had to a freedom "to" embrace what is our path in an ongoing journey in love.

The fundamental dimension of the "yes" professed in the vows of marriage and religious life grounds the ups and downs, the dark passages and the successes, the health and the illness, the acceptances, the misunderstandings, and the ordinariness in the life of the religious and the married couple.[6] Not everyone approaches marriage with a faith perspective, nor do all religious move beyond the formalities of their lifestyle to take a spiritual journey. Even though all people who enter both vocations do not

---

[2]Judith A. Merkle, *Sensing the Spirit: Toward the Future of Religious Life* (London: T&T Clark, 2023), 99–100.
[3]Anthony J. Godzieba, *A Theology of the Presence and Absence of God* (Collegeville, MN: Liturgical Press, 2018), 183.
[4]For a reflection on marriage as a vocation, see Kent Lasnoski, "Marriage and Householding in Christ," in *Catholic Perspectives: Sex, Love and Families*, ed. Jason King and Julie Hanlon Rubio (Collegeville, MN: The Liturgical Press, 2020), 59–67.
[5]Carpentier, "Evangelical Counsels," 277.
[6]See Bertrand Dumas, "The Sacrament of Marriage in Postmodernity: Struggling with 'Spectacularization,'" *Marriage, Families and Spirituality* 27, no. 2 (2021): 175–95. Dumas comments that the mystery of the love of a marriage is made into the spectacular, and the ordinary is lost in the attempt to make it conform to the remarkable. This mentality feeds a consumer approach to marriage, which makes it just another "experience to be enjoyed and then set aside in the search for maximizing the potential for happiness," at 184.

perceive a counsel impacts their commitment in the same way, the spirit of a counsel is related to the ultimate obligations of both.[7] St. Thomas claims that Christian perfection is contained in the Great Commandment of charity: love God with your whole heart, mind, and will and your neighbor as yourself. But the counsel shows "in a special way" (*LG* 42) how they are made realities and given their full symbolism and embodiment. The counsel advises having an attitude of faith-filled generosity and giving in a concrete way in key areas of personal living. The search for love and meaning in life is the expressed or unspoken desire of adult vocational choices, and the counsels offer paths for this search in a secular society.

A Diversity of Gospel Counsels

From the earliest times in the Christian community, it was known that the counsels were free (Acts 4:32). Both marriage and virginity were counsels (1 Cor. 7:25) and one was free to choose between them. During the early centuries of the church, the church held consistently to the teaching of the counsels. Christians were simply taught to follow Christ—the only law is Christ. The good news of Jesus was preached (Acts 3:42), which meant that Christianity was presented in terms of the counsels. All were taught the ideal of the eucharistic community, essentially a relationship of *agape*. This was joined by the *koinonia*, the sharing of goods (Acts 2:42–44). These postures together were later called the *vita apostolica*. This was not a community without private property, rather a practical readiness to share one's goods. Christian marriage was seen as penetrated by the spirit which also inspired the state of virginity.[8] One finds in the Epistles of Paul and early documents of the church other references to moral practices, such as lists of virtues which reflected both pagan philosophy and the Hebrew scriptures. However, the charismatic impact of the Christian life was the following of Christ which normed and gave meaning to the other languages of the good life.

Law and Spirit

For the early church, the relationship between the Law and the Spirit was pivotal in the new covenant with God they experienced in Jesus. They were not saved by the Law, but the law was still essential in their relationship with God. Instead of the letter of the law, they searched for the Lord's presence revealed in the law. Christ's own self was meant to shine through the law. We hear in the Epistle to the Galatians, "Bear one another's

---

[7]The traditional thinking in the church is that marriage flows from nature. While true, commitment to modern marriage seems equally linked to freedom, as the capacity to commit, as marriage today is not inevitable in intimate relationships.

[8]Carpentier, "Evangelical Counsels," 278.

burdens, thus you will fulfill the law of Christ" (Gal. 6:2). However, today, religious and married Christians may question whether the church's law regarding their lives is redundant or intrusive. Modern people tend to see themselves as laws unto themselves, so how a broader institution enters into the details of their lives may seem remote. The charismatic and personal sources of married and religious life seem sufficient, and many are aware that their day-to-day experience does not rest on norms alone for direction. Yet do norms have any value? Does the church have any right to make them? These questions are fundamental to inquire about religious vows in a new age. How the church intervened in the interpretation of marriage over the centuries is beyond the scope of this writing.[9] Yet, we will touch on major turning points in its dialogue with religious life.

Church as Institution and the Counsels

The following of Christ, which was preached to the whole church, was the basis of some Christians taking on a voluntary and closer *koinonia*, or community or fellowship, along with virginity and the sharing of goods. A fifth-century sect known as the "Apostolics" was reproached by the church when they tried to make the above the "rule" for the whole church. The church charged they were wrong since they made a precept out of a counsel.[10] In the early centuries of the church, the separation from the values of pagan society did not require a flight to the desert. Persecutions, exile, and death were frequent realities of the Christian life. However, as Christianity melded into the wider society, it took on its distractions. In response, people tried to find greater solitude, living on the edge of communities or in the desert to find separation from what was felt to be a world hostile to the values of a gospel.[11] Hermits in the desert simply continued the *vita apostolica* when it became too difficult for the whole community, which was involved in the tasks of survival in a harsh environment as well as the distractions of their times.

The monasticism which developed during the fourth and fifth centuries in the Mediterranean world was a development of these early attempts at an alternative way of living. It did so in a context where few were affluent and many enslaved and uneducated. However, the wealthy, aristocratic, and socially prominent also became monks.[12] When St. Benedict wrote his rule, he drew from various monastic traditions, as monastic life was not uniform. He also addressed some of the excesses of drifting and indulgences which had arisen in monastic practice. Not all those who attempted to live religious life did so with excellence. Benedict wanted the structure he set to continually call members to fidelity. Benedict did not envision religious life for the exceptional. He wanted it to be

---

[9] See Waldemar Molinski, "Marriage," in *Encyclopedia of Theology: The Concise Sacramentum Mundi*, ed. Karl Rahner (New York: Crossroads, 1982), 905–31.
[10] Carpentier, "Evangelical Counsels," 277.
[11] Merkle, *Sensing the Spirit*, 36–45.
[12] Peter Brown, *The Body and Society: Men, Women and Sexual Renunciation in Early Christianity* (New York: Columbia University Press,1988), 410.

a life an ordinary person could enter and be happy. Monastic life was not only to express a love of God but also to enkindle it, therefore its structure was important. When he wrote his famous *Rule of St. Benedict* he intended that the monk, by keeping the Rule, would be led by the Spirit of the counsels to Christ.

In the Middle Ages, monastic life focused on the Rule as a school of love and in community. Community life was meant to support the monk or nun and help them learn to love God by loving and desiring to be loved by their monastic brethren. By the twelfth century, the three vows of poverty, chastity, and obedience were established, which gave shape to this experience of the following of Christ (*LG* 43, *PC* 2). Monastic groups of the Middle Ages did perform social services: they ran monastic schools and cared for the sick and the aged, but they were not usually founded for that reason. Their main "work" was saving souls; the byproduct of evangelization was other charitable practices.

The Reformation no longer saw monasticism as the special place to experience God; rather, God was seen to be present intensely in all of life.[13] All men and women were called equally to holiness within their everyday lives; the ideal of a separate and superior religious state was not a focus. Catholics were challenged by the Reformers who questioned the traditional spirituality, which focused on the religious life practiced in the Middle Ages. Founders and foundresses of new religious orders, however, combined active service—teaching, nursing, and caring for the poor—with spiritual practices and exercises in accord with their approach to the Christian life. Ignatius of Loyola, Vincent de Paul, and Angela Merici, for example, pioneered a new form of religious life within Catholicism. For several hundred years after the Reformation, a hybrid form of religious life developed, focused on both the spiritual life and external service to the wider community. This was essential to the social interventions of the wider social mission of the church. The church in the West wished to address the social dislocations of an industrializing Europe and North America. During the nineteenth century, the number of new active orders grew enormously, and those orders that continued to follow the traditional, contemplative version of Catholic religious life steadily declined.[14] The difference between the social works of these orders, and the good works of the monastic communities of previous centuries, was that the service dispensed was not by individuals on a one-to-one basis but through large-scale institutions maintained by members. A key pastoral strategy for the church to carry out its mission and support its members in a new industrial society was Catholic Action. The goals of Catholic Action impacted religious communities, as they shaped their own ministries with the mission of the entire Church. The aims of this movement were to repair or reconstruct Christian civilization where it had been injured or destroyed through the forces of modernization. Its three strategies were to disseminate a better knowledge of Catholic social principles and ideals, as well as the Catholic faith itself; to reorganize the public life of individual nations in

---

[13] Patricia Wittberg, *From Piety to Professionalism and Back: Transformations of Organized Religious Virtuosi* (Lanham, MD: Lexington Books, 2006), 5–6.
[14] Ibid., 6.

accordance with Catholic standards. Lastly, to counteract the poverty, insecurity, and material misery of the laboring population.[15]

The Charismatic Church and the Counsels

When Vatican II began in 1962, the expression of religious life formed up to this point was already in transformation. In 1943, Pius XII wrote *Mystici corporis* which called upon the interpretation of charism in St. Paul. It stressed that the charismatic as well as the hierarchical dimension belonged to the basic structure of the church since both are directed to the building up of the Body of Christ.[16] Later, Karl Rahner developed theologically the charismatic dimension of the church and supported an ecclesiology with a distinction between the interior charismatic order of grace and its external sign and cause in the institutional order.[17] This theological insight later reinforced pastoral questions concerning religious life which arose after the Second World War. Pius XII in 1947 wrote *Provida Mater Ecclesia* recognizing those in secular institutes. These members of the church were living the spirit of the *via apostolica* of the early church, but without public vows, and living other forms of association than congregational life.

By the 1950s, there was a growing awareness that some congregations which arose in the nineteenth century, unlike many before them, did not bring forth a variety of charisms, rather found their identity more in the works they adopted. Congregations simply adopted rules in place which suited their ministry, drew upon popular devotions of their times, and followed the basic prayers required of religious. Canonist Enid Williamson notes, "But a particular spirituality—a distinct expression of one facet of devotion which issues in a way of reacting and acting toward the apostolate as well as in prayer life—seems never to have been an intrinsic part of their structure."[18] Their founding was focused on a needed ministerial work which they listed in their constitutions, with less mention of their charism or spirituality. They stressed the institutional and legal perspectives of religious life, rather than its charismatic dynamism as expressed in their specific group. A juridical atmosphere also impacted much of religious life founded in earlier periods, giving it an unnecessary universality. Therefore, in 1950, Pius XII asked religious congregations not only to come to Rome to launch an assessment of religious

---

[15]Hubert Jedin, "Pope Benedict XV, Pius XI, and Pius XII," in *History of the Church in the Modern Age*, ed. Hubert Jedin (London: Burns and Oates, 1981), 26. Edward Cahill, SJ, "The Catholic Movement: Historical Aspects," in *Readings on Moral Theology, No. 5 Official Catholic Social Teaching*, ed. Charles Curran (New York: Paulist Press, 1986), 5.

[16]Danielle Peters, "Charism and the Consecrated Life in the Twentieth and Twenty-First Centuries," *Marian Library Studies* 31 (2013): Article 19, 47–72 at 49. https://ecommons.udayton.edu/ml_studies/vol31/iss1/19.

[17]Karl Rahner, *The Charismatic Element in the Church* (New York: Herder and Herder, 1961), 12–83. See also *The Shape of the Church to Come*, trans. Edward Quinn (New York: The Seabury Press, 1971), 113.

[18]Enid Williamson, "The Notion of Charism in Religious Life," *Studia Canonica* 19 (1985): 1:99–116, 102–3. As quoted in Peters, "Charism and the Consecrated Life," 50.

life but also to return to the original spirit of their institutes and to adapt to the changed conditions of the post-Second World War world.

Some would say that it is the fault of the magisterial church that religious life became so institutional and restrictive before Vatican II. On the one hand, it is true that the canon law revision of 1917 maintained standards of religious life that stressed more its legal and institutional boundaries than its charismatic spirit. Growing lay associations were not given approval as part of religious life due likely to interpretations of secular life which were not compatible with a religious state identified as "leaving the world."[19] On the other hand, Peters notes that political conditions in Europe around the First World War made it impossible to really assess the state of religious life worldwide. Needs were critical and groups responded as best as they could. The development of the congregation beyond traditional practices of its spiritual identity and service to others was left untended.

The Role of the Church in Religious Life

When asked about the role of the church in religious life, it is common for religious to immediately assume the church has an overly juridical mindset and more than often provides an institutional minefield to cross for a congregation to receive support. Hopefully, that is not always the case. It needs to be recognized that the church has both a right and a duty to foster and protect the charism of *vita apostolica* of the early church and guide its continued unfolding in new circumstances. It also has a responsibility to religious themselves to see that the affirmation of their congregations, once given, remains true, and the congregation itself is acting in the best interest of their life and mission.

In today's church, Pope Francis in *Laudato Si* offers the perspective, "everything is interconnected." This lens proves true when considering the short history we have reviewed of religious life in the church. The interpretation of religious life in any period is connected to a theology of the church, and its interpretation of the Christian moral life. Is it highly legalistic, ascetical, more thematic and virtue-centered, or humanistic? Does the church need a call to poverty as in the time of St. Francis of Assisi, to turn to the poor as with St. Vincent de Paul, or care for immigrants with Frances Cabrini? Also involved is the posture of the church toward the modern world, how the church understands its mission, the role of gender in decision-making in the church, and the defined role of the laity and the ordained—just to name a few issues. Often all these theological realities are not always in sync in any given period of history. For example, today people ask do religious belong to the clergy or laity. The two-tier system the church currently provides is inadequate. When the church identifies religious through the lens

---

[19] For instance, a hundred years before their Vatican approval, secular institutes were emerging.

of the clerical side or the laity side, it leans toward a clericalization of the church or a secularization or laicization of the church.[20] This type of separation in practice can give rise to priests being devalued or the laity made supreme. The Synod calls on the church as the People of God, emphasizing baptism as the source of the mission of all sectors of the church. Religious life, in this perspective, can assume the role of bridge builder between laity and clergy. While some religious are clerics, ordination is not essential to religious life. Those who are neither clerical nor lay still have a role, as that of the spirit, building up the community in the People of God. Through their corporate sign as a community, they offer a unique witness to the role of the Christian life in a secular society. *Fratelli Tutti* calls for social friendship, the relationship of brothers and sisters, or fraternity, as the kind of charity needed in the world today. Religious congregations have a unique opportunity to be this witness.

This recognition of the charismatic dimension of religious life and concern for its care is not new in the church. Evangelical law, or the rule of religious congregations, according to the commentary of St. Thomas (I-II, Q. 106 to 108) is not a code that is given by the Holy Spirit and is spiritually more elevated and demanding than the Old Covenant. On the other hand, more lenient. It is not a code, an external norm; it is a new interior principle, a dynamism: the Spirit.[21] And in no case, St. Thomas observes, should the written laws for religious be too numerous or too detailed. During the period of experimentation in religious congregations called for by Pius XII, and promoted by Vatican II in *Perfectae Caritatis*, Paul VI in an audience (July 9, 1969) reinforced this tradition in the modern church.

> We shall have, therefore, a period of greater freedom in the life of the Church and of her individual members. It will be a period of fewer legal obligations and fewer interior restraints. Formal discipline will be reduced; all arbitrary intolerance and all absolutism will be abolished. Positive law will be simplified, and the exercise of authority will be moderated. There will be promoted the sense of that Christian freedom which pervaded the first generation of Christians.[22]

Vatican II also called attention to a way the Holy Spirit guides the Church as well as religious congregations in new moments as "reading the signs of the times" (Mt. 16:3, GS 11).

Vatican II

Vatican II continued to renew the interpretation of *vita apostolica* of the early church by recognizing the foundations of a religious vocation in Christ and in the Church. It

---

[20] Alexandra Diriat, CSJ, "Le tiers incommode," *Vies Consacree*, no. 2 (April 2022): 29–38.
[21] Gerard Dubois, "Evangelical and Monastic Obedience," *Cistercian Studies* 8, no. 2 (1973): 87–106 at 98.
[22] *The Pope Speaks* 14, no. 2 (1969): 95.

stressed the importance of defining the vocation in terms beyond "leaving the world" and a perspective centered on personal salvation.[23] One "sign of the times" was that modern culture was calling for a re-thinking of how religious life "fit" modern life—by holding freedom and autonomy as such high values.[24] Shifts in thinking made at the council impacted the understanding of religious life. The role of responsibility in the Christian life is not only to be sinless in the world but also to fashion it in peace and justice was proclaimed. The awareness of diversity, of the world church, and of the impact of culture on the religious experience of individuals was voiced. The turn to the person as a hearer and bearer of revelation, and the move toward a liturgical life in the vernacular marked a key change. The universal call to holiness to all people in the church, and the setting aside of religious life as a "state of perfection," challenged traditional understandings. The awareness of the common origin of hierarchical and charismatic gifts in the church stimulated a charismatic renewal movement. The continued effort to recognize the role of charisms in the church was evident in many documents. The charismatic gifts of the laity were recognized. Even though the council did not set up adequate structures to receive these charisms, formation of the laity began at new levels. The council clarified that charisms are not given automatically through baptism, nor are they part and parcel of the sacrament of ordination; they are likewise not to be reduced to a personal gift or talent one has received.[25] For religious, specifically, the stylized and ritualized ways of living, dressing, and apostolic service were viewed as secondary to the call to renew and adapt to changing times. This was a clear call to move from a juridical approach to religious life to focus on its deeper identity. A commitment to the life of the counsels of poverty, celibacy, and obedience were described not as an end but a means, a witness to the love of God and neighbor. The council clarified that it is the perfection of love, rather than the three vows themselves, which distinguishes the impact of the image of God within and the response of the person to the call to holiness. The question then arises, why does one make vows?

Why Do We Make Vows?

It is not unusual today to hear a young person ask, "Why get married? Marriage is just a piece of paper." The person commenting might not be irresponsible but someone searching for meaning. At some level, questions concerning the social institution of marriage and a social institution which formalizes the charismatic *vita apostolica* respond to the same quandary. Does personal commitment need institutional support? In his study of charisma and institution, sociologist Max Weber claimed charism will die out

---

[23]Merkle, *Sensing the Spirit*, 30–4.
[24]This is the general question of Judith A. Merkle, *Committed by Choice* (Collegeville, MN: The Liturgical Press, 1993).
[25]Peters, "Charism and the Consecrated Life," 54.

unless it is incorporated into an institution.²⁶ The institution takes the innovation of the charism and routinizes it into the patterns of daily living so that its reality is preserved.²⁷ Both marriage and religious life have an institutional and stable dimension which is not their complete meaning yet also cannot be left out of an understanding of their reality. While we cannot explore this dimension of marriage in this writing, we can comment on the presence of both charism and institution in religious life. Even the formation of monasticism was a charismatic expression of the Spirit. Through charismatic action, the Spirit continues to form the church and the People of God within it.²⁸ The vows find their identity in the matrix between the charismatic and the institutional in the church, and the freedom of the baptized.

Charisms and the Vows

Theologian John Haughey remarks that while "charisms are notoriously elusive," we can reflect on some patterns they share with other creativity in history.²⁹ First, charisms are God's ways of building up families, communities, parishes, schools, hospitals, agencies, the church, but also business, neighborhoods, cities, and even international relations. Charisms function where there are human needs. The charisms in the church today, including those of marriage and religious life, go beyond Paul's mention of them solely in an ecclesial framework (1 Cor. 12:7). Vatican II clarified that charisms can be expressed in wider society as well as in the church (*AA* 3). *Lumen Gentium* clarifies that charisms belong to the essence of the church, along with its hierarchical nature (*LG* 4. 7.3, 12, 30, 50). Charisms are more than personal gifts or talents that have been received. Believers who have received a charism are to channel this calling, not just for their personal growth but also for the life and development of society and the church. Without charismatic stimuli "from below," one author comments, "the life of the church would often subside into torpor, many wounds would go unhealed and many crises unresolved."³⁰

Religious life, as we know it as an outgrowth of monasticism, belongs to the charismatic structure of the church. Its beginnings in the Christian life gave the church a language to speak of charism not simply as a possession of individuals, a dimension of the church, but as a structure in the church. It seems that *vita apostolica* was a pattern of response

---

²⁶Merkle, *Sensing the Spirit*, 64–8.
²⁷Weber examined charisma as a social phenomenon, not as a theological reality. Judith Merkle, *Discipleship, Secularity and the Modern Self: Dancing to Silent Music* (London: T&T Clark, 2020), 64–6.
²⁸This is also a theological assumption of the synodal movement in the Church. See Serena Noceti, *Reforming the Church: A Synodal Way of Proceeding* (New York: Paulist Press, 2023), 9–11.
²⁹John Haughey, "Charisms: An Ecclesiological Exploration," in *Retrieving Charisms for the 21ˢᵗ Century*, ed. Doris Connelly (Collegeville, MN: The Liturgical Press, 1999), 1–2.
³⁰Friedrich Wolf, "Dogmatic Constitution on the Church, Chapter VI: Religious," trans. Richard Strachan, in *Commentary on the Documents of Vatican II*, 5 vols., ed. Herbert Vorgrimler (New York: Herder and Herder, 1967–1969), I:273–81, 278. As quoted in Peters, "Charism and the Consecrated Life," 54.

to the gospel but not a structure in the church. Early monastic communities were seen as charismatic communitarian expressions within the church and as something new.[31] Both marriage and religious life are seen as stable lifestyles in the church. In the case of religious life, its identity is both charismatic and institutional, as well as congregational in many of its forms. The ecclesiastical state of the evangelical counsels characterizes religious life as both a religious and social entity. As a social entity, however, its identity is love as practiced in the gospel, rather than the rule of law as seen in other societies.[32] Because its identity is tied to the social imperatives of the gospel, and it expresses these imperatives also in the wider society, as one way the church expresses itself to the world, it needs a public juridical organization to order the practice of the counsels.

While the three vows of poverty, celibacy, and obedience are the usual form of the vows, the point is, the profession of vows is not defined by either of the vows as such or by specific vows. Profession is the act of definitive self-consecration to Christ.[33] Each of the vows has been understood in the history of the faith community as a primary mediator of the God-quest, which is at the heart of religious life. Pursuit of each of these counsels of the Gospels is meant to foster union with Christ and the trust in God and service of neighbor which is at the heart of the Christian life. Since these vows are lived in a concrete community, the people with whom the religious shares life are part of living out this covenant. The charism of the congregation to which one belongs also shapes the style of response to the gift of a religious vocation.

The Church recognizes the charismatic quality of each congregation by requiring it to express its unity and identity in its own law, and by recognizing it as an organization which has its own rules. These are expressed in its constitutions and other significant statements. The wider church recognizes this blend between the charismatic and institutional elements of a religious congregation by requiring certain elements in every law. Yet it fosters the independence of congregations to live out their own charism through the practice of exemption. Here a local bishop may exercise appropriate authority, when necessary, over a congregation but does so in tune with the autonomy the congregation has through their recognition by the wider church.[34]

Vows and Wholeness

Today, the multiplication of the possibilities for giving shape, substance, and direction to human moral and spiritual lives has significantly altered the context for understanding

---

[31] Merkle, *Sensing the Spirit*, 62.
[32] Even in many civil societies, a religious congregation is seen as a "benevolent institution."
[33] See Sandra Schneiders, *Selling All: Commitment, Consecrated Celibacy and Community in Catholic Religious Life* (Mahwah, NJ: Paulist Press, 2001), 101. See also 112–13.
[34] Carpentier, "Evangelical Counsels," 278.

the contours and structures of religious life.[35] Religious life faces the same complexities as any religious identity in modern life. The question—is marriage just a piece of paper, is paralleled in questions regarding the relevancy of vows. Both arise from a similar sense of ambiguity seen in culture surrounding the importance of institutions, which contributes to a climate of randomness in everyday life.

Karl Rahner explains the nature and source of this sense of contingency in church and society. Society today no longer sets concrete guidelines for all its groups. Secular society in the past, while not identical to the Christian life, was more in harmony with it. Society itself was homogeneous, hierarchically structured, and with common enough public opinion to shape people's individual decisions about their lives. The impact of society on individuals was less ambiguous than today. In this broader socially constructed society, Christianity possessed a certain official status. The Christian character of society was a product of and an element in the unity and homogeneity of a type of secular society which encompassed it. Even though people had to make a personal act of faith within this culture, the culture itself was formed by more amicable factors outside Christianity.[36] Religion today struggles to find a place in a world where the assumption that the religious realm is superior to the secular realm is no longer generally held. The significance and witness of the vows are related to this situation. It is in the secular world where the whole Christian community seeks to express what it knows about life and its meaning. Jose Casanova puts it this way: "If before, it was the religious realm which appeared to be the all-encompassing reality within which the secular realm found its proper place, now the secular sphere will be the all-encompassing reality, to which the religious sphere will have to adapt."[37] Faith and its expression in this world is an option, not a necessity.[38] A religious vocation, more easily supported in the homogeneously structured culture after the Second World War, is lived and interpreted under new conditions. This requires a fresh capacity for an interior self, a "within" of conviction. Rahner claims ordinary mysticism is needed to sustain a graced religious presence in secular society. This witness is evidenced in self-awareness and freedom, responsibility, discernment, and capacity to collaborate with others. The vows are meaningfully interpreted for many when tied to these qualities of life and the needs of the times, centered in the heart of discipleship.

---

[35]Phillip Rossi, SJ, "Contingencies of Grace: Hospitality, Otherness, and the Enactment of Human Wholeness," in *Seeker and Dwellers, Plurality and Wholeness in a Time of Secularity*, ed. Philip Rossi (Washington, DC: Council for Research in Values and Philosophy, 2016), 285–300 at 285.
[36]Karl Rahner, "The Situation of Faith Today," in *The Practice of Faith: A Handbook of Contemporary Spirituality* (New York: Crossroads, 1983), 29–32. See also Merkle, *Sensing the Spirit*, 146–52.
[37]Jose Casanova, *Public Religions in the Modern World* (Chicago, IL: The University of Chicago Press, 1994), 15,
[38]Hans Joas, *Faith as a Option: Possible Futures for Christianity* (Stanford, CA: Stanford University Press, 2014), 71.

Lonergan and Autonomy

Bernard Lonergan provides a language which unveils the capacities needed to make a profession of vows: either in marriage or religious life. Ideally, for both, the person has reached a certain level of personal development. Lonergan explains that a critical and decisive stage in life is reached when one finds out for oneself what he or she can make of oneself. When one decides for oneself what one is to be. When one lives in fidelity to one's self-discovery and decision. He remarks:

> It is the existential moment that the drifter never confronts. He thinks as everybody thinks, he says what everybody says, he does what everybody does, and so do they.
>
> The mass of unauthentic humanity lacks the courage to take the risk of thinking things out for themselves—they might very well be wrong if they did. It lacks the resoluteness that decides and the fidelity that stands by its decisions. But the development that reaches its goal in the existential decision and in fidelity to that decision is the emergence of the autonomous subject.[39]

He continues that in life we pass through two significant periods. The first concerns objects: we learn to do things for ourselves, decide for ourselves, and find out what we need to know. One develops habits and becomes a certain kind of person through his or her actions. But there comes in this process a moment when we realize we have developed not only through a type of mastery but through these efforts have made ourselves. He remarks, "There arises the question of finding out for oneself what one is to make of oneself, of deciding for oneself what one is to be, and of living in fidelity to one's decision. Such existential moment is a disposal of oneself."[40] This capacity requires a certain intentionality or development of the capacity to enter into such a decision and consciousness of self and all the dimensions of human life which come through human development. Human development for Lonergan is the mediation of autonomy, or the growing capacity to be self-determining. So, while some former impressions of religious life suggest one ceases in it to have this core autonomy, Lonergan's perspective claims the opposite; yet this autonomy is given a purpose in the life of the vows.

Within human life, even such disposal is not absolute. In spite of the fact that one makes a firm resolution, the choice to continue a path is made over and over. One can dispose of oneself, but one still must be faithful to it, and it can seem at times as if one has never made the resolution in the first place. Lonergan places this disposing of oneself within a community. It is done as a choice within the three fundamental areas where love is expressed: love of family, of one's fellow human beings, and of God. These

---

[39] Bernard Lonergan, "The Mediation of Christ in Prayer," *Philosophical and Theological Papers, 1958–1964*, Vol. 6, ed. Robert C. Croken, Frederick E. Crowe, and Robert M. Doran (Toronto: University of Toronto Press, 1996), 160–82 at 171.
[40] Ibid.

loves represent three levels of consciousness of what comprises the wholeness of one's life. One disposes oneself in love, in fidelity, and in faith. In this light, a vow serves the pursuit of this loving autonomy and its detours over a life course. A vow in the Christian life is a sacred promise or commitment, made freely and publicly with the approval of the church.[41]

The profession of vows begins the journey of religious life in a new manner than the explorations and testing that went before it. Vows can have a time limit to test whether their orientation is life-giving for the member and if applicants are a good "fit" in a community. Lonergan's depiction, however, of self-disposal is attuned with final profession. This casting of one's lot within a concrete community confirms a *process* already begun.[42] It makes a community both a context of becoming and a group with its own mandate of manifesting itself because of its place in the church. The community too must follow a path of fidelity by how it lives, solves its problems, realizes its successes, works toward common meaning, and handles both development and breakdown. People leave religious life today, not always because of a breakdown of their commitment, but because their congregations seem to have given up their mandate.

The community does not make a person authentic. A person who makes vows is autonomous in a community. We remain what we make of ourselves. Lonergan reminds us, "But because his/*her* present resolutions cannot predict his/*her* future decisions, he/*she* is always until death a piece of unfinished business. Consequently, his/*her* living is the manifestation, the mediation of his/*her* existential decisions."[43] Yet, a person's autonomy is not the whole story of the vowed life; his or her community is a reality in this process. Her concrete possibilities, the constraints that hem him in, the opportunities that call her forth, and the psychological, social, and historical achievements and abnormalities that make up any situation mark the existence of the religious. In turn, the working out of the individual autonomy of members marks the history of the community. The individuals in a community are their greatest resource. The bonds between the individual and the community are not the primary object of the vow but are included in the life direction expressed. These realities require communities today to also take responsibility for providing a climate for flourishing for all members to live out their commitment. With the aging process in many congregations, this requires a very generative spirit in all the members.

A vow is commonly understood to be a resolution that has no exception, that closes off choices which do not foster its path. It differs from a good intention or a goal which expresses a desire for a time. Because a vow has no exception, it does not mean it always regulates behavior or performance; we can fail to follow it. However, it marks such behavior as breaking the vow, or permission can be granted to be freed from a

---

[41]Canon 1191 *1. A vow, that is, a deliberate and free promise made to God about a possible and better good, must be fulfilled by reason of the virtue of religion.
[42]Here, we are referring to the form of religious life within a congregation.
[43]Italics added. Lonergan, "The Mediation of Christ in Prayer," 173.

vow. However, behavior contrary to a vow does not change the definition of the vow. The vows of religious life are one expression of a path of life to love God and neighbor. There are both clear boundaries to the vows as well as indeterminacies as members, and communities, grow in awareness of their significance and ramifications in the context in which they live. Vows in religious life are usually public.[44] They outline perimeters of a lifestyle which sets a path of personal transformation and links it to the transformation, needs, and healing of others in concrete situations. For a religious, vows are a public declaration of the style and contours of how one will live the Christian life, in respect to sexuality, possessions, and use of one's freedom in collaboration with the mission of one's congregation or the mission of the church. Vows are fundamentally an expression of hope that the desires of one's heart will be fulfilled in the mystery of the journey of one's life with God and others.

Finally, the canonical definition of a vow mentions it must be fulfilled by means of the virtue of religion. Encased in this juridical language, however, is a deep truth of religious life. Religion can appear to be one choice among others, as any other choice. In the context of a consumer society, religious identity can seem like other choices, a preference for a style of faith, or a selection among options.[45] On the contrary, Hans Joas argues that the will which responds to religion is distinguishable conceptually from a rational choice between preferences. Faith is itself a state of grace: humans can aspire to it but cannot coerce it.

Religious faith involves an experience of self-transcendence, of being moved beyond the self by another, a situation, or a personal recognition of something of which one was previously unaware. The will expressed in this situation is one of surrender. One is now in a new place, experienced as a better self, a truer self, or a hidden self that is not as positive as once thought but is integrated into a fuller sense of self—as one measures by a different standard. One is moved or seized by something: one experiences a self-surrender to "more."

It is common that people may know they have experienced something religiously, but they may not know what it means. The experience of being moved requires interpretation. Religious experience is not something which flows from previous cultural or religious interpretative patterns. Rather it demands continued interpretations to be meaningful to people of the times. This highlights the importance of meaningful community experiences, prayer, liturgy, and service over the lifetime of a religious to integrate faith with the experiences of living. It also confirms the importance of religious relating religious life to the society in which they are embedded, as well as remaining open to other cultural expressions across the globe.

William James describes the faith of a religious person not as holding onto something to be true in the cognitive sense, a belief that might be shaken by discursive argument,

---

[44]Canon 1192 *1. A vow is public if a legitimate superior accepts it in the name of the Church; otherwise, it is private.
[45]Hans Joas, *Do We Need Religion?* trans. Alex Skinner (London: Paradigm, 2008), 29.

but rather as an attitude toward reality underpinned by the sure sense that a greater power is present. Like someone who falls in love, the beloved affects one's life, even when not physically present.[46] Vows, ongoing conversion, and prayer all share a common source. All are marked by a certain non-volitional character, even though they involve serious personal choice. At heart, all are ways one participates in the power from which an individual's life force flows. One does not create this power; rather, one touches into it and is moved by it—one touches into wholeness. Prayer and all the elements of one's spiritual life is a witness that something real is there.[47]

Vows and the Counsels in Postmodern Life

The great plurality of lifestyles which exist in modern society can appear to be an obstacle to religious vocations, since there are so many things one can become. This sense of plural options is coupled in society with a weakening of the institutions of marriage and religious life. Many of the paths offered in our pluralistic society reflect a life course based on the power of self-sufficiency in an immanent frame. These models evidentially lose their appeal when the life they promise does not emerge as envisioned or when the challenges of life transform their carefree image. Personal tools to face obstacles, even for the fortunate, often seem to be missing. Modern culture is silent about an option of a life requiring commitment, sacrifice, and self-discipline. Rather, life seems to be defined by a career path focused on a function to be performed if there is a desire in the wider society for it to fulfill. Who needs a church which makes demands when our culture urges us to look at only one side of life, the sweet without the bitter? When human life is understood and liberated on its own terms, there is no need for God. We can save ourselves.

Belief in something beyond self-offers to a person not simply a match for aptitudes or desires, but a potential for becoming which is comprehensive enough to incorporate all of life with its twists and turns, and its deeper needs for love and significance. Religion must be able to point to something in its living that is not simply a religious legitimation of the values of the society in which it lives.[48] Religious life, and Christian marriage, among others offer this more comprehensive and realistic path. The vows do not exhaust what is involved in either vocation. The vows of religious life, based on the tradition of the counsels, only find their purpose in union with Jesus Christ, in a love like his own.[49] After Vatican II, it was debated whether the use of the counsels themselves, which so decisively characterized the self-understanding of the religious orders of the past,

---

[46]William James, *The Varieties of Religious Experience* (Cambridge, MA: Harvard University Press, 1985), 66. See also Merkle, *Sensing the Spirit*, 68–9.

[47]Ann and Barry Ulanov, *Primary Speech: A Psychology of Prayer* (Louisville, KY: Westminster John Knox Press, 1982), 126.

[48]Johann Baptist Metz, *Faith in History and Society* (New York: Seabury Press, 1980).

[49]St. Thomas Aquinas saw the merit of the counsels, not so much in the "thing in itself," as their capacity to lead to a transformation to love (his words, as instruments of perfection) ST. II-II, 183–9. See Anil D'Almedia, SJ,

could still be maintained in the post conciliar years.[50] This question is often raised by religious who claim the vows need new names. Poverty, chastity, and obedience do not cover their experience of discipleship as religious. Our exploration will recognize that the use of aptitudes, personal development, and capacities both for God and to be with others are all part of the sense of wholeness which the vows embrace (*PC* 1). The focus of this text is not to pursue new names for vows; rather, it will attempt to highlight their multidimensional character as well as relationship to central dynamisms of the human personality and life journey. The emphasis of "touching wholeness" as a lens to view the vows is not to replace them, rather to unfold their character as doors to true transformation. For that reason, in the following development of each of the vows of obedience, poverty, and celibacy, we will weave together how the vows embrace the dimensions of a well-lived life in Christ and the transformations which are incorporated on the journey of wholeness. We hope these ponderings lead the reader both to recognize these passages in their own lives and to add to these insights, but also, to own how the path of the vows provides and can bring forth the wholeness they desire for themselves and the world. This is their witness to those who follow. If the vows need to be renamed, we will leave that to others. This text aims at a reflection on the significance of a life formed through the vows in the world today.

"Vocation to Live Religious Poverty in India," *Vidyajyoti Journal of Theological Reflection* 82, no. 9 (September 2018): 654–78.
[50]Peters, "Charism and the Consecrated Life," 56, note 38.

PART II
THE VOWS OF RELIGIOUS LIFE IN A SECULAR WORLD

CHAPTER 5
OBEDIENCE
THE CHALLENGE OF AUTONOMY AND PLURALITY

The journey of life is not meant to be traveled alone; rather, we are meant to walk with others (Gen. 2:18). Though faith commitment is free and personal, God calls us in community, as the People of God (*LG* 9). Just as God called the people of Israel his own people and made covenants and transformed them, we as the "new people of God" are invited into this relationship through the Holy Spirit. The congregation to which a religious belongs is integral to how he or she participates in the community of the church and beyond. Both the religious and their community are called at this time of transition, to the covenantal and transformative relationships to which God draws them. Obedience is central to their response.

Formators in religious congregations often say obedience rather than celibacy is more difficult for new members to understand. In a culture in which autonomy is such a high value, this is not surprising. It seems fair to say even longstanding members of religious congregations struggle with the meaning of obedience today.[1] The interpretative framework of one's culture impacts an understanding of obedience. Today, we find that groups where authority has a central role, like family and church, are often disparaged and seen in tension with personal fulfillment.[2] Moderns often assume that a "perfect community" is marked by the type of organization which creates conditions where everyone can do their own thing without interference. Autonomy, as the capacity for self-determination or to direct my life as I want, suggests the directives of another are totally unnecessary for its realization. If the main goal of life is maximum possible self-determination, then the idea of obedience is superfluous. Instead, moderns often consciously or unconsciously hold the hope and desire that there will exist such a complementarity among their desires and those of others that a harmony of action will follow. Some assume that God or nature will bring us to a stability and peace in life without any reliance on the intervention of the restrictive authority of institutions or structures. These appealing but deceptive hopes of modernity are likely to impact the modern person's first thoughts about obedience.[3] Goethe's advice that the master is

---

[1] John P. Langan, SJ, "The Good of Obedience in a Culture of Autonomy," *Studies in the Spirituality of the Jesuits* 32, no. 1 (January, 2000): 1–32.
[2] Judith A. Merkle, *Being Faithful: Christian Commitment in Modern Society* (London: T&T Clark, 2010), chapter 5 on church and family, 79–98.
[3] Langan, "The Good of Obedience for a Culture of Autonomy," 4.

shown by working within limits seems absent from the modern imagination. So, how do we make the vow of obedience intelligible today?

As we approach obedience, we will treat it, as we will poverty and obedience, with a set of questions which hopefully will suggest to the reader its importance and meaning today beyond traditional formulas. First, we will look at obedience simply as part of the maturation process of human life—obedience as a human challenge. As in self-mediation, here obedience impacts how we seek to understand ourselves and the world around us, by learning what is real and valuable in life and developing the skills of human living. Second, we will examine the lived reality of obedience in adult life, as religious. Since we develop not alone but with others, in mutual self-mediation, we take responsibility for the traditions which have been given to us and offer their wisdom to the coming generation. We commit ourselves to a path, forge a life together with others, and use our gifts to collaborate in meeting the needs of the world and church and make the changes necessary to adapt our lives to the needs of the gospel. Third, we will reflect on obedience as a spiritual capacity and way of life. Obedience is the posture which both grounds this search, promotes bonding and collaborative life in community and ministry, and links daily life to relationship to the person of Jesus Christ. Obedience has another dimension, as a mutual self-mediation with Christ, not just self-mediation through another. The intellectual, affective, moral, and religious conversions which enter the life of a religious through obedience make concrete their life with Christ, as well as their life with Christ shapes their response. As we discuss obedience, we will focus on issues which seem particularly important in this time of transition and leave the rest to the reflection of the readers and their communities.

Obedience and Secular Culture

It is not just religious who confront the reality of obedience in modern life. In fact, a former understanding of obedience in religious life as simply following orders might be a criterion for employment in a corporate office, a health care facility, a brokerage, or the key to upward mobility in a political party. "Obedience" can be a cloak for cowardice and a signature of someone who lacks a sense of personal integrity. St. Augustine once said that even a band of robbers have community. This suggests the dynamics of authority and obedience are necessary even to a life of crime. Augustine alerts us that many religious realities, like obedience, have an instrumental value, but their true meaning goes beyond these superficial appearances.

Obedience seems out of fashion in the modern world. Moderns have been attracted for centuries to a world in which individual desires are easily harmonized and satisfied. This "dream" is often an impetus for those seeking to be set free from traditional societies and customs. John Langan reminds, "the ideal of the individual set free from artificial or irrational bonds and empowered to become autonomous and self-determining emerges as one of the most powerful and most attractive objectives of an enlightened or modern society."⁴ Popular culture echoes these sentiments as encouragement to "do one's thing" is often joined with criticism of institutions believed to impede personal fulfillment, defined by the individual. The possibility that society can be organized so that each can do precisely what they want, without interference of others, remains in the background of modern cultural horizons.

What further complicates this situation is the impact of a *nova effect* on secular society: an explosion of ethical, religious, and atheistic options that offer explanations of a meaningful life. Most approaches limit themselves to only what is possible in this life and leave the question of transcendence unaddressed.⁵ While influenced by this culture, the meaning of obedience in religious life rests on an alternative vision of life. Life's meaning extends beyond the natural scope of life, from birth to death, and there exists a transformation beyond that of human perfection. Langan offers an example of the Christian approach by citing St. Ignatius. His vision calls for a life marked by engagement, strenuous activity, and obedient service. Personal projects are not rejected but they do not stand alone; they are subordinated to gospel ideals of the Kingdom. The goal setting involved goes beyond the ordinary aspirations of the energetic and ambitious, good in themselves, like career, winning a marathon or climbing Mt. Everest. While these goals require a program of preparation, practice, and execution, they have a path to successful accomplishment that is well known. The goals of Ignatius, on the other hand, are compatible with a wide range of means and intermediate conditions and require other capacities than know-how to accomplish. They are goals that are not primarily within the scope of human agency and human planning. Yet they are not just generic or abstract pie in the sky. They have a major influence in making decisions and providing direction to choices. The expectation is, "individuals will be willing to join their lives and their projects under an authority capable of coordinating and integrating their individual efforts into the larger but less than ultimate purposes of meeting the needs of the Church and the various communities it serves."⁶ The human dilemma of obedience today, the tension between autonomy and plurality, is impacted by the multiplicity of options in society. However, its origins as an alternative view of life have been encountered by all in history who have followed it.

Charles Taylor contributes another insight into obedience in secular society by pointing to two highly desired values in modern life: autonomy and authenticity and their relationship. Autonomy is the state or condition of self-governance—leading one's life according to the reasons, values, or desires that are authentically one's own. Taylor charges that human autonomy cannot be reached in isolation, as often held in society. Rather, the self is defined in part by communal boundaries. For instance, people cannot become autonomous without the language learned in community. We learn in a community the meanings and values necessary to live peacefully and reach a sense

---

⁴Langan, "The Good of Obedience for a Culture of Autonomy," 4.
⁵Charles Taylor, *A Secular Age* (Cambridge: The Belknap Press of Harvard University, 2007), 3–20.
⁶Langan, "The Good of Obedience for a Culture of Autonomy," 5.

of personal identity among others. Part of the human condition is the desire to belong somewhere. The need to belong spurs human activity. We require agreement in some form. We enact values, we argue about them, sometimes we even fight about them. Yet, their significance is never reached alone. The more important relationships are to us, the more impact they have on this process. We define our identity always in dialogue with, and at times in struggle against, the things our significant others want to see in us. Even after we outgrow some of these others, and they disappear from our lives, the conversation with them continues within us as long as we live.[7]

Since autonomy is formed in interaction with others and life itself, it requires our involvement. We confront things which are contradictory which must be rejected, complementary which expand our horizons, moving and discouraging which engaged our energies, or just "different" which and must be integrated into our other priorities. Taking responsibility for oneself, self-creation, is the first step in life; it continues throughout our lives and requires others. Hence, in a puzzling way, autonomy and plurality are related. The one thing we have in common with those who appear "other" in our lives is they too have a "self" and a reason to be. Karl Rahner claims that the real commitment of obedience is not constituted by a promise to obey the commands of a superior; rather, it consists in binding ourselves to a definite and permanent mode of life, in accord with the evangelical counsels—religious life. With "one wild and precious life," one makes a choice throughout the whole of life.[8] This mode of life involves a concern not for transitory things but for things of God. It implies the sacrifice of significant values such as the independent orderings of our life—made possible through the possession of material goods or the freedom to act as we would through the founding of a family. It requires a measure of religious activity such as prayer and ministry. Obedience, in religious life, is the acceptance of the common good in imitation of Christ according to a constitution that the Church has approved as a path of Christian living.[9]

To integrate the timeless insights concerning the *vita apostolica* in scripture and tradition with awareness of contemporary life and culture to gain insight into obedience requires a type of dialectical thinking. It is a type of thinking which can draw from multiple perspectives and arrive at a reconciliation of seemingly contradictory information and postures. We do this knowing no one thinks exactly as the societal ideals of a meaningful life we have depicted. Terms used to describe general directions in thinking are "ideal types," not the mindset of any individual, who is far more complex. In dialectical thinking, there is a combination of the concrete, the contradictory, and the dynamic. The Christian life today requires the capacity to balance these realities. The

---

[7] Charles Taylor, *Multiculturalism and the Politics of Recognition*. The University Center for Human Values (Princeton, NJ: Princeton University Press, 1994).
[8] Mary Oliver, "The Summer Day," in *New and Selected Poems* (Boston: Beacon Press, 1992).
[9] Karl Rahner, *Christian in the Marketplace* (New York: Sheed and Ward, 1966), appendix. As quoted in Gerard Dubois, "Obedience: Evangelical and Monastic," *Cistercian Studies* 8, no. 2 (1973): 87–108 at 102.

dynamic principle that moves us beyond the apparent opposing choices is love. In this territory, the vow of obedience dwells.

Obedience as a Human Challenge

Erik Erikson and the Life Cycle

All three vows impact human development. Our response to life, marked by the successes and limitations of our personal growth, influences the capacity to live the vows, as well as experience the joy and meaning they promise. When Jesus said "I came so that they may have life and have it more abundantly" (Jn 10:10), it seems fair to say Jesus included in his desire for us the integration of life described by the psychologist Erik Erikson. We will call on his developmental theory to gain insight into the personal transformation involved in all three vows, and here in obedience.

In the early 1950s, Erikson envisioned the creation of the self as occurring through a lifelong sequence of developmental stages. Each person goes through eight stages in life. Each stage involves a crisis or conflict, whose resolution is crucial for continued development. The eight stages are the following: trust-mistrust (ages 0–1), autonomy-shame and doubt (1–3), initiative-guilt (3–5), industry-inferiority (5–12), intimacy-isolation (18–40), generativity-stagnation (40–65), and integrity-despair (65+).[10] The ages assigned are common times in which these issues arise, as the crises characterize the predominant psychodynamics of that age. However, the crises are not restricted to these periods alone. Throughout our lives, we return to these conflicts if our life situation engages the emotional conflicts they involve.

One works through each crisis by finding an appropriate ratio between the positive and negative poles of the struggle. In the crisis of trust versus mistrust, the goal is not to eliminate mistrust, but to have trust predominate over mistrust in one's life orientation. At each crisis we must reorient our lives and relate to the world in new ways. Social demands and physiological changes in our lives require adaptive emotional, perceptual, and cognitive responses. These crises do not arise because of our choices; rather, they present themselves without our permission. For instance, aging and its issues are not self-selected, nor are we presented with the option to skip our adolescence. We are vulnerable at each transition, as what "worked" at a previous stage is no longer adaptive to the present challenge. As we leave one state of nuclear conflict and enter another, anxiety can arise.[11] Over time, we develop vital strengths from effective negotiation of the crisis. Yet, at a later juncture, we may experience the same crisis, but from a different perspective of experience.

---

[10] Erik H. Erikson, *Childhood and Society*, 2nd rev. ed. (New York: W.W. Norton and Co., 1963) (1950). A study of the vows relating them to Erikson's insights is developed in: Judith A. Merkle, *A Different Touch: A Study of the Vows in Religious Life* (Collegeville, MN: The Liturgical Press, 1998).
[11] Don S. Browning, *Religious Thought and Modern Psychologies* (Philadelphia: Fortress Press, 1978), 220–4.

Erikson claims human development follows an "epigenetic principle." All advances to later stages of development, leading to independence, maturity, and responsibility, carry forward lower levels of development. Without the earlier, the later stages are not better or stronger—just repetitive. Later stages of development become strong, rich, and stable by including and restating earlier levels of development.

In our study of obedience, we will suggest the psychosocial crisis most engaged in the life patterns the vows encounter. Erikson's insights intersect also with Lonergan's intellectual, affective, moral, and religious conversions in the life of a religious. Together they offer a heuristic device to gain insight into life issues which the scope of the vow embraces. All connections cannot be made, but some will be noted by way of example.

Trust-Mistrust

The path of obedience plunges one into the human dynamism of trust and mistrust in a new way.[12] Over the course of a lifetime, obedience involves a trust-mistrust relationship with one's community and church, as well as state and civic institutions. All are connected to a relationship with God.[13] The conflict between trust-mistrust is engaged in infancy when dependency on caregivers to fill basic needs is tested. Through interactions with them, the infant learns whether life is dependable or filled with betrayal and abandonment. The ideal connection between trust and mistrust is a balance between the two.

Someone whose trust has been betrayed repeatedly may bring higher expectations to the community or greater needs for consistency of life and response from others. During these times of transition and uncertainty in religious life, in church and society, this need can escalate.[14] The conflict of trust-mistrust elicits inner strength of character through the tension between the negative pole of gluttony, which can stagnate growth, as well as healing potential of hope. Hope is ultimately "saving" and leads to wholeness. Obedience poses for a religious both possibilities. The goal of trust-mistrust is not to trust everyone. The task is to develop appropriate trust in others, in oneself, and in life, as well as a suitable distrust of what is not trustworthy and ultimately brings harm. Gluttony is an act of mistrust as well as indiscriminate trust. Gluttony is a desire for more than we need: more attention, sex, or its substitutes in food and drink or other addictive behaviors. Anticipation of future deprivation makes one overly demanding in the present. The gluttonous person is indiscriminate and places trust in substances, processes, or food and drink to satisfy present wants. Gluttony ignores the dangers of attending to the real consequences of its wants. Rowan Williams depicts gluttony as the urge to absorb and

---

[12]Merkle, *A Different Touch* 205–20.
[13]One cannot ignore, for example, the impact of the sexual abuse practice—a breach of trust—on church practice and attendance.
[14]Merkle, *Sensing the Spirit*, 157–9, on uncertainty in contemporary times.

consume, centered in a self-oriented picture of oneself. It is healed as we acknowledge we are created, therefore in need of others.[15] To maintain relationships, we need to respect boundaries. Living this realization requires that we begin with trusting someone.

Congregations too can adopt gluttonous patterns. They can make too many demands on members. They can focus so much on the immediate satisfactions of members that they fail to hope for and plan a future. The virtue of the trust-mistrust conflict is hope. Hope is the capacity to believe that one's wishes can be fulfilled in spite of the deep urges and rage that mark the beginning of existence and continue through life.[16] Rahner relates hope to the call of obedience. Hope "forbids us to invent our own happiness and struggle for the paradise we like. It jars us out of all our life's evidence, plausibilities, and comfortable securities, and shoves us into the infinite darkness of God, which we can only behold with God's eyes."[17]

Initiative versus Guilt

The crisis of initiative versus guilt is centered in a new child's capacities for language, mobility, and capacity for more activity. Initiative is a sense of ambition and purpose. Guilt is the negative pole of this crisis, the anxiety produced when boundaries have been crossed. Initiative involves the capacity to cooperate with others, not just to take charge. Initiative, rather than conformity, draws one into the common purpose of religious life. The virtue-vice struggle of this crisis is between purpose/dedication and greed. Both potentials are developed through interaction with others and both involve negotiating of boundaries.[18]

Initiative involves the capacity to include the will of others in cooperative efforts. Purpose and dedication form the capacity to imagine and pursue a goal, face defeats, deal with limited opportunities, and overcome fears. Dedication is the capacity to set aside certain tasks and focus on them, rather than trying to do everything. Purpose and dedication bridge the gap between desire and competence.

Greed is the desire to possess or acquire something in an amount far greater than needed. Instead of testing the world and seeking to act in accordance with its laws and movements, greed seeks to make the world conform to its desires. Greed in this sense is related to the negative pole of this crisis, guilt. Healthy guilt is the awareness that one has trespassed legitimate boundaries. In contrast, unhealthy guilt squelches initiative and can become a mechanism of social control.

---

[15]Rowan Williams, *Passions of the Soul* (London: Bloomsbury Continuum, 2024), 58.
[16]Erik Erikson, *Insight and Responsibility* (New York: W.W. Norton and Co., 1964), 118. In relationships to congregations, see Merkle, *Sensing the Spirit*, 154–9.
[17]Karl Rahner, "Hope," in *The Practice of Faith: A Handbook of Contemporary Spirituality* (New York: Crossroad, 1983), 249.
[18]Merkle, *A Different Touch*, 209–11.

Greed for power can block legitimate outlets for initiative of members and can lead to paralysis in a congregation. Greed or avarice is a longing for control over others, over the circumstances of life, and over one's image. It feeds a false image of life that such control will bring personal happiness. Instead of an openness to a reality beyond my own selfhood, greed offers an elusive picture of myself and the world.[19] Members controlled by guilt expect leadership to do everything for them and lack proper initiative of their own; hence, their needs are never satisfied. Controlling others through inflicting guilt is an evasion of the hard work to motivate and collaborate on common efforts. Greed limits affective bonding and the sense of collaboration and belonging it represents. While initiative envisions outcomes that are realistic, greed is based on distorted thinking and dismisses information that does not conform to personal desires. The practice of guilt and greed are ways to avoid the challenge of initiative. Greed is a deadly sin because it distracts us from what is important, the very object of the vow of obedience. Purpose and dedication build bridges to the future. For this reason, the tension between purpose/dedication and greed is a dynamic of the vow of obedience, especially in this time of transition.

Industry versus Inferiority

Erikson claims that the crisis of the school age is not bound to physical changes, as in earlier periods. The challenge of industry versus feelings of inferiority is created by the need to be useful and productive. This need extends over the lifetime of a religious. Industry is the capacity to sublimate personal disappointments in the interest of being productive. It involves taking pleasure in the completion of projects through attention and perseverance.[20] Industry involves the capacity to face limits and failures yet be productive. Sooner or later, we measure our capacities against others and come up short. Feelings of inferiority set in. Competence and envy are the virtue-vice poles of this crisis, as both are responses to the challenge of industry. Envy is the discontent and ill-will that surfaces in the face of the possessions or advantages of another. Envy is the desire for these possessions for us, not necessarily the will to invest in the work it takes to acquire them. Competence, on the other hand, is the acquisition of skills. It involves the discovery of what works in a situation and gives its own self-verification. This comes from successful experiences with the outside world. It involves dexterity, intelligence, and discipline.

Instead of doing the hard work of competence and risking failure, in envy we seek to feel competent by bringing the other person down to our size. Envy is the shortcut to industry. The human spirit can hold the delusion that the accomplishments of another diminish its own. Envy can control a person so that they avoid productive situations

---

[19] Williams, *Passions of the Soul*, 61–7.
[20] Donald Capps, *Deadly Sins and Saving Virtues* (Philadelphia, PA: Fortress Press, 1987), 39ff., 91 ff.

completely. However, in the life of a religious, these self-imposed restrictions are not those of obedience or humility. One can be highly competitive, employing envy, using criticism and detraction regarding others, rather than engaging them. Envious people convince themselves of boundaries they set themselves and others find these very difficult to overcome or challenge. Envy partners with the negative pole of this crisis and feeds an inferiority which covers up an unwillingness to put forth effort or risk failure.[21] Spiritually, envy looks at another rather than at Christ who goes ahead of us in our life journey.[22] The developmental task of industry-inferiority is to use and enjoy our real capacities, to accept others that may be brighter, faster, or more accomplished, to find joy in the true satisfaction of using one's own gifts. The vow of obedience further orients this process under the guidance of the Spirit. However, the initial task of being productive is a human capacity upon which grace builds.

In the community, most people share both sides of the industry-inferiority equation. They are competent in some things and inferior in others. Envy can cripple members through submission to the paralysis of being envied. On the other hand, envy can be productive. It can be a signal that another has a skill or a quality that I want for myself. If used correctly and used as impetus for competent action, it can be a signal to grow.

Most people wish to feel useful and productive all their lives. The vow of obedience taps into this core human desire. The virtue-vice characterization of these various life crises in Erikson's developmental theory shows that the accomplishment of the core elements of life tasks, shared by all, builds human strengths, and that avoiding the challenges of these passages harms our very person. Regarding the capital sins only as moral failures suggests that letting them rule our lives has no negative effect on our happiness or person. Some think our "sins" affect God but not ourselves. Others think even the notion of sin is artificial, a vestige from the past, having no relevance today. A psychological reading of these struggles does not erase their moral content but frames them in the deeper meaning the tradition has always intended. Virtue was for our own good as humans deeply loved by God, not a test to measure our worthiness. Erikson offers us one language of this path of human wholeness and its course. St. Irenaeus said, "The glory of God is a human being fully alive." For this reason, we recognize that the path of the vows engages in the challenges of being human we meet in the first part of our lives and return to often as we grow and mature. The vow of obedience draws the real person we are, no more and no less, more deeply into the mystery of life with Christ.

---

[21]For a study of envy, the envied, and envying, see Ann and Barry Ulanov, *Cinderella and Her Sisters* (Philadelphia, PA: The Westminster Press, 1983).

[22]Willams, *Passions of the Soul*, 90.

Obedience as a Lived Reality

Obedience enters our relationship with others, but not through a loss of our own will, as some interpretations of obedience suggest. An absence of will is not capable of the initiative required to be productive. Obedience checks a "proprietary" or a "possessive" will that looks only after its own interests, a will that is not available to the lead of the Spirit or the needs of others, especially the common good.[23] Obedience is not just a posture toward an authority figure. Rather, it impacts our life with others more as an interior disposition, an attitude toward oneself, God, and being in the world. It raises the question: Can I give way for the common good? Will I collaborate to make a way? Can I walk with others on the way? Do I seek the Spirit leading on the way? An authority figure cannot force any of these dispositions; they must arise from within. Obedience calls both the person who holds formal authority and the members to look for the common good.

Obedience does not require a person always to do the contrary of what they want, to be continually frustrated. This mistaken posture toward obedience makes an absolute of obedience as "freedom from" one's own judgment. Gospel living is meant to create a "freedom to" which flows from an awareness of God's love for us and letting ourselves to be loved. This creates the freedom to take initiative, to sustain difficulties, to integrate both successes and failures in our lives, and to offer one's judgment when elicited. Obedience is lived in modern life not just in receiving orders. Often today permission is given for a project or ministry placement a member initiates, rather than one created "from above." The risk level for the individual is higher since the initiative came from them. Obedience is more than simply functional. "obedience, conceived as a social instrument for allocating resources and as an institutional means for effectively carrying out tasks, does not give us an adequate appreciation of the religious meaning of obedience."[24] Obedience involves a respect for conscience in the midst of a search for the will of God and a desire to give oneself to causes, values, persons, and communities that are seen to be of greater worth than the individual self. A holistic sense of obedience goes beyond the model of autonomy in society just recast in religious terms.

Obedience is not a religious excuse for inappropriate control of others; nor should religious collude with forces in church and society with this aim. Religious today cannot partner with movements that are authoritarian and rest on manipulation of others through fear and subtle social control. Religious obedience should model a healthy response to the needs of our world. Peace and harmony require a society which has strong enough resolve to withstand authoritarian measures, domestic and international, which operate through unnecessary coercion under the "sheep's clothing" of return to values and standards. The public witness of religious today can exhibit a balance between conscience and collaboration needed for a stable global society. They must avoid demonstrating the behaviors of a negative authoritarian institution that people no

---

[23] Dubois, "Obedience: Evangelical and Monastic," 92.
[24] Langan, "The Good of Obedience in a Culture of Autonomy," 7.

longer trust to protect important values or concede to the individualism of the culture that cannot maintain the institutions which ensure personal freedom. The practice of obedience in these cases transcends its personal good to offer public witness.

Power, Autonomy, and the Limits of Agency

While autonomy holds great prominence in the values of modern life, it is often associated with qualities which are highly criticized: individualism, subjectivism, and relativism. Autonomy, as understood at the core of obedience, is identified in a different manner. A broader vision of autonomy includes the importance of social respect and moral finitude. This comprehensive vision offers members and those in positions of authority with new challenges. It fosters a capacity and a witness to better human relationships necessary in the world order. The building blocks of a holistic sense of obedience go beyond a zero-sum equation of "power over." Instead, the realm of obedience involves the coordination of responsible freedoms among diverse perspectives and persistent uncertainty, or contingency.[25]

A modern concept of obedience is not centered in passivity but in initiative for the good. The fact we are limited in our understanding of good, as well as our capacity to be effective in bringing it about, does not diminish human dignity; it makes it all the greater. The heart of ongoing moral conversion is the desire to keep trying. Its motivation is not to appear all-powerful and capable, "to be like gods," but springs from the desire to do the right thing. Obedience is the exercise of autonomy within a community of finite people trying to do the same thing. Recognition of finitude is at the heart of the mutuality of a life of service and of community life.[26] God's affirmation of us is greater than any of us can attain on our own. Obedience is to foster the mutual recognition and respect we give to one another, despite the fragile and vulnerable freedom we each possess. Without this, the affective bond in the community is not sustainable. Our freedom is fragile not just by the inconsistency of our intentions, or by inattention and banality impacted by the everyday, but also by the violence and violation members encounter through the misuse of power, and the difficulties of life of their own life course.[27] Pope Francis recognizes human vulnerability on a wider scale in *Fratteli Tutti*. He points to the "shattered dreams" caused by "reductive anthropological visions" that allow injustice to persist (*FT* 22).[28] Such vulnerability, and its admission, is crucial to the hospitable welcome to the

---

[25] See Phillip J. Rossi, SJ, "Faith, Autonomy, and the Limits of Agency in a Secular World," in *At the Limits of the Secular: Catholic Reflections on Faith and Public Life*, ed. William Barbieri (Grand Rapids, MI: Wm B. Eerdmans, 2014), 226–49.

[26] A community examen might be: Is it possible for members, as well as those with positional authority, to admit mistakes without the consequence of losing power?

[27] Rossi, "Faith, Autonomy, and the Limits of Agency," 233.

[28] See Marcus Mescher, *The Study Guide to the Encyclical Letter of Pope Francis: Fratelli Tutti: On Fraternity and Social Friendship* (Mahwah, NJ: Paulist Press, 2021).

other that shapes the witness of religious congregations in secular society. Obedience in this sense contrasts with self-interest, disregard, mistrust, and discord that flow from a culture of autonomy, with its goal of standing alone superior to the other.

Power

Power at its core has three dimensions. At its basic form, power is persistence in being before difference, an aspect of the tension between autonomy and plurality. We do not just exist, but people can examine us, question us, even try to define us—but we remain ourselves. The difference is external—our autonomy is called into question from the outside—yet it endures. "Power is unity of being with itself despite a difference, the presence of future being in present being."[29] This is the power of persistence. Second, there is the power of self-determination, the power to act toward a future. This is the power of self-preservation. Third is the power of giving, where one acts upon another and impacts their welfare. This is the productive, creative power of being itself. This power of becoming, among others, is reflected in the developmental crises of trust-mistrust, initiative-guilt, and industry-inferiority.

Political or social power is the will of individuals or groups exercising a determining influence on the communal life of a number of people within a common living space or organized structure.[30] Here a sense of power interfaces with obedience. In the church and religious life, there are individuals who have positional power. They operate on the basis of the role received and the jurisdiction and responsibility involved in the role. Besides positional power, they might employ transactional power, by having the power to offer incentives and enter into negotiations. Theologian Serena Noceti argues, "Both types simply manage what already exists or else implement slow, incremental changes"[31] Both types of power are helpful in the coordination of any group, but neither type can foster a collective identity or contribute to a "common reason" for strengthening ecclesial or communal relationships.

Both authority and obedience are practiced by all who share in the lived reality of obedience. While those with positional authority have designated roles, most situations call for the collaboration and participation of members. Members can cooperate, exercise their authority negatively through non-cooperation, or creatively through dialogue and collaboration. Sometimes there is a need to resolve problems of coordination; other times policies need to be adopted to implement values in the community life or ministry of members. Not as frequently, there are directives to individuals regarding serious

---

[29]Klaus Hemmerle, "Power," in *Encyclopedia of Theology: The Concise Sacramentum Mundi*, ed. Karl Rahner (New York: Crossroad, 1982), 1263–6 at 1264.
[30]Ibid., 1263.
[31]Serena Noceti, *Reforming the Church: A Synodal Way of Proceeding* (Mahwah, NJ: Paulist Press, 2023), 84.

matters in the expectation that they will be obeyed.[32] How authority and obedience involve these situations is impacted by their purpose and gravity. Our first thought regarding authority-subject relationships is that the authority is always a designated elected individual. However, that is not the case. There can be designated roles others assume to meet the needs of the group. Those who do assume positional authority are also under obedience to the community rule and the common good; their autonomy is not Absolute. Today, other structural forms of engagement are involved in meeting the needs of the lived reality of obedience: committees, chapters, staff positions, and the like. Consultations also engage non-members, such as advisory boards, hired firms, health care representatives, and state officials.

It has become obvious that for a wide range of decisions, open discussion and formal and informal consultation are necessary. When tasks are complex, a model of information traveling up and decisions traveling down are often not effective. It can happen that those with delegated authority know less about a project than those with expertise among the membership. More important is the participation of the membership in a decision, as far as possible, so that there is the necessary consensus to make a good decision and implement it. This requires a different kind of leadership and membership than what is required for obedience today.

Transformational Obedience

A type of leadership and membership is needed today which can go beyond managing what already exists. This calls for decisions to nurture a practice of obedience and leadership which can foster collective identity or contribute to a "common reason" for strengthening communal and church relationships.[33] The church, as well as religious communities, have traditionally relied on the "hard power" that is linked to authority roles in both organizations. This "power of role" has historically been given high social recognition and established both entities as effective bureaucratic organizations. Since Vatican II, congregations of religious women have experimented with their governing structures. They sought a governing style based more on mutuality. They attempted to integrate principles regulating relationships under the image of church, not solely as an institution but as the People of God, into their structures. This was an attempt to move from a type of monarchical model of organization, which impacted both church and congregations, to one more attuned to the equality of the baptized.[34] In religious congregations, there was also a need to shift how authority was used to heal the wounds

---

[32]Langan, "The Good of Obedience in a Culture of Autonomy," 9. The third example is likely the one most related to the canon law directives regarding obedience.
[33]Noceti, *Reforming the Church: A Synodal Way of Proceeding*, 84–5.
[34]Sandra Schneiders, *Buying the Field: Catholic Religious Life in Mission to the World* (New York: Paulist Press, 2013), 426.

felt by some members who were harmed by an overly institutionalized approach in the pre-Vatican era.

The call to a transformational style of leadership is more than a continuation of even this approach of renewal. Transformational leadership suggests the ability to inspire desired changes, motivate people to work for the common good, mobilize energy to move from individual to collective interests and actively involve intermediate groups and bodies, comprised of members and non-members. It constantly calls everyone through an authentic witness of life and meaningful verbal and symbolic communication, to the final objective. It does not just rely on role power, yet it still involves role distinction and jurisdiction. Transformational leadership uses emotional intelligence, empathy, and the ability to hear and recognize the needs of individuals. It has a pastoral tone. However, it is also capable of leading the transformation of an organization, not simply maintaining the status quo. It can deal with the ambiguities of an age of contingency: it can adjust to different contexts, use good timing, take advantage of current trends, adapt current strategies, and engage others in the rhythm of joint action.[35] The outcome of transformation, however, does not just require a renewed approach to leadership; it is dependent on the engagement of membership.

This type of leadership assumes an obedience of collaboration. Since many congregations are made up of mainly elderly people, it requires a willingness to overcome a natural reluctance to change or leave the task of carrying out any real change to those who will come later. However, no one will come later unless there is a movement forward. Middle-aged members, who are often considered "young" in aging congregations, also must move beyond their "sidelined" role in congregations. Often, members in older generations have continued to serve longer in central or support roles than in the past. This stems from their place as the dominant generation; there are fewer people to replace them; there are needs requiring immediate action; and some feel the adaptation after Vatican II is sufficient renewal. There is no openness to further change which could be initiated by a new generation. Because of changes in structures, younger members have ministered in contexts unknown to their community, leaving doubt in their community of their leadership capabilities.[36] Many have exhibited leadership elsewhere, but members have not witnessed it. The challenge of collaborative obedience for those in underrepresented generations, races, and cultural groups is to move beyond past hurts and alienation, and a comfort zone of non-participation, to step forward to serve when they are able.

The call of the synod calls for a different practice of obedience in the life of the church. Participation and responsibility for the life of the church, invited by baptism, evokes a new style of leadership and membership as "walking together" (*DSC* 11). For those with positional authority, this involves more the power to persuade rather than

---

[35]Noceti, *Reforming the Church: A Synodal Way of Proceeding*, 84–5.
[36]See Merkle, "The Niche of Religious Life," in *Sensing the Spirit*, 35–58.

a style of command and obedience.[37] It requires members to be willing to explore the consequences for people's lives if any side of a debate prevails. It expects of all the desire to remain open to the decision which best serves the common good.[38]

Transformational obedience requires new skills. The Word of God speaks in scripture, prayer, liturgical life, personal traditions, the teaching of the church, and the lives of the saints. Many would add the witness of those with moral courage in their own time. The existential world speaks through personal experience, other people, as well as the world events and daily situations.[39] Obedience is to foster attention to the truth; the truth is to promote "freedom from" biases and attachments to "freedom to" loving responsibility. If moral life, in its deepest sense, is the result of a new inner dynamic, the Spirit, and not just the result of the external constraints of the law, then the practice of transformational obedience requires both a deepening spirituality and attention to the tools which offer understanding of the world—economics, the social sciences, as well as psychology. Congregations since Vatican II have overcompensated for a lack of attention to the balance required by the above. Some tended toward over-reliance on a business model of organization, which does not speak to members' sense of purpose. Others have limited themselves to spiritual-theological categories, which seem unrelated to modern reality. Members and those with a position of authority in a model of transformational obedience are called beyond present impasses to attend to the need to consult, to commit to explore one's charism, to foster the needs of the church, and to discern what is required by the Spirit to move to the future.

Obedience as a Spiritual Capacity and Way of Life

How does awareness of contemporary societal pressures, like the tension between autonomy and plurality, or conflicts detailed by the social sciences, unveil any new understanding of the spiritual path of obedience? Psychology shows that the spiritual path of obedience includes normal development in conformity with the laws of growth— from outer-directedness to inner-directedness. The spiritual tradition, though, goes beyond a vision of human development as a conquest of self and the regulation of one's life. It enhances the path of obedience with the goal that no decision is made under the guidance of any inordinate attachment. The spiritual tradition affirms that the pluralism of one's life, which most divides our intentions, is not always that which comes from society, but from the multiple conflicting desires of our own heart. The book of Genesis

---

[37]Bernard J. Lee SM, "The Social Matrix of Religious Obedience," *Review for Religious* 67, no. 3 (2008): 290–303 at 295. Lee explains unilateral power as the capacity to influence, guide, adjust, manipulate, shape, control, to advance one's own purposes, and to be affected as little as possible in the process. Relational power presumes the ability to both produce and undergo an effect, since the capacity to absorb an influence is as truly a mark of power as is the strength involved in exerting an influence. This person is willing to be influenced by others in a climate of mutuality.

[38]Ibid., 301.

[39]Kathryn Fitzgerald, ACJ, "By Obedience to the Truth," *Review for Religious* 42, no. 5 (1983): 770–3.

outlines a deeper dimension of the struggle of autonomy and wholeness. The first human beings wanted the fruit of life (represented by the tree of life) themselves, taken by force, even if it was forbidden. They wanted to grasp this divine condition—you will be like gods—by their own powers alone. Jesus, however, took another way. He emptied himself of this condition, setting aside even what was permitted. Matthew states, "Then he said to his disciples, 'Whoever wishes to come after me must deny himself, take up his cross, and follow me. For whoever wishes to save his life will lose it, but whoever loses his life for my sake will find it'" (Mt. 16:24-25). To listen, which is at the heart of obedience, is not a giving up of self. A person without a sense of self does not feel the tension in waiting and listening because they desire another to assume responsibility for their self-direction. They are relieved of the stress of decisions. Rather, the ability to wait and listen, to look for God's will, is a recognition that our salvation is not at all in proportion to our strength and striving but is God's gift to us.[40] We are given wholeness by God, and it is in trust in God's love we strive for wholeness in our lives. Jesus' command to his followers can seem like double talk unless we can embrace the depth of connection with God it invites. It is not a command we ever accomplish, but it is a path of invitation which leads to our deepest desire. Doing God's will can never be separated from clinging to God's love for us and being willing to continually open our lives to that love and its consequences, as Jesus himself opened his life to the love of his Father. This is having a capacity for God to change one's life course. It impacts one's intersubjective dealings; it becomes a structural relationship in making decisions; it penetrates the emotional quality of relating to those with positional authority; it subordinates one's will to another in a voluntary way even in a community of equals. "The vow forms a gift of certain aspects of self. The subject, like the superior, remains a person who has responsibility for his (her) own growth as a moral and religious person, who has obligations of conscience, and who has to determine the shape and the meaning of his (her) own life."[41] Its motivating force is love, love shared, and love shown in deed.

Law of the Cross

Obedience is often connected to a notion of self-sacrifice as a goal in itself, as a following of the crucified Christ. However, this interpretation misses the point of obedience, as the law of the cross is overshadowed by the law of perfection. The renunciation of obedience flows from the self-sacrifice required by all love. A love which only requires self-sacrifice and nothing else is questionable and is not love identified with wholeness or discipleship. Attempts to understand the mystery of obedience only through the social sciences also fall short. Psychological and sociological studies of obedience offer insight into relationships, commitment, and human development; however, evangelical

---

[40]Dubois, "Obedience: Evangelical and Monastic," 92.
[41]Langan, "The Good of Obedience in a Culture of Autonomy," 17.

obedience can only find its true meaning in the essence of the Gospel.[42] Philosophical underpinnings of obedience assist in understanding the integrity of human life and the meaning of self-determination, but this too only highlights what encompasses obedience rather than defining it. Obedience is the heart of a listening and waiting for, and response to an encounter with God; a hearing which touches one's heart and calls a person to a new place, internally or externally. Obedience in this sense is tied to a life of prayer, where one becomes attuned to God's word and learns to recognize and allow its impact. All obedience leads to Christ and responds to his invitation, come, follow me (Mt. 4:19). This frames obedience beyond the work religious do, to the why they do it. This does not diminish the professional or ministerial quality of what is done; rather, it highlights the love behind it.

The religious meaning of obedience grounds all its other dimensions. It unveils the human energy, goodwill, and love involved in becoming with its ultimate purpose. The emotional trust-mistrust of human development moves to a new realm of trust in the Spirit. The challenge to use one's gifts of industry-inferiority unfolds in a witness in mission. This is not a superficial relationship, as Jesus said, by their fruits you will know them (Mt. 7:20). Rather obedience expresses itself in a style of integrity in both successes and failures, collaborations and confrontations, peacekeeping, civilities, outreach to the margins, and prophetic outcry. Graced obedience is marked not just by what one does but by how he or she does it, with the fingerprints of the gospel or the marks of self-interest. The energy of initiative-guilt moves from projects to the less clear journey of self-knowledge. The obedient person meets not just an ideal self but one's true self in ongoing conversion.

The conversion of St. Paul involved more than a spectacular religious experience. It began a self-confrontation, a period of blindness, where the murder of Stephen and his personal self-righteousness in interpreting God's call to the Jews had to be named for what it was. The embrace of the sin and finitude of one's inner journey is as sound a witness to the church to what it means to follow Christ as one's outer journey of accomplishment and service. One who has been obedient to the truth of one's own life, in its light and darkness, is more likely to hear the call of God manifesting itself in the signs of the times and the lives of others. The listening of obedience, which can hear the false claims of popularity, honor, superficial upward mobility, and how to "get by," will distinguish false voices elsewhere. An honest person can allow prayer and the Word of God to have an impact and can also affirm goodness in the people and situations of life. This is authenticity. One learns honesty in the dark night of self-discovery through naming the forces internally which contribute to a false self. Persons of true gospel obedience then can discern how claims to happiness counter to the gospel in modern life distract one from the call of God. They can recognize in their culture patterns and initiatives which are in harmony with the sustainability God wills for all creation.

---

[42]Vito Arresto, FMS, "On Obedience and Mission," *Review for Religious*, January-February 1989), 65–73 at 67.

Gospel obedience is centered in the gestalt of religious life, the following of Christ, who is the only evangelical counsel. It flows from a consecration of one's whole existence, not just an embrace of three obligations.[43] Only Christ can make a religious capable of the journey of obedience. Jesus draws the religious to himself, and in this grace, it is possible to find one's way and touch wholeness. The Law of the Cross, the paschal mystery, is best understood as all grace, as something which moves in us, from an intellectually known reality, something known about, into our conscious living, our spontaneous living, and our deliberations, through a growth in prayer. Lonergan explains:

> if one is in the state of grace, if one keeps out of sin, if one does good deeds. One does all this only by the grace of God. But it's occurring only by the grace of God is not something which has a label on it. It is a life within us that goes on, that is promised to us by Christ, that fructifies in us. Our ideas about it can be as vague and inconsequential as the ideas of Topsy: when she was asked how she came into the world she said, "Ah 'spect ah just grow'd." But this life within us becomes habitual conscious living.[44]

By "habitual" Lonergan means one is not thinking of it all the time, but one reverts to it. One can be distracted by worldliness yet return to it in a spontaneous manner, as one who is in love can be engaged in much activity yet is distracted from everything except the beloved. Perhaps this is what the ancients termed being in the presence of God. One is not in constant self-study or analysis; rather, it is a living, developing, and growing consciousness, "in which one element is gradually added to another and new whole emerges."[45] This transformation, which can be applied to the posture of obedience, is the manifestation of something which has already been given as a gift to us, as we are temple of the Spirit, members of Christ, and adoptive children of the Father. It is the manifestation of this inward gift to the outward witness of our lives. While the vow of obedience does not lead to perfection in this transformation, our touch into this wholeness, already given, is a product of its path.

We manifest this gift of grace in our acts of obedience. Our response, however, is to a universal call to all. All are called in the gospel to pray without ceasing, to love our neighbor, to seek to be a good Christian and in this pursuit love Christ. Every thought, action, word, omission we do in life unites the growth of our whole person to a life whose focal point is Christ. We choose by looking at Christ's example, thus interpreting Christ through our own personality. Lonergan reminds us that we do not witness to the Christ of

---

[43] Rene Carpentier, "Evangelical Counsels," in *Sacramentum Mundi*, Vol. 2, ed. Karl Rahner (New York: Herder and Herder, 1968), 276–9 at 278.
[44] Bernard J. Lonergan, "The Mediation of Christ in Prayer," *Philosophical and Theological Papers, 1958-1964*, Vol. 6, ed. Robert C. Croken, Frederick E. Crowe, and Robert M. Doran (Toronto: University of Toronto Press, 1996), 160–82 at 170.
[45] Ibid.

Paul or John.[46] "We put on Christ in our own way, in accord with our own capacities and individuality, in response to our own needs and failings."[47] Everything is the mediation or means by which this process occurs—everything turns back to Christ in one way or another. Because the focus and style of our search for wholeness are centered in Christ, our personal development is not just our human quest, but one done in relationship to a person. Attention to this reality is the vow of obedience.

Since Christ himself, as a man, developed and acquired human perfection, he too had a choice of how he was going to proceed. Christ could have chosen other than he did; this possibility is a dimension of being fully human. Jesus took the path not of honor, esteem, and riches but of poverty, humiliation, and suffering because of us. "We think of the way of the cross primarily as a cross of Christ. But primarily the way of the cross is the way fallen human nature acquires its perfection."[48] Christ, through his own autonomous choices, chose to find wholeness by thinking of us and what we needed to be able to find wholeness ourselves. The counsels, the precepts, the example of Christ are what we rely on to find wholeness through Christ. On the path to wholeness, we recognize that the human condition involves suffering, the suffering required by love, rather than its avoidance. We attune ourselves to the principle of overcoming evil with good and transforming it into good, but above all, we have the example of Christ himself on our journey. We choose the path of Christ in the cross because it is Christ's path. "If any want to become my followers, let them deny themselves and take up their cross daily and follow me" (Lk. 9:23).

A life of prayer opens us to the path of obedience in reference to Christ. In this process, what is already in us as gift is expressed in our personal development, in community, its structures and its life in mission, and manifested in society.[49] The choices we make in this process unite us to Christ.[50] We become then in reference to Christ, as Christ became in reference to us. Lonergan summarizes, "In both cases the fundamental theorem, as it were, is transforming evil into good, absorbing evil of the world by putting up with it, not perpetuating it as rigid justice would demand. And that putting up with it acts as a blotter, transforms the situation, and creates the situation in which good flourishes."[51]

A commitment over a lifetime, through the vow of obedience, is accomplished in situations and with people who bring both joy and the cross. "Walking together" is an image of a synodal church, and this image rather than walking alone describes an obedience which is transformational. Leadership is called to be among rather than above others, and membership is to be with and not against any movement not initiated by

---

[46] In an analogous way, each Christian is a gospel, as he or she seeks to put on Christ.
[47] Lonergan, "The Mediation of Christ in Prayer," 180.
[48] Ibid., 181.
[49] See Merkle, *Sensing the Spirit*, 59–83.
[50] The challenge today is creating a balance between these aspects of religious life. "Obedience experienced as submission to totalitarian authority predictably led to excessive individual independence." George Aschenbrenner, "Prayer, Mission and Obedience," *The Way Supplement* 37 (1980): 50–61 at 52.
[51] Lonergan, "The Mediation of Christ in Prayer," 182.

oneself. An incarnational obedience, located in real processes in community, offers the affective bond with one's community. Mission means a member does not send themselves but is sent by the community as an expression of their mission.[52] In the last analysis, obedience involves interaction between people, structures, and processes which are both fallible and salvific at the same time. Persons involved are fallible in knowledge, limited in their sympathies, and imperfect in their progress to the fullness of life in Christ.[53] Obedience channels yet does not terminate processes of reflection, questioning, and interpretation on the part of all, whether they hold positions of authority or draw on the authority of their membership. Jesus' own paschal mystery is expressed in the account of both his ministry and passion as an expression of obedience to the will of his Father. Obedience draws us into this same paschal mystery, as well as the joy of being a disciple.

---

[52]Aschenbrenner, "Prayer, Mission and Obedience," 53.
[53]Langan, "The Good of Obedience in a Culture of Autonomy," 17.

CHAPTER 6
POVERTY
THE CHALLENGE OF AGENCY AND FINITUDE

Jesus said, "No one can serve two masters. He will either hate one and love the other or be devoted to one and despise the other. You cannot serve God and mammon" (Mt. 6:24). While this seems to be a clear directive, questions about the use of material things and their relationship to ultimate matters, the subject of the vow of poverty, are given diverse responses in the gospel. Mammon in Arabic means "that in which one trusts." In the passage above, scripture scholars stipulate it refers to dishonest wealth.

Often, we limit our understanding of the practice of poverty to decisions to live simply or a type of self-restraint regarding material things. The gospel indicates, however, that these external practices should flow from a deeper foundation. Luke cautions against trust in dishonest wealth primarily in terms of its effects on the one thing necessary, love. He focuses on the blindness the pursuit of wealth can bring to the needs of others and links it to its ultimate consequences. The parable of the rich man and the poor man (Lk. 16:19-31) illustrates the impact preoccupation with wealth has on the lasting assessment of one's life. We find that Luke does not limit his message about the import of material things simply with a caution to be fair in economic exchanges with others. The parable of the dishonest steward urges the prudent use of one's material goods in light of the imminent crisis of the coming of the end of the age. (Lk. 10:1-8). This suggests the necessity of keeping one's "eye on the prize," the ultimate one, is even more important than offering a lesson in honesty. Matthew echoes this attention to attend to the foundational issues behind the use of material things. The parable of the talents, or the money given in trust (Mt. 25:14-30), rejects cowardice and praises productivity. Matthew steers away from a pursuit of self-perfection as the essence of fidelity. His approach challenges a simple interpretation of the vow of poverty as thriftiness.

The gospel offers a helpful focus for religious to consider the significance of a vow of poverty in secular times. Religious often live in a life situation where sufficiency is not a question. They likely have a roof over their head and food on the table. Jesus puts his hearers, in the parable of the talents, into a world not of sufficiency, rather one full of complications, harshness, and predatory behavior. The deeper message is that people who are immovable, who cannot risk, who want to make themselves secure, who would delay rather than to act, will not find success in the world of the Kingdom God wants to create.¹ Gerhard Lohfink is even more to this point discussing the parable of the Crooked Manager (Lk. 16:1-13). Behavior that traditional Christian sensibilities about material things would condemn simply through a reading of the ten commandments is left untouched. The story of the manager who unscrupulously uses his master's property to secure his own future is not offered as a bad example of material management by Jesus. The outcome of the behavior is simply left out. An inevitable prison sentence is not mentioned. This story of a scoundrel does not lead to Jesus' evaluation of his crime, but to praise the determination with which he rescues his own existence. Lohfink interprets Jesus' point as "You must act in just the same way . . . in light of the reign of God. It is offered to you: now, today. But it will come to you only if you apply your minds, your 'smarts', your imagination, your passion—your whole existence."²

Religious facing the current crisis in religious life can gain insight from these gospel passages as to what the vow of poverty might be calling them to today. Attention to the core values of poverty in light of the coming of the Kingdom takes us beyond debates such as, do we need to change the name of the vow to one of simplicity or care for creation? These diversions are well-meaning yet might distract from the matter at hand. Others to avoid are those which focus on deprivation as perfection. Even less convincing is a shallow interpretation of the vow which would equate any refrain from enjoying the beauty of art, music, literature, or learning as somehow pleasing to God. These anti-world, anti-body, and negative views of the ordinary pleasures of life are attitudes which have at best been a detour from the real call of the vow. If the vows are to foster a life in which one is to serve God and their neighbor with their whole heart, their whole soul, and their whole mind, we need to ask where to look for direction in a secular world.

The Economy of Poverty

While the choice between God and mammon is perennial in the Christian life, religious today seek to make this distinction in new circumstances. They live in a capitalist society with one foot in an economy of capitalism and the other in an economy of gift.³ Religious live in different economies and in various classes within a world system with many who have unequal access to material things. Unease concerning the name of the vows certainly gathers around poverty because of the nature of the economic world in which many live. Religious in the first world interact in an economy where a CEO earns about 300 times as much as his or her average employee. The rationale for such inequality is that people deserve what they get in a capitalist economy through the operation of

---

[1] Gerhard Lohfink, *The Forty Parables of Jesus*, trans. Linda Mahoney (Collegeville, MN: The Liturgical Press, 2021), 166–73 at 172–3.
[2] Ibid., 173–8 at 177.
[3] George Scialabba, "What Were We Thinking: The Intolerable Inequalities We Take for Granted," *Commonweal*, January 2023), 20–5 at 22.

supply and demand. A Catholic hospital system which seeks to attract good leadership, in a competitive market, must ask to what point can they require candidates to live in an economy of gift.[4] Religious communities, who seek to pay a fair wage to their employees, must ask the same. A gift economy stresses using one's gifts for the common good, giving one's best efforts at work, following one's dreams, sharing in the "common" of family life, making a contribution to the arts or the sciences, building culture, and establishing the world as a better place, saving the earth.[5] Religious live with one foot in a capitalist economy and one in a gift economy; as do many others. The challenge is to blend the two.[6] As mentioned in other places, John Paul II called for the need in life and ministry to mix a sense of transcendence and the culture as compenetration.[7] This is the challenge to make concrete an essentially religious ideal, one that cannot be totally validated through rational terms, into the very life of church, society, and culture. Attention to this mandate is a first step of direction in the interpretation of the witness of the vow of poverty.

Today many religious live a middle-class lifestyle, which includes various modern conveniences. Religious are not dualists—those who see material things as lacking in value before spiritual realities. They want to experience, and for others to experience, the most natural and human good possible and to be set free from practical want and suffering so as to give themselves to more spiritual pursuits and more effective service. Most have access to enough money to develop maturity and freedom and to exercise responsible stewardship and generosity. The challenge is the attachment of our hearts to the situation this control over things creates and its seductive capacity to draw us away from God and others into our own world—the world we can control.[8] We can be living within the financial boundaries of our communities yet bring our iPhones to dinner to avoid being present to others. Just like in families, our use of material things can draw us apart or bring us together. Perhaps this offers a second direction in our interpretation of the vow of poverty: How does it build community?

Poverty and Finitude

Key to the human experience of finitude is the awareness of a void within each person that only God can fill. To live as if that contingency, or uncertainty, is not there requires

---

[4]Regina Wolfe Wentzel, "CEO Perspectives on Morality and Business," in *Business Ethics and Catholic Social Thought*, ed. Daniel Finn (Washington, DC: Georgetown University Press, 2021), 9–24.
[5]Nindyo Sasongko, "A Caravan of Solidarity: An Asian Constructive Theology for a Triune Economy of Gift," *Exchange* 44 (2015): 381–402.
[6]"Pope to Business Leaders: Use Gifts to Promote the Common Good," *Vatican News*, October 21, 2022. https: www.vaticannews >news.
[7]Judith Merkle, *From the Heart of the Church: The Catholic Social Tradition* (Collegeville, MN: The Liturgical Press, 2004), 236.
[8]Emmanuel Mansford, CFR, "Love Does Silly Things: The Prophetic Power of the Vow of Poverty," *Religious Life Review* 53, no. 286 (2014): 133–45 at 138–9.

constant distraction. We keep filling it, often with things, power, and relationships. Religious are not dualists; all these aspects of life are good in themselves. It is when we try to fill what only God can fill that we stray from what is most important, the one thing necessary. To make room for God therefore requires that we examine our desire for "more" and ask, is it more of God, and what is of God or more of stuff and position? It is human to experience inner emptiness; it is illusionary to think we can fill it with a thousand things and "touch the wholeness" of the one thing necessary. Perhaps a third direction in living the vow of poverty today is to ask how does it help me pursue what I set out to pursue in seeking religious life?

It is not the case that the asceticism of former practices of poverty is without merit. Most religious experienced during their formation the movement from an average family life to a congregation as an adjustment in the use of material things. One learned to live with less or to restructure one's access to material goods. We note the realism of Pope Francis, who does more than exhort us to embrace the high ideals of an economy of gift, but also sets limits to check the pressures of an economy of greed. Rules and regulations regarding material things are not vestiges of the past but support needed for realistic movement to the future. Recent international news notes the Pope limits the gift a member of the Vatican can receive to 50.00 in order to prevent the unchecked corruption which has happened in the past.[9] William Schweiker expresses how easily the reality of greed can impact our lives.

> Greed is a passion, a human desire, to draw some socially defined material or ideal value (money or power, etc) into the self and thereby to undercut the domain of social meaning itself. Greed works to isolate the self by breaking the necessary bonds of human community. One could see greed as a form of inverted narcissism in which the self is not elevated to the center of the world (pride), but, rather, seeks to consume the world and lose itself in what is desired and consumed. Yet, in doing so, greed also undercuts the fragile bonds of social concord.[10]

The Challenge of Agency and Finitude

Schweiker links greed to the rejection of one's human finitude in a way which makes such behavior more than a personal failing, but rather one which has social and cultural consequences. This insight helps us see the vow of poverty as one which goes beyond a practice of a "life of perfection" to one of significance for a secular age. Moderns often view human agency as encumbered by a sense of God. They reason that certain

---

[9] "Pope's Anti-corruption Decree for Vatican Limits Gifts to Forty Euros," *Reuters*, April 29, 2021. https://www.reuters.com >europe.

[10] William Schweiker, "Reconsidering Greed," in *Having: Property and Possession in Religious and Social Life*, ed. William Schweiker and Charles Matthews (Grand Rapids, MI: Eerdmans, 2004), 249–71 at 256.

life goods can be more naturally attained if they are not related to a divine source. To offset a religious outlook on life, they define the potentials of a human person within nature itself.[11] This design does more than simply subtract religion from life; rather, it reinterprets life goods themselves. The source of the life goods which make life worth living is within, not centered in any transcendent factor. The first source is one's own agency—the person's own powers of rational order and control, together with the power of expression and articulation. The second is found within nature itself, in its order, but also in nature within, in what wells up from one's own nature, desire, affinities, and sentiments.[12]

A life with a faith-orientation in secular society can share these values, as they are perspectives of current thinking and the world in which moderns live. However, these aspirations stop short of what is necessary to ground a vow of poverty or to understand it. The powers of agency, human reason and will for a believer are God-made and part of God's plan. They constitute the image of God within the human being. In exclusive humanism, these sources lie only within; they form the basis for an independent nontheistic morality. Nature itself is the prime moral source; however, this is human nature without its author. Initially, these concepts were theistic, but over time people shifted to believe human agency was only empowered if free of any relationship, consideration of, or submission to God. Many persons of faith also value the inner powers of being human, but they do not see them as apart from their relationship with God.

The difference between the two views surfaces when life goes awry. A sense of contingency in modern life is hard to avoid. It enters as the human experience that the world does not always work as it should.[13] The experience of contingency and finitude touches us in our desire to understand, with the awareness, we cannot know everything. We cannot control the weather, or the irrational behavior of a friend or neighbor. Disease challenges our best medical efforts, and drive-by shootings defy the desired order as well as a sense of justice. The threat that we can destroy creation as we know it tempers all surety of a peaceful world ahead. Our capacities of human nature include not only the power to create, innovate, and express ourselves but also the facility to conceal from ourselves our own finitude and inner motives. What we often miss in our assessment of

---

[11]Charles Taylor, *The Sources of Self: The Maker of Modern Identity* (Cambridge: Cambridge University Press, 1989), 319.
[12]Ibid., 314. See also Merkle, *Discipleship, Secularity and the Modern Self*, 42–3.
[13]Edward Schillebeeckx calls this a contrast experience. Good people see things amiss in the world and in the church and say, this should not be. Yet, implicit in this "no" to how things are, is a "yes" to something better. *Church, The Human Story of God* (New York: Crossroads, 1990), 22. Their initiative to make things better, to overcome obstacles, to work toward a solution is a drive toward the wholeness of life, the "more" of the Holy Spirit, that which we both seek and possess in seed in our hopes and dreams. Faith implicitly places our confidence in a center beyond ourselves and in a future we do not yet possess. Both believers and unbelievers have the experience of contrast. For believers, the response is linked to the risk of faith and a sense of purpose that, at the level of modern life, is unverifiable. We sense we are on this earth for more than the everyday measures of a good life.

life is our human dignity is irrevocable, not in spite of our finitude but in virtue of it.[14] For believers, the reality of grace tips the balance of life in our favor.

Grace and Finitude

Grace enables the power of our human agency in a world of contingency. Grace enables freedom rather than impedes it. In modern life, dependency is seen as a negative. Autonomy and agency are imagined in American society as upward mobility gained through personal achievement. One advantage of upward mobility, in the American mind, it that it brings with it a personal life space, where the individual needs to depend less and less on others. The ultimate goals of a good life are viewed as matters of personal choice alone; it follows, values, and priorities cannot be justified by any wider framework of purpose of belief.[15]

When the individual and his or her agency become the center of reality in such a radical way, relationship with the truths of nature, interpersonal reality, common tradition, and religious meaning have no integral connection to living. A sense of responsibility can be reduced to an assessment of "success" or measuring whether the priorities we have chosen are achieved.

Theologically, however, the relationship between God and a human person is characterized precisely in contrast to any dependence otherwise met within the world. Acknowledgment of and surrender to God in love has its own mystery. Self-possession and dependence increase in direct but not inverse proportion. It is God's movement of love toward each person itself which causes a genuine difference from God and creates what is independent, and has its own being, the human person.[16] When a human being acts, exercises his or her agency, God enables this freedom, yet it is the freedom to say yes or no. God is precisely what makes the person free. In turn, God transfers this power to the person's own responsibility for itself. God and the human person therefore co-exist in freedom yet in difference. That which provides human agency with its fundamental moral range and depth is that it is exercised in a purely human manner. God can do much that we cannot. The very acknowledgment of our finitude—that God is God and we are ourselves, creatures—opens the door to our agency. Denial of finitude leaves us caught in the tension between the limits of our reason and the very dynamism driving us to surpass those limits. While it is good for us to always seek to surpass limits in our knowledge of life and nature to learn new things, this is theoretical knowledge only. This

---

[14]Philip J. Rossi, "Faith, Autonomy, and the Limits of Agency in a Secular Age," in *At the Limits of the Secular: Catholic Reflections on Faith and Public Life*, ed. William Barbieri (Grand Rapids, MI: Wm B. Eerdmann, 2014), 226–49 at 230. I borrow from Rossi's insights in the following.
[15]Robert Bellah, *Habits of the Heart: Individualism and Commitment in American Life* (Berkeley, CA: University of California Press, 1985), 8, 22.
[16]Karl Rahner, "Grace and Freedom," in *Sacramentum Mundi*, Vol. 2, ed. Karl Rahner (New York: Herder and Herder, 1968), 424–7 at 424.

drive can impel us to "be like gods" and feel we can control the operations of life itself. "It would be easy to acknowledge that not controlling the world is part of being human, were it not for the fact that *things go wrong*. The thought that the rift between reason and nature is neither error nor punishment but the fault line along which the universe is structured can be a source of perfect terror."[17] To cover up this terror we engage in idolatry, confusing God with other beings. Jesuit Phillip Rossi comments,

> our finitude is so deeply constitutive of the moral shape of human agency that, were we to convince ourselves that we had succeeded in overcoming the moral limits of our finitude, we would not thereby have made our agency more "godly"; we would, instead, have deflated its capacity to engage the play of contingency that stands at the core of the human moral enterprise.[18]

This leads to a fourth sense of direction in the interpretation of the vow of poverty, does it foster a poverty of spirit, or ground us in our place before God in the real world in which we live? The interface of grace and freedom is the heart of the vow of poverty. In making room in one's life for God through the letting go required by the vow, we receive our true selves, the gift of wholeness, and know what we give back to God is an element of the gift itself.

Francis of Assisi sums up the relationship of poverty to the pursuit of holiness as wholeness. "Holiness is not a fulfillment of self nor a plentitude we give ourselves. It is first a void we discover and accept and that God comes to fill inasmuch as we open ourselves to His plentitude. Our nothingness, you see, if it is accepted, become the free space where God can still create."[19] For Francis, a person is who he or she is before God, and no more, and certainly no less. Poverty "in fact" is meant to foster a detachment from all that hinders a person from enjoying this freedom.[20] Rules surrounding poverty are there to help focus and strengthen our desires, especially when we are distracted or weak. The spirit of poverty is to lead us to inner and outer freedom. It is to foster in us the capacity to allow our moral tastes to change so we can increasingly find happiness in values other than things, be happy with whatever we have, and to be concerned that others have enough. St. Paul reflects on his own journey. "Not that I say this because of need, for I have learned, in whatever situation I find myself, to be self-sufficient. I know indeed how to live in human circumstances, I know also how to live with abundance. In every circumstance and in all things, I have learned the secret of being well fed and going hungry or living in abundance and of being in need. I have the strength for everything through him who empowers me" (Phil. 4:11-13).

---

[17] Susan Neiman, *Evil in Modern Thought: An Alternative History of Philosophy* (Princeton, NJ and Oxford: Princeton University Press, 2002), 80–1.
[18] Rossi, "Faith, Autonomy, and the Limits of Agency in a Secular Age," 231.
[19] As quoted in Mansford, "Love Does Silly Things," 140.
[20] See moral tastes in Merkle, *A Different Touch*, 166–9, 208.

Poverty as a Human Challenge

Religious life is a framework which structures our relationships to God, self, others and the world. Just as in other adult vocations, it involves face-to-face living and role expectations, which involve mutuality, responsibility, trust, and communication. The religious enters a matrix of relationships and roles which impact the development of his or her person. A religious faces the same psychosocial challenges as any adult, within the context of their lifestyle. Therefore, we will continue to use Erikson's psychological insights as one way to examine how the vow of poverty relates to human growth and development. Poverty, the transformation we undergo in order to find the love we truly desire, is not only one vow, but characterizes in its own unique way the entire project of the vowed life. The two life passages most associated with the dynamics of the vow of poverty are autonomy versus shame and doubt, a challenge of early life, and the crisis of integrity versus despair, which comes at the end of life, evoked by the struggle with death.[21]

Autonomy versus Shame and Doubt

Moderns assume that financial independence is key to the broader goal of autonomy and the wider agency that money enables. For Erikson, the struggle for autonomy begins long before we have checking accounts. He awards the psychosocial crisis of autonomy versus shame and doubt to early childhood.[22] This crisis emerges as we gain new physical control over our bodily processes. "Holding on" and "letting go" become stances which transfer to dealings with people, especially parents, in the life of a child. The "no" of the two-year-old is a statement that parents no longer have all the power; the child has some also. The autonomy sought is the recognition that we have this right. Genuine autonomy occurs when we do not allow our will to be broken, but also do not always need to have our own way. We "resolve" this crisis when we are young, yet we revisit it throughout our lives.

The negative pole of this autonomy crisis is shame and doubt. Greater mobility opens us to the possibility of failure. We make bodily mistakes, soil ourselves, spill things, fall down—all sources of feelings of humiliation and being exposed. We doubt ourselves and our abilities and encounter the world as less supportive than we hoped. Holding on and letting go transfer into relationships. We share not only things but also express our will and share power. Some modern theories view the construction of the personality as an attempt to restore equilibrium to a young self, struggling with doubt in the face of this crisis.[23]

---

[21] Merkle, *A Different Touch*, 176–85.
[22] Donald Capps, *Deadly Sins and Saving Virtues* (Eugene, OR: Wipf and Stock, 1987), 33–45, 73–86.
[23] Helen Palmer, *The Enneagram in Love and Work* (San Francisco, CA: Harper and Row, 1993), 7.

Will and Anger

The virtue-vice struggle in the autonomy versus shame and doubt crisis is between will and anger. The negative potential associated with this crisis is anger, as an emotional response of agitation caused by displeasure. Anger in these situations is aimed at persons and situations that block our will. Here, anger is considered not just a necessary emotion but as a deadly sin. A deadly sin is a destructive human capacity which gives rise to other self-destructive behaviors.[24] Anger as a deadly sin is a drive toward vengeance which manifests itself in rejection of love, relationships, communities, and even self-care, which is essential for our flourishing. The end course of anger is isolation and the personal bondage it fosters. Righteous anger, anger aimed at an evil that ought to be combatted, is a positive use of its energy. It can shake us out of indifference. However, Cassian argues that anger is tricky. We tend to call all anger "righteous," whereas anger often causes blindness to our own self-serving. He uses the example if a leaf covers our eyes, whether it is of lead or gold, it still blinds us. "The gold of righteous, transforming anger and the lead of self-serving, sullen, resentful anger, have the same effect of limiting what you can see."[25] Appropriate anger can easily slip into self-righteous anger, a passionate habit that serves illusions about ourselves.

With gluttony, anger partners to perpetuate a self-created image of ourselves.[26] Will is the positive quality and outcome of this crisis. Will is related to acceptance of finitude and vulnerability. Will is the determination to act on our desires coupled with acceptance that our freedom is limited. Will requires the courage to engage the world, even though it is full of contingencies and capable of evoking fear and pain. Through will we determine what desires are essential to our sense of self and our goals and what desires can be let go. We learn to "chose our battles," exert judicious self-restraint, and work toward what we really want. Courage and will engage the world despite its capacity to hurt. Anger blames and isolates and is paralyzed by the opposing wills of others. Here self-doubt wins and the desire for true autonomy is weaken.

Integrity versus Despair

The psychosocial challenge that comes at the end of life is evoked by the struggle with death. Death is the greatest "letting go" that any human being must face. The crisis of integrity versus despair opens in an ultimate way the meaning of the transformation of desires which poverty evokes.

---

[24] William E. May, "Sin," in *The New Dictionary of Theology* (Collegeville, MN: The Liturgical Press, 1990), 954–67, at 966–7.
[25] Rowan Williams, *Passions of the Heart*, (London: Bloomsbury/Continuum, 2024), 50–1.
[26] Ibid., 58.

The crisis of integrity and despair is a response to the loss and the inevitability of death which comes at the end of life. Loss of opportunities, positions of influence, disappointments with others, diminishment of physical and cognitive abilities, the curtailment of our autonomy, necessary dependencies, and pain and chronic illness are real.[27] Poverty in old age is not an option; it is a way of life. The adage "Old age is not for sissies" likely has many defendants.

Integrity is the human capacity for order and meaning in the midst of diminishment. Integrity is the ability to be whole and centered in the face of decline. We can stand in this wholeness because we can find our place in a larger sense of meaning. Through integrity, we chose to keep connected to people who have become important to us. It offers perspective on our past, not dwelling on lost opportunities but on the contributions we made to others. Integrity is the link to a meaning system which takes our contribution and gives it a place in values which outlast our lifetime. Integrity involves the acceptance of our one and only life course and the people who have become significant to it. Integrity is more than a quality of personal character. It is a pathway to the center and order of life which is there for the seeing. It is certainly an encounter with touching wholeness. In this sense, Erikson notes that our latter years call us to transcend the self we have developed through our lives to identify with the heart of life which holds everything together. Perhaps it is only in these last decades of life that we understand, "no longer I, but Christ lives in me" (Gal. 2:20).

Some try to defend against the real losses of old age through nostalgia or mythologizing their lives or those of their congregations. The better defense is to see life in relation to those who have gone before us and those who will come after. This requires the asceticism to let go of resentments and the capacity to hold onto the deep linkages which give life meaning. This will not come easily for those who have not engaged the challenge to hold on and let go earlier in their lives. Yet even for those who have met these challenges, earlier learnings will be restructured and reframed before the concreteness of aging. It will not be the same holding on and letting go of earlier decades, but one which only the conditions of later years can evoke. Gospel poverty finds a new matrix of transformation in the crisis of integrity versus despair. The transformation of our desires in this crisis is expressed in a new capacity for wisdom and its ability to offset melancholy.

Wisdom and Melancholy

Wisdom and melancholy vie for our energies during this last stage of our lives. Melancholy is more than sadness; it involves hate and ill will. Melancholy robs a person of the capacity to look back on his or her personal or congregational life with a sense of

---

[27]Capps, *Deadly Sins and Saving Virtues*, 63–73, 110–18.

order, meaning, and coherences, or sense of integrity. The capacity to think is weakened because it is filled with resentment. In this way, melancholy creates a blindness far deeper than physical blindness.[28] The result is a person can no longer affirm. One can only denounce and repudiate. Unlike mourning, melancholy cannot transcend loss to discover a more universal meaning in which to find new ways of loving. This includes a new and different kind of love for significant people, for those of other generations, for new ways of living, and for oneself as a "good enough" person who has faced the successes and failures of a particular life cycle.

Wisdom offsets a melancholic pull. As "detached concern," wisdom is knowledge that comes from responsible renunciation. Wise people maintain their interest in the problems of everyday. The older person enters into their solutions, however, less from self-interest and more from a viewpoint which considers problems in their entirety, from the whole of life which one sees when death is approaching. It is not that older people have answers, but they have a perspective which comes from having turned against disgust, despair, and hopelessness as the answer to life's dilemmas. Wisdom responds to loss, the sense that one did not do everything, nor become everything, with a different posture than the melancholic spirit.

In face of loss and diminishment, wisdom holds on to the truth that one's life has an essential wholeness, even though it has not been perfect. To the next generation, the person of wisdom communicates that life can be held together in spite of losses. While the melancholic are at odds with themselves, the wise witness to the essence of the spirit of poverty, that there is more to life than anything can take away (Rom. 8:18). Letting go of loss and holding onto God and the goodness of life continue to express the first promise of the vow of poverty to give all to God and count on God for everything. This promise, by the end of life, has made its way into deep levels of the self and impacted all who touch the life of a religious.

Poverty as a Lived Reality

The vow of poverty, like celibacy and obedience, is a renunciation.[29] Renunciation in this sense is not just the giving up of any good, as one would follow a diet to maintain a proper weight for ballet. Or even the choice to practice a moral good, like to contribute to a foodbank by giving cash one might use for a night out. The renunciation of the vow of poverty, together with celibacy and obedience, is understood as a permanent form of life. It involves a renunciation which is more comprehensive than that needed to live a "good" life as understood in broad Christian terms. It is not a renunciation of something which can deter one from a good life or is wrong. It expresses a love of God and neighbor

---

[28]Ibid., 63–70, 110–16.
[29]See Karl Rahner, "Reflections on a Theology of Renunciation," in Theological Investigations, Vol. III, trans. Karl H. and Boniface Kruger (New York: Crossroads, 1982), 47–57.

beyond ethics or a normative sense. As a calling, it renounces positive values and goals of this world. These values are not just lesser values which must be forsaken for higher ones, such as recognition when one is offering one's talents in a common enterprise and might be overlooked. Rather, these values have meaning in themselves. In Rahner's words, "For such values include the marital union and the freedom of development of human existence by being able to decide for oneself about the material presuppositions and autonomy of one's existence (i.e., riches and independence).[30]

The Transformative Effect of Living Poverty

Since the vow of poverty in many forms of religious life is meant to be lived communally in a congregation, elements of its practical demands require thought beyond personal practice. Pope Francis remarks in *Laudato Si* that a lack of attention to our collective life leaves us with too many means and few institutional ends.

> So many things have to change course, but it is we human beings above all that need to change. We lack awareness of our common origin, of our mutual belonging, and of a future to be shared by everyone. This basic awareness would enable the development of new convictions, attitudes and forms of life. A great cultural, spiritual and educational challenge stands before us, and it will demand that we set out on the long path of renewal. (*LS* 202)

What might such a transformational living entail? How does it impact our understanding of the vow of poverty? Response to this challenge requires each congregation to ask, what is the world we want to foster? We cannot do everything, so what will we do? What does our charism call us to do? What steps are needed so our long-term hopes can be realized? What are we willing to let go of and what must we hold onto to do what we are called to?

Often the topic of poverty is raised when creating a personal or community budget. A budget is a plan for the coordination of resources and expenditures. On its own, it has no normativity or values. A transformational budget, on the other hand, expresses a desire to shape the future mission and utilize the agency of the congregation for social goals. This requires a long-term perspective to the degree possible for the group. Rather than accepting drift and accommodation to over-spending to protect the status quo, a community can ask, if we cannot meet a need due to a lack of personnel, how can we enable the project? All congregations seek to support their members adequately and especially care for the elderly. However, the lack of any vision for the future, coupled

---

[30]Ibid., 50.

with a lack of will to change patterns, practices, and collaborative associations, can limit a vision of the vow of poverty simply to a simple lifestyle and saving money.

A budget is a place where our economic responsibilities and faith commitments are reconciled and balanced. It is where we navigate what it means for a congregation as a group to live a mission in this world, the secular and global world. The bottom line for a religious congregation must be more than solvency. While there is no mission without solvency, only with it, there is no transparent purpose for a congregation to exist. The deepest question of a transformational poverty is how charism, faith, and mission call us to rethink categories like impact, success, and what is essential for us as a congregation.[31] Authors Clemens Sedmak and Kelli Hickey say it clearly: "The loss of solvency is bad but the loss of mission is worse. The loss of material assets is bad, but the loss of faith and love is worse."[32] Deciding what this means for each congregation is a practice of transformational poverty. Practices of personal poverty of members are linked to this vision and make sense only in light of it.

Gathering the Fragments of Direction

In an economy of consumption and abundance, as well as one of scarcity, the Great Commandment, love God with your whole heart, mind, and soul and your neighbor as yourself, translates into assuming responsibility for respecting and enhancing quality of life for all. Religious living in first-world economies face the challenge of interpreting the vow of poverty in light of the moral and economic problem of how to live rightly in an age of runaway consumption.[33] They do so in a culture where there is little discourse about inordinate desires or the language of greed.[34] Religious, however, can draw from significant theological currents since Vatican II to gain perspective on their use of material things. Liberation theology criticized market capitalism for its deficiencies in its acquisition and distribution within a globalizing capitalist order. The ecological movement has alerted us to the consequences of human excess in a finite biosphere upon which the whole array of biological and material forms relies for survival. Virtue ethics has promoted a return to a simple lifestyle and personal and social practices which reflect a more communitarian and organic lifestyle.[35]

---

[31] Covid certainly called all institutions to ask, what are essential services, and how do we maintain them?
[32] Clemens Sedmak and Kelli Reagan Hickey, *Counting the Cost: Financial Decision-Making, Discipleship and Christian Living* (Collegeville, MN: The Liturgical Press, 2023), 106.
[33] Some in developing countries experience this cultural shift emerging in the urban areas of their society. See Anil D'Almeida, SJ, "Vocation to Live Religiously Poor in India," *Vidyajyoti Journal of Theological Reflection* 82, no. 9 (September 2018): 16–40.
[34] William Schweiker, "Reconsidering Greed," in *Having: Property and Possession in Religious and Social Life*, ed. William Schweiker and Charles Mathewes (Grand Rapids, MI: Eerdmans, 2004), 249–71 at 254.
[35] Christine Firer Hinze, "What is Enough? Catholic Social Thought, Consumption and Material Sufficiency," in *Having: Property and Possession in Religious and Social Life*, ed. William Schweiker and Charles Mathewes (Grand Rapids, MI: Eerdmans, 2004), 162–88.

The Vows of Religious Life in a Secular Society

All these approaches point to aspects of a transformational vow of poverty, which surpasses an asceticism that simply glorifies self-denial or disciplines the body. Rather, each of these approaches sheds light on how a vow of poverty can witness to the new situation of today. They point to a joyful and life-affirming engagement in and with the material world, as they reflect on the wholeness of what it means to be fully human, in the context of the challenges our current situation presents.

A New Asceticism

It is not enough today to interpret the vow of poverty through the lens of the world-denying asceticism cited by Max Weber of the nineteenth century and embraced also Christian practice.[36] The asceticism of the twenty-first century, however, cannot simply give religious legitimation to cultural biases regarding material accumulation. Wholeness of life requires engagement in the material world without expecting too much of it. To the degree that religious witness to the use of material things in a manner which makes clear their ends transcend any worldly achievement, they question the modern assumption that salvation is *immanent in this world* alone and challenge the expectation that it is found solely there. The gospel caution, you cannot love God and mammon, extends to a cultural ideology of exclusive humanism, that this world is all there is and all that is needed for human flourishing is found there. Charles Mathewes finds in Augustine's "use paradigm," or sense of stewardship, an approach to the world, a helpful clarification. This traditional way of thought "acknowledges that our ends transcend any worldly achievement, but are yet vectored by this world toward a transcendent God beyond."[37]

Religious enter into a new assessment of their vow of poverty in an ecclesial climate where the market has often been viewed as an impediment to the just distribution of material goods. In its most extreme form, this approach has identified economic injustice with capitalism, making weighing the choice between God or mammon beyond the reach of Christian morals and reasonable evaluations. Yet Christian ethicists, along with church leadership, have reopened the question of the moral assessment of the market in ways which surpass simplistic answers and offer a language for more holistic approaches. Pope Francis links the market, technology, political power, and

---

[36] Weber's view of the world was rather negative. It was a place of temptation and filled with sensual pleasures which divert one from the divine. The world had enough "satisfactions" that it fosters in the religiously average person a type of complacency, distracting them from the necessity of "those things necessary" for salvation. Therefore, a withdrawal from the world was necessary. In Weber's terms this is "world-rejecting asceticism." Judith A. Merkle, *Beyond Our Lights and Shadows: Charism and Institution in the Church* (London: Bloomsbury/ T and T Clark, 2016), 122, See also Max Weber, *Economy and Society*, Vol. I, ed. Guenther Roth and Claus Wittich (Berkeley: CA: University of California Press, 1978), 543.

[37] Charles Mathewes, "On Using the World," in *Having: Property and Possession in Religious and Social Life*, ed. William Schweiker and Charles Mathewes (Grand Rapids, MI: Eerdmans, 2004), 189–221 at 191.

ecological destruction when he cites the illusions of the technocratic paradigm. This is the worldview that tends to see all of reality as a problem awaiting an application of scientific and technological power, thus deluding us into thinking we can become powerful enough and wise enough to apply our power to all things (*LS* 63, 200, 106–109). The market shares in this deception in its assertion that it can resolve every material problem through its magical theories of "spillover" and "trickle." There are those who would have the world believe that the freedom of the market is enough to keep everything secure (*FT* 33). The road forward requires the work of continued ethical reflection on transnational systems, institutional and political analysis, and the requirements of justice. But it also must include inquiry into how human desires, values, and motivations forge the bonds of human society or destroy them. The vow of poverty engages this more holistic vision of "touching wholeness," as it interprets its goal as a critique of the limits of our societal vision of economic and human fulfillment. Religious do so as they also witness to alternative patterns of community and material involvement. Pope Francis cautions that unless we recover the shared passion to create a community of belonging and solidarity for our time, all our energy and resources will come to nothing. If we allow ourselves to be fed by misleading global illusions that economy alone will save us, we will be led to a collapse that will leave many in the grip of anguish and emptiness. He goes on to say,

> Nor should we naively refuse to recognize that "obsession with a consumerist lifestyle", above all when few people are capable of maintaining it, can only lead to violence and mutual destruction. The notion "every man for himself" will rapidly degenerate into a free-for-all that would prove worse than any pandemic. (*FT* 36)

It is imperative that the lifestyle of religious serves the church as a witness to economic wholeness. This means they need to foster an understanding and assessment of the stimulation of desires brought by consumerism which are necessary for the functioning of economic systems as well as their dangers. They need to assist the church to reclaim and revise a language of human desire necessary to live responsibly in a culture of consumption. The witness of a vow of poverty in these times lies at this nexus. Modern commerce has created social goods like freedom from destitution, increased income, innovation, education, better health care, and international cooperation. These are the very goods we desire for those who do not have access to them. Yet institutional reform is constantly needed so these goods serve human ends rather than feed a system of exploitation built on a rapacious desire for more goods or wealth than one needs or deserves. The witness of the vow of poverty today engages congregations in legislative, educational, and prophetic actions that censure new institutional devices which exploit the very service industries of health care, education, food provision, and housing meant to foster human growth. Awareness of and involvement in these concrete measures place religious at the forefront of the promotion of human wholeness economically by their lives and their mission.

How Much Is Enough?

Charles Taylor reminds us that moderns try to find the fullness they seek through immanence; they look for love, meaning, and significance-a quasi-transcendence, through this world alone. If this world is all there is, material things inevitably hold an importance which they cannot deliver. Perhaps it was the desire of Jesus to keep us from this deception in his admonition, you cannot serve God and mammon. When there is no higher purpose to human life in the imagination, the question of what is enough dangles in a space where only practical limitations can evoke a response.

For those who cannot imagine life without the over-confident promise of unrestricted and increasing access to material things, times of inflation, shortages, and financial downturns can reveal a personal fragility from which they are usually buffered. Shifts in the cultural imagination bolster this deception. The absence of a "higher purpose" or a good that transcends human flourishing often reduces God's providential role to a simple "economic" ordering of creation to our mutual benefit. The absence of a sense of mystery, or the assumption that humans can see everything and solve every problem, even the mystery of evil, fosters a vision of life where God has no place, since even the highest spiritual and moral aspirations can arise without God. Taylor remarks, "With growing confidence, reflected in the new harmonious, economic-centered order, neither grace nor God's power in us seem all that indispensable."[38] There is also a lack of concern regarding our final destiny. People deny that God plans a transformation of human beings, which takes them beyond this life to the next. This shift in cultural imagination explains the remark of a student when a religious came to his classroom to explain the practice of religious life, "Why would you do that?"[39]

Looking for direction for a transformational living of the vow of poverty involves more than a new budget. Yet it must be as concrete as one.[40] It is to take up the role religion has to overcome; what Pope Francis calls a culture of indifference. Some indifference stems from the inability of our human finitude and apathy to meet the ideals of our modern age. Moderns promote a desire for universal benevolence; however, when it conflicts with our material wants, we lower expectations through indifference. The vow of poverty is lived today in a world where the moral imagination of those with enough suffers from both "too much" and "too little," caused by the impasse of maximal demand.

Maximal Demand

The modern person today faces the "dilemma" of demand, how to meet the moral obligations which seem beyond those held in previous generations. Modern society is not

---

[38]Charles Taylor, *A Secular Age* (Cambridge, MA: The Belknap Press of Harvard University Press, 2007), 234.
[39]Mansford, "Love Does Silly Things," 133–45.
[40]See Sedmak and Hickey, *Counting the Cost: Financial Decision-Making, Discipleship, and Christian Living*, 107–34.

without a sense of ethics. While public morality tells moderns they are to be concerned for the life and well-being of all human beings on the face of the earth, they are to further social justice among peoples, they are to subscribe to universal standards of human rights, it leaves unanswered how are we to respond to these demands. Society does not address how these demands are compatible with vision of human fulfillment offered by its own narrative—that significance is drawn from unrestricted and increasing access to material things, through the unrelenting cycle of desire and fulfillment.[41] Does the actual but sometimes hidden truth of their incompatibility exact a high price in terms of wholeness? Taylor asks a similar question: How do we respond to these demands, and what resources do we draw upon? Does awareness of them leave us feeling inadequate, bad, or guilty for not being able to meet them?[42] Do we seek havens from the persistent feeling of being overwhelmed and having failed? What happens when human efforts fail even when they address a social problem, or even their success uncovers a further challenge which seems insurmountable? What about the suffering of the world which appears to have no redeeming value? Where do we go with the dead ends that war, famine, epidemics, and hunger leave us as we admit their existence and impact on our world?

Charles Taylor charges that today, "a higher calling," a heroic demand, has been placed on modernity itself without the deeper constitutive values to carry it out. It is no surprise that indifference exists in the face of the fact that values beyond expediency are not only disregarded but lack foundations. The moorings of higher values collapsed because of an Enlightenment critique which accused religion of denying the ordinary fulfillments humans naturally seek regarding material things. They charged that religion was counter to wholeness as it questions what nature requires: embrace of pleasure and the avoidance of pain; the realization of ideals of spontaneity, creativity, and awareness of feelings as guides to well-being. Happiness through production, material gain, or "bettering one's condition" became goods in society which seemed opposed to the goals of religion. As early as the early twentieth century the church and theologians wrestled with both the acceptance of these modern values and their limits. They urged integration of biblical values such as the love of one's neighbor and its links to righteousness, rather than total rejection of material things. John Ryan, a Catholic social ethicist at the beginning of the 1900s, wrote on questions such as "The Fallacy of Bettering One's Position," "The Duty of Distributing Superfluous Wealth," and "Minimum and Maximum Standards of Living."[43] Modern Catholic Social Thought has constantly criticized the value of "having" over "being" in consumer culture throughout the various cycles of capitalist expansion in the last centuries.[44] These efforts have impacted the interpretation and living of the vow of poverty in modern religious life.

---

[41]See Christopher Lasch, *The True and Only Heaven: Progress and Its Critics* (New York: Norton, 1991).
[42]Charles Taylor, *Sources of the Self: The Making of Modern Identity* (Cambridge: Cambridge University Press, 1989), 495–521.
[43]See Hinze, "What is Enough," 165–71.
[44]See *Compendium of Catholic Social Doctrine of the Church*, Pontifical Council of Justice and Peace (Continuum International Publisher, 2006).

The dialectic of adaptation to the economic culture yet critique of it is reflected also in the church's rejection of the key interpretive framework of modern life, a theory of progress. This explanation for the future of society claims that the modern economy, propelled by human greed, holds the secret of progress. The desires of one generation become the necessities of the next; this cycle is inevitable. Therefore, economic decisions are to be made solely according to mutual benefit.[45] On the contrary, the church challenges the order of mutual benefit as the only norm of social and material exchange because its vision of life upholds a higher order. It promotes self-restraint and holds that natural desires can be satiated. We find in the heart of the tradition in Aquinas not the rejection of desire, but an understanding of virtue as "desiring aright." This means a redirection and reshaping of desire toward authentic human well-being (ST I-II, 1.55, art. iv.), or in the terms of this writing, wholeness.

An ellipse of our final destiny in modern society, and a capacity for a relationship with God in this life, leaves out a perspective which can order and enjoy all other things—a sense of the purpose of life, which includes the common good. This vision is also necessary so that nature itself can be preserved, and desires toward authentic human well-being can be fostered (*LS* 81). Religious life, as a witness to the presence of God, has significance in upholding the ultimate destiny and meaning of human life. Taylor charges this perspective is not "anti-modern," but is the same destiny which grounds the most valuable gains of modernity, such as the primacy of rights and the affirmation of life.[46] Lack of this grounding just perpetuates the cycle of maximal demand and indifference.

A Map for a Living Poverty in a Time of Transition

How does a religious congregation foster the witness of the vow of poverty today amid the challenges of economies of abundance and scarcity? If we want to understand the human dilemma of agency and finitude in its relationship to the vow, we cannot limit our understanding of its practice simply to personal practice and simple living. A transformational living of the vow of poverty must embrace three foci: (1) focus on personal and social virtue; (2) fostering practical agendas for institutional renovation through advocacy and legislation; and (3) prophetic witness to ideological critique and deeper structural transformation. Religious live the vow of poverty in a world where an alternative moral horizon exists. The measure of witness or counter-witness no longer exists in a world where both belief and unbelief benefit from the unchallenged security which religious faith and its denial enjoyed in earlier epochs. Moral sources today need

---

[45]Merkle, *Discipleship, Secularity, and the Modern Self*, 43–4. "Since the ideal of polite society follows the modern moral order of mutual benefit, those who live in a disenchanted world can still experience moral fullness, without reference to God within the range of purely intra human powers." at 44. See also, Taylor, *A Secular Age*, 244–5.

[46]Charles Taylor, "A Catholic Modernity," in *Dilemmas and Connections: Selected Essays* (Cambridge, MA: The Belknap Press of Harvard University, 2011), 167–87 at 181.

to be expressed, not only in reference to God and religious language but in the new frontiers of the modern self. John Paul II referred to this as the *humanum*, the true dignity of the human person, which includes both practical ramifications in the contours of global life and a vision of the human person which includes a trajectory of growth toward otherness and depth inherent in its nature (*SRS* 14, 17, 18, 49). This is a vision beyond the *homo economicus*.[47] Religious are to participate in shaping the policies and movements which support the *humanum*; and in this witness both to the transcendence which grounds their life and the modern values of the dignity which attaches to our own powers of reason and creative imagination and the depths of nature both within and without.[48]

At this juncture, religious in first-world situations and those in advanced developing economies cannot take for granted the know-how to put into practice the threefold approach to living the vow of poverty mentioned above. Religious themselves have faced new economic conditions. In the years following the Vatican Council, with its growing attention to material insufficiency across the world, Europe, the United States, and other regions experienced unprecedented and widespread economic growth and abundance, and in some instances, struggles with excess.[49] At the same time, a new stress and option for the poor and active solidarity replaced simple charity toward the poor, as many European-American Catholics transcended their working-class roots to become comfortably ensconced in the middle classes.[50] Some religious orders lost contact with the working class and found themselves cultivating the wealthy in efforts to support ministries and a growing aging population. Others simply aimed at solvency in a climate of decreasing new entrants and rising costs of care. Both efforts were well-intentioned but an insufficient path for the future. Furthermore, the challenges of increased individualism in religious orders make it difficult to act or speak as a group politically on behalf of the poor. Lack of personnel to offer direct services impacts a congregational "footprint" in poor areas. Communities have developed creative approaches to continue to offer service to the poor without a fee. Yet, they recognize that lifestyle changes, such as fewer living in community, offer new challenges. Some struggle to balance inclusion in the professional and life patterns which enable them to serve and avoid the expectations of the same living standards. Since the economic situation in which we live shapes our desires and expectations, these challenges have no easy answers. They require ongoing support, conversation, and discernment in congregations going forward. No single approach—be it personal virtue, advocacy, or prophetic action—is adequate to confront the questions surrounding consumption and sufficiency in a globalizing twenty-first

---

[47]See Anthony Annett, "The Economic Vision of Pope Francis," in *The Theological and Ecological Vision of Laudato Si: Everything is Connected*, ed. Vincent J. Miller (London: T&T Clark, 2017), 160–74.
[48]Merkle, *Discipleship, Secularity and the Modern Self*, 50.
[49]For example, the state of some Catholic Universities in the United States that are grappling with the question of what the cost of survival is and for what purpose, while others look for an apologetic to support a tuition cost which is out of reach for a growing number of applicants.
[50]Hinze, "What Is Enough?" 173.

century. Each one taken alone offers only a trajectory filled with bias and lacunae, offering a "poverty fundamentalism" that misses its spirit. "If I give away everything I own, and if I hand over my body over so that I may boast but do not have love, I gain nothing" (1 Cor. 13:3). Fulfillment of the gospel calls concerning material goods requires the creative counterpoising of these three mutually correcting directions of thought and action together with a fidelity to the leanings of a congregational charism. This path, which goes beyond the legalistic framework of the vow of poverty, offers a way to the conversion of heart which the vow is meant to foster and the wholeness it seeks to offer.

Poverty as a Spiritual Capacity and Way of Life

The vow of poverty is not a goal in itself; rather, it is a way of living to help us to remove whatever makes us less free to receive God's goodness and love. It is to attune our capacity for God by the slow but concrete process of letting go of whatever replaces, hinders, or cripples our openness and response to God's love in our lives. Poverty in society evokes visions of either the grinding poverty of the masses or a way of individual perfection removed from worldly affairs. Religious poverty is neither, it is chosen "for the life of the world" to foster the coming of the Reign of God. In its lived expressions, poverty offers a sacrament of hope for others. As with each of the vows, poverty leads us to a world beyond our fingertips, out to the other, whom we may not encounter if left to our own devices and preoccupations. Anthony Gittens clarifies, "In order to be both altruistic, and generative, my *religious poverty* must turn my life inside out, direct it at my neighbor (and my God), and help in some fashion to give life to the world."[51]

In this journey, we experience the pull of our desire for agency and control and meet the limits of our finitude. Through prayer and discernment, we become aware of our mammon, those things in which we place our trust, and learn to let go. When we can allow our trust in God to stir our consciousness, we find ourselves in the posture of the women in the gospel, who reached out to touch Jesus' garment in order to be healed (Mk 5:28). We find the grace to engage the emptiness in the self that only God can fill, our existential poverty. The wholeness that poverty touches is the truth of our reliance on an infinitely loving God and God's trustworthiness in all circumstances. Because of the life of Jesus who took on the human condition, we can embrace the poverty of human life among others "on their way," as well as the limits of ourselves. Relying on God's love, we can be generous in giving our gifts of self to others, being available and "disposable," working toward bringing about the Reign of God with others, with hope.

For this reason, poverty is not just spiritual but incarnational. Choices of poverty are concrete. As religious, our choice of poverty and simplicity of life is part of the common life of all Christians, but as congregations, we have a public witness to it. People have a

---

[51] Anthony J. Gittens, CSSp, "Poverty for Life," *Religious Life Review* 53, no. 284 (2014): 5–16 at 7.

right to expect something from us. They can expect us to be friends and advocates of the poor. They can refuse to accept our miserliness in replacement for an open-handedness to the poor and those who rely on us in all classes. They can judge us if we do not reach out beyond our own kind. And they can help us redirect the plenty of some to others in need. They have a right to look to us for efforts to close the gap between the haves and have-nots, and join with us to make possible education, health care, significance, rights, and recognition in society and the church community for those on the margins. We recognize that others have the right to assume we are in solidarity with those who are overlooked and forgotten. Above all, they should be able to see us as interrelated as a community, not as individuals alone on a personal journey, and know we act in our own realms always with the whole in mind. The vow of poverty is not just a choice with which we begin our religious life, but an ongoing commitment which impacts our choices over a lifetime with real people in actual communities. In this time of transition, the vow of poverty is also our public commitment to be people of hope who will hold onto what is necessary to plant the seeds for the future of religious life and to let go of that which simply fosters comfort and the familiar. In this, we will likely face the greatest challenge of poverty in religious congregations: that is, to foster what is necessary so that the next generation may continue to fashion the witness of religious life in the Church.

CHAPTER 7
CELIBATE CHASTITY
THE CHALLENGE OF SINGULARITY AND THE OTHER

A crossfire of interpretation surrounds any discussion of human sexuality today. It stems from wider debates concerning the meaning of human life and sexual expression in secular society. Some understand celibate chastity through the lens of what it is not—"not being sexually active"—rather than what it is. Religious are not the only people who choose to be celibate. Celibate chastity is distinguished, however, from other motivations as it is religiously motivated. Celibacy is an adult sexual stance within the complex arena of human affectivity, generativity, and love. For religious, it is not just a temporary decision, but one of a permanent life course. Since it is lived over a lifetime, it is able to be examined through many different lenses.[1] Human sexuality marks all the decades of life, while different aspects of sexual awareness and integration have prominence in particular periods. For this reason, specific issues for the celibate at one moment of life may be less significant at others. Since understandings of human sexuality in society and Church are undergoing evolution and debate, it is not surprising that understandings of celibate chastity are impacted. On the one hand, celibate chastity is not porous to contemporary discussions, since it involves a promise of permanent continence. On the other hand, celibacy shares with marriage a need for a more adequate language of human sexuality and its significance for wholeness. Those examining Church language regarding Christian marriage remind us that the meaning of human sexuality is not exhausted with the language of total self-gift or self-giving love under the conditions of marriage. Marital love is certainly marked by self-giving love, but its path also involves the experience of self-fulfilling love and friendship.[2] Some find that considerations of sexual life in marriage and celibacy are too often marked by a pre-Enlightenment tradition of linking sex to renunciation and control. While there are certainly important life lessons and habits to be learned under this lens, maintaining only this perspective limits meaningful dialogue about sex in society. Modern notions of sexuality have positive orientations

---

[1] Sandra M. Schneiders, *Selling All: Commitment, Consecrated Celibacy and Community in Catholic Religious Life* (Mahwah, NJ: Paulist Press, 2001), 109.
[2] Charles E. Curran, *Catholic Moral Theology in the United States: A History* (Washington, DC: Georgetown University Press, 2008), 193. While this reference refers to a more comprehensive view held by those who want to expand an understanding of marital love, it seems appropriate to include how those same qualities also can be understood, through different means, in the sexual integration involved in celibate chastity.

as well as blind sides.[3] Negatively, society elevates sexual pleasure to an absolute good; positively, it upholds the goodness of natural impulses and sentiments, the importance of the natural course of family life and heritage, and the good of pleasure in well-being. If one's theological language only stresses self-gift, control, and renunciation, conversations between church and society can seem like two ships passing in the night.

The aim of this reflection is not to offer a new language of human sexuality in the church; that task is better left to others. But it will assume that religious life is able to contribute something to the common search for meaning of human sexuality, rather than just be considered as a "non-player." More importantly, this dialogue is important for religious life, so that its meaning in secular society is better understood. Sandra Schneiders remarks that the discussion of religious life is no longer solely focused on its role in the church; rather, its meaning has shifted to a broader focus. "The question about the life itself is one about its wholeness, its integrity, its authenticity as a way of being in this world."[4] Certainly, the meaning of celibate chastity falls into this category.

Our discussion of the vow of celibate chastity will affirm, as it has with obedience and poverty that the witness of religious life to the wholeness of life is not limited to the service it offers. The argument that religious life frees a person from the duties of family life to more freely serve others is true, but it is insufficient to ground the vow's value. Religious life will not be presented solely as a life of self-giving because this is not a complete description. It also offers the possibility of self-fulfilling love, intimacy, and friendship, within a life of service through an alternative adult sexual stance. Celibate chastity can be a path of touching wholeness, but each vow alone, as stated with obedience and poverty, is not a value in itself (1 Cor. 13:3). Even celibate chastity is not a matchless value. Celibate chastity is an aspect of an entire lifestyle in which it finds its meaning.[5] The hope is an inquiry into a range of issues surrounding celibate chastity will highlight its significance for religious life, church, and society in secular times.

The Challenge of Singularity and the Other

In modern society, from the time we are born, the special character of being oneself is highlighted.[6] In contrast to the time period before the nuclear family—when children were sent to a wet nurse and returned to the family when able to work—children today are told, you are special, unique, one like no other.[7] The notion of singularity, or the incommensurability of the person, refers to this experience. In the Christian tradition,

---

[3]Sara Coakley, *The New Asceticism: Sexuality, Gender and the Quest for God* (London: Bloomsbury, 2015).
[4]Schneiders, *Selling All*, intro., x.
[5]See Josef Fuchs, "Chastity as Vow in the Jesuit Life Project," *The Way Supplement* 19 (Summer 1973): 96–104.
[6]Often, this sense, in war-torn countries, those controlled by dictatorship and violence, or devastated by environmental disaster, is experienced "in contrast" in the inability to adequately honor children's rights and unique dignity because of survival needs.
[7]See Edward Shorter, *The Making of the Modern Family* (New York: Basic Books, 1977).

it is the absolute worth of the human person before God.[8] Since we become ourselves in relationship to the world and other people, singularity involves its inverse experience, encounters with the pluralism and difference of the other. Discussion of the place of celibate chastity in secular times involves this rather abstract, but real, issue of the relationship of singularity and the Other.

The philosopher Soren Kierkegaard claims that the ancient world and the biblical worlds have very different concepts of the self.[9] Socrates had no concept of the self as the single individual who has come historically into the world. The truth of the self, for Socrates, is eternally hidden in such a way that it can neither be sought nor known. He equally had no concept of the other as the single individual—as he or she also lacked the singularity of coming historically into the world—in other words he had no concept of the neighbor. Ancient thought, in contrast to biblical thought, therefore seemed to lack a way difference between the self and other, the challenges of plurality and universality, the relationship between the individual and the universal were met. Kierkegaard argues that biblical thought has as its intention to hold these apparent diversities together.

Overcoming what appears to be an opposition between self and others engages us in a journey of faith. Human faith is the capacity to go out of ourselves in love rather than into self in egotism.[10] Faith, in Kierkegaard, is different from other ways we respond to what is other, whether our neighbor or the world itself. At one level we simply respond. We react to life coming upon us by seeking pleasure, having interest, or expressing boredom—simply as a response. At a second level, we respond to life by calling on principles, or ethics, to make decisions as our response. Faith, however, requires going beyond these first two levels yet ultimately incorporates them. Faith involves a paradox, as a commitment to put one's trust in something eternal and Absolute, beyond what we can see or reason. It is a search for the truth beyond just our impressions of it. The biblical narrative names this Absolute as God.[11]

---

[8] "Singularity" is also a term in physics, mathematics, and quantum theory. We are using the term here heuristically to portray the fundamental relationship between the self and the experience of the other.

[9] See Avron Kulak, "Between Singularity and Plurality: Kierkegaard and the Paradox of Absolute Difference," *Journal of Kierkegaard Studies Yearbook* 26, no. 1 (January 2021): 223–39 at 227. This article addresses how in a pluralistic world, with no master narratives and no narratives that are non-controversial, there must still be, according to Kierkegaard, a singular principle in light of which we are commanded to respect the narrative of the other. For an example of diverse concepts of the self, see Mary Frohlich, *Breathed into Wholeness: Catholicity and Life in the Spirit* (Maryknoll, NY: Orbis Books, 2019), 75–98.

[10] Psychologist Erik Erikson claims such faith is necessary for human development. Erik H. Erikson, *Childhood and Society*, 2nd rev. ed. (New York: W.W. Norton & Co., 1963 (1950)). See also Juan Luis Segundo, *Faith and Ideologies*, trans. John Drury (New York: Orbis, 1984).

[11] Judith A. Merkle, *Discipleship, Secularity and the Modern Self: Dancing to Silent Music* (London: T&T Clark, 2020), 57–9. See also Charles Taylor, *Sources of the Self: The Making of Modern Identity* (Cambridge, MA: The Belknap Press of Harvard University Press, 1989), 449.

Celibate Chastity and Belief

Kierkegaard sheds light on how the difference between belief and unbelief enters the process of response to what we experience as Other.[12] Instead of moving from one finite thing to another, embracing the good to be found in life, a person goes deeper. In faith, a person chooses in the light of infinity. In making important choices, like a vow of celibate chastity, a person chooses two things. First, she/he chooses what kind of person one wants to be, oriented toward what is good, or simply what is convenient or self-serving. The second choice is to express in a concrete action the intention of their first choice. A vow then is an action to express this wider intention or desire. Such an action expresses love of God and the People of God; both offer new possibilities for intimacy in shared lives and ministry.[13] A vow of a religious responds to a call in grace to which a person answers with a specific action—a life choice as a religious.[14] Kierkegaard notes that in making a concrete choice of the good, the man or the woman also choose themselves. The choice is infinite; it is not for the sake of any finite thing but on the contrary, all finite things get their value and significance from this choice. All things in one's life may be the same, but if they are chosen in light of the infinite, they are no longer absolutes, as what defines one's final goal—they are simply relative to a wider life project. On the surface, it may be that the detail of one's life does not change. However, why the person chooses what they do changes. They now live for the infinite. This change is purely inward but expressed outwardly through vow. It is a change which transforms a merely outward life and gives it inwardness. Celibate chastity, in this instance, becomes a mark of one's singularity.

The way we overcome the opposition between the incommensurability of self and the other is through love of neighbor; there is no other way. In fact, the development of our true self, our singularity, depends on it. "single individuals are absolute and incommensurable only insofar as they stand in absolute relation to the neighbor as absolute and incommensurable."[15] If I am a unique human being worthy of respect, so

---

[12]We note people may choose celibacy for a variety of reasons. A vow of celibate chastity is made for religious reasons. See Schneiders, *Selling All*.

[13]Celibacy represents the possibility that genital sex need not be at the heart of every profound human relationship, and that sexual intensity, lived celibately, can empower the human person as a whole. See Margaret Farley, "Celibacy under the Sign of the Cross," in *Changing the Questions: Explorations in Christian Ethics*, ed. and intro. Jamie L. Manson (Maryknoll, NY: Orbis Books, 2015), 222–40 at 235.

[14]This does not imply choosing a life of marriage is self-serving. Every authentic way of life incorporates relationships that are intrinsically good and hence constitutive of the fullness of life toward which they are also a means. Rahner notes, it is false to say that "two loves, the love for God and Christ on the one hand, and the human love which finds its fulfillment in marriage on the other, are opposed to one another as rivals." "On the Evangelical Counsels," *Theological Investigations*, VIII, trans. David Bourke (New York: Herder and Herder, 1971), 148. It simply means for this individual, this is a response to a personal call. See Merkle, *Discipleship, Secularity and the Modern Self*, 76. It is also a call to a lifestyle recognized in the Church. Lifelong celibacy, chosen for the sake of the reign of God, has from the early Christian centuries been valued in part as a witness to an unlimited future—an embodiment of eschatological hope in a world to come (*LG* 43, 44). While both vocations are responses to this baptismal call, religious life does this in a unique manner, specific to its charism.

[15]Kulak, "Between Singularity and Plurality," 228.

is every other. The biblical narrative states that no human being is excluded from this dignity. Kierkegaard concludes that the single individual can exist as a single individual only in light of viewing all others as single individuals—as incommensurable—as neighbor.

Celibate Chastity and Creation

For the ancients, like Socrates, the truth resided in the eternal and therefore never could be known. The role of the teacher was to show students their ignorance of the truth, which was not fully accessible to them or to the teacher. However, the biblical narrative testifies to a God who entered time and did not remain only in the eternal. Kierkegaard argues that if we are to be delivered from an ignorance of the truth, of knowing ourselves or our neighbor, of awareness of our singularity and its existence in the plurality, then we must ground our beginning in something different than the ancients. This is our creation by God—"in as much as the learner exists, he is indeed created, and, accordingly, God must have given him the condition for understanding the truth."[16]

One can forfeit this relationship and live in untruth, or sin, through free choice. However, to go beyond the ancients, we must go to the biblical narrative of the incarnation, and to Genesis, with its witness to creation and original sin. It testifies when God entered time in the incarnation of Jesus Christ, he brought us the condition we have forfeited. Awareness of our singularity is recovered through alertness to how we forfeit it before others by undue focus on apparent and unsurpassable differences between ourselves and others. The future of congregations and the health of the Church at a time of great diversity rely on this insight. We hear it echoed in the Synod. Are we willing to be drawn beyond mutual incomprehension and suspicions of each other?[17] Love of neighbor is the only way to overcome this impasse. At its foundations, the vow of celibate chastity engages us in this core human movement from our singularity to the Other.[18] Charles Taylor concurs that our movement toward another is a "leap." "Loving the world and ourselves is in a sense a miracle, in face of all the evil and degradation that it and we contain,"[19] Central to the Christian tradition, therefore, is that people are transformed through being loved by God. This is a love they mediate to each other. The movement toward the other is the means through which all bring transformation to the families, communities, hospitals, schools, neighborhoods, boardrooms, corporations, and churches of society.

---

[16]Ibid., 231.
[17]See Timothy Radcliff, OP, "Synod Retreat Meditation: Conversation on the Way to Emmaus," *Vatican News*, October 2, 2023.
[18]Kulak, "Between Singularity and Plurality," 239.
[19]Taylor, *Sources of the Self*, 452.

As we relate to and conceive of human beings, so we relate to and conceive of God.[20] Religious ground the vow of celibate chastity in the presence and Absolute reality of God who sustains them in the totality of their commitment. They learn and make real, through their living and ministry, the meaning of truth, love, equality, and the absolute value and dignity of all human beings in real time. Religious life is incarnational; it is a response to the presence of God in real time. The vows, as a leap of faith, are also a witness to the wholeness of existence in the life of every human being. The lifestyle of a religious is to reflect the presence of the goodness of God amid the ups and downs of their lives and those of God's people.

While today there are many conceptions of self, the biblical narrative indicates the criterion which allows their differences not to stand in contradiction, but to allow their diversity and pluralism to express a more adequate language of wholeness within the human community. As communities, religious are to stand against all use of religious or absolute language to ground action which oppresses, invalidates, or annihilates the other in the name of establishing a singularity of national, economic, cultural, racial, sexual, or religious identity.[21] The common journey of the human community is also the journey of those who vow celibate chastity.

Wholeness and Contradiction

According to theologian Edward Schillebeeckx, we do not find salvation, or wholeness, primarily by means of a correct interpretation of reality but by acting in accordance with the demands of reality.[22] We meet God and become fully ourselves through encounter with challenges in life and our own human condition, not despite them. We encounter these challenges in our own singularity, in encounter with others and in the context of our lives and societies. For Schillebeeckx, this dynamic occurs most clearly in "contrast experiences." These are situations in which the contradiction between what is and what "should be" cannot be ignored. Good people refuse to give evil an equal footing with good. The discontinuity experienced stirs a response—something must be done. Hidden within our "no" to a situation is a "yes," hope for a better world, and a commitment to take steps to make it better.

A similar struggle presents itself in the relationships and inner drama of our personal lives. Reality as "other than I thought or intended" interrupts. At times reality reveals to us an aspect of ourselves we have not imagined. To be human is to come up against the limits of all our experiences of knowing and willingness. To choose "more" is a choice

---

[20]Kulak, "Between Singularity and Plurality", 234. The liberation theologian Juan Luis Segundo affirms: what we say of God, we say of human existence. *Grace and the Human Condition*, trans. John Drury (Maryknoll, NY: Orbis Books, 1973), 127.

[21]Gorski, Philip S. and Samuel L. Perry, *The Flag and the Cross: White Christian Nationalism and the Threat to American Democracy* (Oxford: Oxford University Press, 2022).

[22]Edward Schillebeeckx, *Christ: The Experience of Jesus as Lord*, trans. John Bowden (New York: Crossroad, 1981), 47.

to grow, to be real instead of relying on appearance, or to change what can be altered. It may mean accepting a new challenge or facing illness or loss. The task of singularity and plurality lies within this very basic encounter with others and the world around us. The paradox is that accepting we are neither the origin of reality nor even the source of our knowing and understanding allows there always can be more. Because reality is grounded in more than myself, I can expect there is more to life than I know. We find meaning through how we respond to this fact. My move against meaninglessness is to find in contradictions and limits which cannot be rationalized or removed, the possibility of a Wholeness of life. I can find in the other, who I cannot manipulate and form in my likeness, a neighbor and companion with whom I can walk. This Wholeness in the reality of the world around me and in the Other is more than I can create or plan, yet its otherness makes all reality possible for everyone and most importantly for me. In human faith, I encounter reality; in religious faith, I encounter God.

Celibacy as a Human Challenge

While the discussion of singularity and plurality might seem remote from the realities of celibate life, John Foley, SJ, acknowledges their connection to the sexual and affective qualities engaged by a celibate commitment. Life is not primarily about having sex, yet sexuality is never absent from life. Sexual faculties serve the wider goal of becoming fully human, becoming increasingly capable of loving relations. When physical sexuality is integrated into this process, it serves the greater project of wholeness.[23] Celibacy and chastity are not the same. Celibates vow to refrain from explicit genital sexuality; chastity is the choice to restrict explicit sexuality to relationships where it is proper, as in marriage. Marital chastity restricts explicit sexuality to one's partner and refrains from sexual relationships outside this union. Married people are chaste but not celibate. It follows that celibate chastity involves refraining from relationships that would naturally imply sexual relations.

Sexual integration is a lifelong task which requires time, patience, honesty, and maturity. As relationships engage our whole personality, relationships with another person widen the scope of my life and require me to include their good into my own. I must make room for them. It requires a balance of my needs and theirs, which entails delayed satisfaction and self-awareness of my own feelings and desires. Foley makes clear that singularity is not selfishness but can be seen as "my own terrain" and necessary for a healthy celibate life. It is a personal territory within, where I am welcomed by my own self. "This is a realm I do not have to wrest away from others—be they lovers, superiors, or rules—in order to be freely myself."[24] It is my own love and confidence in myself; its

---

[23]John B. Foley, SJ "Stepping into the River: Reflections on the Vows," *Studies on the Spirituality of Jesuits* 26, no. 4 (September 1994): 1–31 at 16–22.
[24]Ibid., 18.

lack causes pain, anxiety, and social maladjustment. Singularity, as my own terrain, is not an enemy of love but necessary to it. The presence of it allows me to be with myself. My sexually affective capacity lives within this terrain, as well as my capacity for sex. "Capacity for sex will still be there if I am someone who lacks a trustworthy internal territory, but it will then become a way of searching for the home and relationality I lack, engaging in truly promiscuous acts for that purpose."[25] If I lack a trustworthy internal capacity, I am more prone to look at sex as a way to find the home and relationality I lack.

Celibate chastity is not just an internal struggle between virtue and vice. It is part of a framework of life. Like marriage and single life, it is practiced within a broader network or web of relationships, duties, and mission. It is lived in the same context of commitments surrounding poverty and obedience. This plurality, of being situated in a world, challenges us to move beyond the core human impulse of appropriation or ownership of people and things and the instinct of self-assertion vis-à-vis others or dominance over them.[26] Here plurality is an encounter with difference and what is other. This does not rob a person of being a whole person, but rather sets the conditions where it is possible. In this wider terrain, all need people and relationships. The reality of personal terrain includes the capacity to be open to others. In Foley's words, "Personal territory means my own way of receiving and letting go; it does not mean 'filling up' or "closing off."[27]

Intimacy

Intimacy is essential for a life of celibate chastity, and it is necessary to enjoy the intimacy offered in religious life. Lynn Levo, CSJ, reminds us that only genital intimacy, such as erotic or orgasmic closeness, is not acceptable in religious life. However, religious life offers the possibility of intimacy on many levels. A celibate commitment involves learning how to move toward and be with others in various ways. Emotional intimacy is necessary for wholeness. Being in tune with one another, having a close bond that involves mutual understanding, trust, vulnerability and communication is the intimacy desired by all people, and it is important to sustain religious commitment. Religious life offers the possibility of meeting others in the world of ideas, or intellectual intimacy, as well as sharing experiences of beauty in aesthetic intimacy. Religious engage in acts of creating together in creative intimacy. They relate through experiences of fun and play in recreational intimacy. Common in religious life is sharing tasks in work intimacy. They cope together and with others in problem-solving and experience pain in crisis intimacy. Religious face and struggle with differences in the intimacy which arises from dealing with conflicts. They share ultimate concerns in spiritual intimacy. All the above forms of

---

[25]Ibid.
[26]See Felicisimo Martinez, OP, "The Virtue of Chastity in Religious Life," *Religious Life* 54, no. 294 (2015): 301–8.
[27]Foley, "Stepping into the River," 19.

intimacy require good communication. Being honest with another and receiving them fosters communication intimacy.[28] Intimacy is possible in religious life to the degree a person can be themselves in community and the communal culture fosters the diversity necessary to receive people in their uniqueness.

Since community is not a given but a task for the members who comprise it, sexual integration engages the celibate in the personal growth necessary to build relationships. The mutuality between the members and the responsiveness of the group creates the conditions to hold relationships together and experience the long-term sense of fulfillment healthy committed relationships can offer. The person who has not yet found themselves may attempt to answer questions of meaning in religious life simply by turning over the life task of their singularity to another. It is not just young people who enter marital relationships before they know themselves sufficiently who do this. A religious can have this intention when they enter a congregation, thinking this simple act will shield them from loneliness, give them an identity or prestige, and take care of the inevitable unknowns and struggles of life ahead. In all states of adult life, there is loneliness, which is a mark of the human condition. Loneliness cannot be dispelled totally by communion with another or even by falling in love. Sexual integration of single, married, and celibate men and women involves accepting these limitations and learning to live with them. All sexual integration includes learning to love people as they are, not our fantasies of them. Movement from our singularity to the Other can be real, fulfilling, and happy while at the same time requiring patience, committed love, and willingness to forgive.

An aspect of being oneself is gender identity. While its significance is a debated topic in society today, those who choose celibate chastity are called to live their lives, their sexual orientation, and emotions with fidelity. All are called to renounce genital affection, live as singles, not as couples, avoid relationships of exclusivity and possession, and live with personal self-knowledge and acceptance of their sexuality before God and others.[29]

Theology and Sexuality

Bernard Lonergan claims that theology mediates between a cultural matrix and the significance and role of religion in that matrix.[30] Certainly in the West, society has held varying views of sexuality which impact understandings of celibacy. Sex has been

---

[28]Lynn Levo, CSJ, as quoted in Maria Cimperman, RSCJ, *Religious Life for Our World: Creating Communities of Hope* (Maryknoll, NY: Orbis Books, 2020), 88.
[29]Friendship involves a type of exclusivity but is not identified by it. There are forms of intimacy that belong to sexual partnerships but not to celibate relationships. Coupling is going through life as a couple rather than being sexually single. Coupling and living situations of religious as dyads or triads are not the same. See Patricia Wittberg, SC, "Dyads and Triads: The Sociological Implications of Small-Group Living Arrangements," *Review for Religious*, January-February 1990, 43–51. For coupling see Judith A. Merkle, *A Different Touch: A Study of the Vows in Religious Life* (Collegeville, MN: The Liturgical Press, 1998), 248–52.
[30]Bernard J. Lonergan, SJ, *Method in Theology* (Toronto, CAN: University of Toronto Press, 1977), xi.

depicted as evil, as well as the primary good. People have charged that life without genital sex is against nature, as well as have assumed celibates are either secretly debaucherous or have a distaste or fear of sex. Yet the human experience of those who lead celibate lives counters these views. "Whether celibacy is chosen or graciously accepted, many of those who live it manifest in their lives not only happiness and wellbeing but the heightened peace that comes with human self-realization and fulfillment."[31] The theology of human sexuality in the church affirms marriage and family life as well as singleness and celibacy. All states of life can express baptismal commitment. Faith, however, serves to foster discernment of an individual's path and assists in weighing cultural norms regarding sexual expression. The church has a role to foster healthy sexual norms in society both by what it teaches and witnesses. In this it must engage the whole church in discerning in what way the tradition can promote a sexual ethic centered in good science as well as responsive to the stresses and possibilities men and women face today. While the church's own failures in the sexual abuse crisis threaten its credibility around human sexuality, it must pull from its best efforts, not its worst representations.[32] As in all interactions with culture, the church needs to discern what to affirm, foster, critique, and contradict. It needs also to apply this method to itself so that the church can move toward the embrace of its deepest values and away from its own cultural limitations and biases.[33] Religious in various cultures, therefore, are to probe the legitimacy of the celibate option and answer its critics in their own circumstances. It is an important task for religious to express their own vow of celibate chastity in terms of changing understandings of human sexuality, marriage, and family, and the call to holiness shared by all Christians.

Celibate Chastity as a Lived Reality

Gerdenio Sonny Manuel, SJ, cautions that focus on the behavioral minefields of psychological dysfunction and clergy misconduct is inadequate to update a treatment of celibate chastity for the secular age.[34] Positive aspects, psychological, social, and spiritual, of living a chaste and celibate life point to how such a lifestyle promotes the

---

[31]Farley, "Celibacy under the Sign of the Cross," 235.
[32]See Stephen Edward de Weger, "Unchaste Celibates: Clergy Sexual Misconduct against Adults-Expresssions, Definitions and Harms," *Religions*12, no. 393 (2022): 1–27. https://doi.org/10.3390/rel1.3050393.
[33]See, for example, Pope Francis' condemnation of clericalism: "Clericalism defiles the face of the Church," *L'Osservatore Romano*, October 27, 2023. For links between clericalism and sexual abuse, see Julie Hanlan Rubio and Paul J. Schutz, *Beyond Bad Apples: Understanding Clergy Perpetuated Sexual Abuse as a Structural Problem and Cultivating Strategies for Change*. Ignatian Center for Jesuit Education (Santa Clara University, 2024), www.scu.edu. The study defines clericalism "as a structure of power that isolates clergy and sets priests above and apart, granting them excessive authority, trust, rights, and responsibilities while diminishing the agency of lay people and religious." For female religious, any system which upholds a style of exceptionalism with its imbalance of mutuality and reciprocity could frame similar, but not identical, dynamics.
[34]Gerdenio Sonny Manuel, SJ, "Living Chastity: Psychosexual Well-Being in Jesuit Life," *Studies in the Spirituality of Jesuits* 41, no. 2 (2009): 1–36.

health of a vocation and impacts the effectiveness of ministry. God's grace touches us by means of our vulnerability throughout our lives as we try to keep in balance not only the goal of celibacy but the wisdom that enables it to thrive. Manuel suggests five active practices to foster healthy celibacy. We will address three of them under lived celibacy and the remaining two at the end of the chapter. These five practices serve as experiential dimensions to living chastity, as well as indications of the basics needed to support it. Manuel lists these practices as follows:

I. Live close to God and our deepest desires.
II. Develop broad and deep interpersonal relationships and communities of support.
III. Ask for love, nurture others, and negotiate separations.
IV. Cope with stress and recognize destructive patterns of behavior.
V. Celebrate the holy in the company of Jesus.[35]

Ministry, Community, and Celibate Chastity

In the past, people claimed celibacy offered greater freedom for ministry and was a means to foster community. This reasoning flowed from a pre-Vatican institutionalization of religious life in which the three vows interfaced uniquely. Poverty was linked strongly with community life and a uniformity of lifestyle crucial to a unity of community life. Obedience was connected to ministry as the way in which individual members were integrated into the mission of the congregation, a mission which was efficiently coordinated by the leadership. Celibacy was less a matter of public attention, many times addressed vaguely and inadequately, and often directed to deportment with family, men, women, children, and one another—usually marked by modesty and reserve in expressions of affection.[36] The religious motivation, union with Christ, was associated more with religious life as a whole than with celibacy.

After Vatican II, religious congregations reappropriated ministry as integral to religious life itself and set aside monastic elements of their life which impeded ministry.[37] A more structured life of prayer was set aside, while retreat, spiritual direction, and the integration of personalism into spirituality enhanced spiritual development, albeit even if it became more privatized and optional in practice. Within religious life and Western culture there was a revolution against authority and institutions. People entered religious life who had never suffered from the excesses and abuses of authority of pre-conciliar times. However, growing up in the transitional culture of the 1960s and beyond, many

---

[35]Ibid., 4.
[36]Schneiders, *Selling All*, 144–59 at 145. I will call on Schneiders' argument for context in the following.
[37]Ministry also became less institutionalized. See Judith A. Merkle, "The Niche of Religious Life," in *Sensing the Spirit: Toward the Future of Religious Life* (London: T&T Clark, 2023), 35–58.

had weaker family, religious, and social moorings than generations before. The need to belong was paramount. New entrants desired to participate in a meaning system beyond self and the desire-pleasure model offered by culture. Schneiders comments that the need for community evidenced by new entrants did not necessarily flow from the more traditional spirituality of total self-gift to Christ.[38] It could become that, but culturally it had a different starting point. For those who were already members of religious congregations, the vast shifts after Vatican II raised new questions. Some saw religious life as a package with celibacy as part of a life of service. However, even if the primacy of celibacy was not explicit from the beginning, it did become a main reason for staying in religious life. With societal and ecclesial changes, opportunities for community, service, and ministry in the church were no longer limited to membership in religious communities, especially for women.[39] It became clearer that the relationship between the communitarian and ministerial dimensions of religious life are not the same as that between celibacy and its mystical/relational identity. When Manuel lists his practices to live a healthy celibate life, he lists, "live close to God and our deepest desires" first and "develop broad and deep interpersonal relationships and communities of support, second. His analysis reflects the reliance of a religious vocation on the presence of a primary relationship to God."[40] We have noted this historical diversion to point out that the establishment of relationships in ministry and communities of support is in a very different context today than pre-Vatican religious life. Establishing healthy relationships as a celibate requires an ongoing religious conversion without necessarily the institutional boundaries set in previous times. For Lonergan, religious conversion is an ongoing fundamental shift in one's orientation toward God, which informs and motivates other conversions. Religious conversion in religious life, therefore, is inseparable from the emotional, cognitive, and moral challenges and development which encompass the whole of religious life as celibate.

---

[38] Schneiders, *Selling All*, 148.

[39] Schneiders clarifies that we best understand celibacy within an understanding of religious life as constitutively both religious and a life. Religious does not mean a generalized spirituality or personal synthesis of various religious traditions. It is Christianity, in its Catholic incarnation (noting other Christian traditions have religious). It is a lifeform which makes it different than joining the Peace Corps, National Organization of women or feminist support group or other organization aimed at service, or advocacy. It involves more than part-time, temporary, and free-will commitment of time and resources. Religious Life makes a claim on the whole life of its members, on the totality of their personal time and their resources. See *Selling All*, 152.

[40] Manuel, "Living Chastity," 7. "Over time and through every dimension of our personal, communal and apostolic life, Jesuits are called "to reverence the divine presence as the horizon in which they live, to apprehend the immanent providence of God that draws them into its own working for the salvation of human beings, and to hold onto God as the purpose that energizes their work—learning thus to find God in all things." GC, "Chastity in the Society of Jesus," 119, no. 245.

Relationships, Celibacy, and Wholeness

As men and women go through the developmental stages of identity, capacity for love, and generativity, they also become capable of communion, union with God as the center of life.

The path of celibate chastity is a unique way to journey through life's passages. Most people in the Christian life do this through marriage and family life. However, celibacy incorporates, rather than circumvents, the challenges of the life passages of all adults. The celibate's whole lifestyle, not just their genital abstinence, impacts how well the vow fosters their path to wholeness. Today, a new style of religious identity relies increasingly on internal agency by virtue of an individual's own authority and cultural or lifestyle preferences, rather than those of traditional institutional or external norms. A religious must be an adult among adults and cannot rely on any form of exceptionalism, either in its male, feminine, or clerical forms. Adult Christians who vow celibate chastity are bound to the sexual boundaries as well as the relational challenges which identify their life in the church and frame it as an alternate sexual stance of marriage and the single life. In this sense, the way a female religious shows affection or a male religious promises friendship should be supported by the living of all three vows and by the demands of community and ministerial life. Vowed celibacy is a framework of love meant to lead to sexual integration. Integration for a celibate occurs through primary and affective dimensions of sexuality and the non-expression of genital behavior.

Sexuality has a wide impact on our lives. It has a primary, affective, and genital dimension. Primary sexuality refers to how men and women are present to reality. All persons, including hermits, have a primary sexual relationship.[41] While many reject the complimentary of men and women, arguing that defining male and female traits often depicts women in a subordinate position, theorists like Jung cite an *anima* and *animus* dimension of every personality that must be integrated into a whole.[42] We develop our primary sexual self through interaction with persons of the opposite sex, nature, fine and performing arts, literature, dreams, prayer, and formation of values. Primary sexuality is involved with questions such as: How do I view my body? How do I care for it? How do I see myself as a man or woman? How do I view men? What are my spontaneous reactions to women and assumptions about them?

Catholic imagination often stops at genital contact or activity when sexual sin is considered. However, negative gender relationships, with no physical contact, are destructive and divisive. Harassment and exclusion of homosexuals, the inability to accept the leadership of women, hatred and distrust of men, and lack of compassion and openness as the church seeks to understand and respond to the needs of the LGBTQ community reflect sexual issues, in the realm of primary sexuality.

---

[41] Merkle, *A Different Touch*, 248-62.
[42] Ann and Barry Ulanov, *The Witch and the Clown: Two Archetypes of Human Sexuality* (Asheville, NC: Chiron Publications, 2018).

Affective sexuality refers to feelings, emotions, or moods that move toward or incorporate some form of intimacy. The spiritual dimension of affective sexuality is a faithfulness and presence that sustains all love, consideration, warmth, hospitality, kindness all are ways our affectivity is shared. Through affective sexuality, we not only seek relationships but those that involve closeness. Transactional relationships, those involving the exchanges our roles in society dictate, are not the same as relationships where people experience us as reliable and caring. In close relationships, affective sexual behavior, a caring look, gestures, a delight, an acceptance, a conversation of personal sharing, can be an end in itself or can be in the service of and part of genital behavior. Certainly, in marriage, affective signs of consideration are the glue of a happy relationship. For celibates, the desire for a life beyond "transactional" relationships challenges them both to be aware of their own affective needs and to make choices to keep their expressions of affection at the appropriate level.

Early in the life of a religious learning to engage in relationships which are healthy and celibate might involve struggle and mistakes. It is by working through these conflicts that maturity grows. However, later in life, it can become more evident how avoidance of relationships in the small and specific ways they are maintained prevents a religious from cultivating healthy relationships and communities of support. Holding oneself aloof from relationships by offering the excuse to oneself and others that the demands of one's job, role, or being needed somewhere else make investment impossible can foster a life of prominence in ministry but not necessarily one of happiness and intimacy.[43] A crisis of intimacy can arise when the promise of position or a life "above the fray" wears off, and one faces illness or the end of life, alone without the support that a habit of relationships could soften. Questions of loneliness and the need for relationships to celebrate the highs and lows of life must be asked along the way. Do I always need to be in a role? Where am I an adult among adults? What relationships in my life claim my attention and why? When appropriate, how do I move from the role of pastoral agent, mentor or teacher to personal friendship? Am I satisfied with the relationships I enjoy? What am I grateful for, and what would I change? How do I initiate, support, and sustain my friendships?[44]

Genital sexuality refers to the behaviors, thoughts, fantasies, desires, and feelings that involve or encourage genital behavior. Genital behavior and genitality are different. Sexual intercourse and masturbation are explicit forms of genital behavior. Feelings and fantasies that do or can activate genital processes are modes of genitality.[45] Genitality incorporates thoughts and feelings that could but need not be expressed in genital behavior. Genital sex, in the Christian life, requires time, place, and commitment—the conditions of marriage. Time means it happens "over time" in the fostering and bonding

---

[43]Manuel, "Living Chastity," 11.
[44]Ibid., 16–17.
[45]See Andre Guindon, OMI, "A Theory of Sexual Ethics for Concerned Christians," in *Readings in Moral Theology, No.8: Dialogue About Catholic Sexual Teaching* (Mahwah, NJ: Paulist Press, 1993), 22–46.

of a relationship and the building of a family. Therefore, in the Christian life, healthy genitality is the capacity to give and receive genital expressions of love as part of a broader love commitment which is emotional, functional, and spiritual, the lifestyle of marriage. The celibate lifestyle is not compatible with the physical presence and spiritual and functional experience of spousehood. Celibates who engage in genital relations are trying to integrate their lives around two all-inclusive commitments. Celibate chastity is a way of loving, not a ministerial commitment alone. Celibates, if they have not fostered real friendships and communities of support, can attempt to resolve the loneliness they feel through seeking a sexual partner.[46] However, the problem is internal. To integrate the passion of sexuality I need to be, at least becoming, a self. Full sexuality requires that I have a sense of my feelings, my specific memories, and my desires. If we hold onto the picture of religious life as an integrated lifestyle, it is easy to see how the search for positions of power and authority, as well as possession of people, things, and control can also be substitutes for the self-possession necessary for a celibate commitment. Celibacy thrives when it flows from the discovery of oneself as lovingly open to others and to God.

The central motivating force in healthy genitality is love, making love concrete. Genital love makes love in marriage immediate and concrete, as well as a loving relationship gives meaning to genital sex. For the celibate, the need for love is met through a deepening spiritual life, family, community, ministry, satisfying interests, and friends. Sexual tension is suppressed, not repressed. Self-awareness fosters the recognition that non-sexual needs can drive sexual behavior. The drive to let go when over-extended, find escape when bored, reach for comfort when anxiety, painful experiences, or depression take over, can frame short-lived sexual experience as an "answer" to these life struggles. The need to feel special, to feel power over another, to express hostility, or to act out from past experiences, such as the substitution of a significant other in one's past, can also be hidden motivations for sexual behavior. Yet, all these issues remain, as a return to reality leaves the same disappointment and emotional confusion unaddressed. People who equate sex with intimacy may try to replace a lack of past interpersonal intimacy in their family or in friendship with an "automatic" intimacy of genital sex. They confuse the mutual knowing and being known of true intimacy with the physical intimacy of sex. Healthy community and the support of prayer can help the need for connective and transpersonal experience. Prayer, communion with nature, love of the arts, and friendship are all possible avenues of fulfillment. Balance in the lifestyle of a religious, regarding mutuality in relationships, equality of the sexes, and collaborative capacity to build community with others, all foster the integration of healthy sexuality.[47]

---

[46]Sometimes, this loneliness is part of life. Other times, it comes from overwork, lack of investment in friendships, ignoring a prayer life, isolation from community, and not enough relaxation and recreation.

[47]See Rubio and Schutz, *Beyond Bad Apples: Understanding Clergy Perpetrated Sexual Abuse as a Structural Problem and Cultivating Strategies for Change*. The study looks at the relationship between sex, gender, and power in clericalism and how it creates conditions predisposed to the possibility of sexual violence. Clericalism in this sense is defined as "a structure of power that isolates clergy and sets priests above and apart, granting them excessive authority, trust, rights and responsibilities while diminishing the agency of lay people and

In this sense, celibate chastity is a relational reality, not a solitary one. It is not a refusal to interact with others or to engage in intimacy, but it involves finding oneself through being open to others and to God. The self-possession and maturity needed to have real relationships with others is core to the path of charity characteristic of religious life.[48]

For this reason, Manuel adds to his list of practices for a celibate life, "ask for love, nurture others, and negotiate separation." Long before we could ask others directly for love, we did so indirectly as we looked to others for assistance and attention. As adults, we often do not want to show our vulnerability to others by asking for help. Yet providing help when needed, especially at times of celebration and recognition, illness, transitions, and bereavement is an important signature of healthy community life today and a fulfillment of the covenant of community life. Awareness of the need to ask for love, nurture others, and negotiate separation gives rise to these questions along the way of celibate loving. Who are the people, family or friends, that we feel we can depend upon for help in small, everyday matters and in times of great need? When and how do we ask God and others for the love and support we need? Do we allow the love of others to free us from sin and shame, or do we expect rejection and therefore do not hope for love to be given.?[49]

Erikson, Celibacy, and Singularity

Vowed celibacy engages the major life crises of adolescence and adult years: identity versus identity confusion, intimacy versus isolation, and generativity versus stagnation.[50] These challenges provide the life situation in which the love of a celibate person takes flesh. Celibates grow through the same passages as other adults, according to their lifestyle. God summons each to growth by these invitations in life.

Identity versus identity confusion involves self-recognition, an experience of oneself as a center of continuity and sameness. Identity involves a type of occupational or ministerial commitment or capacity to take responsibility for a productive social role. Identity confusion is simply the opposite; the person cannot "take hold." There is a lack of a sufficient sense of self. Since people do not know who they are, others cannot count on them. A stable sexual identity is part of this sense of self and necessary to make a celibate commitment.

---

religious." Anyone (ordained, religious, or lay) can be clericalist or anti-clericalist. This is not an attempt to demonize priesthood or priests but to question how relationships are institutionalized in the church. The focus of this study is not on clericalism as a personal problem of an individual but as a structure in the Church. This is also the approach of Pope Francis and his criticism of clericalism. *Ignatian Center for Jesuit Education*. Santa Clara University @ www.scu.edu. The dynamics of clericalism can be present in many relationships where there is unequal authority and power.
[48]Foley, "Stepping into the River," 20.
[49]Manuel, "Living Chastity," 20.
[50]In this, I am indebted to Erikson and Capps as previously cited. See Merkle, *A Different Touch*, 266–76.

A virtue-vice struggle engaged in arriving at a sense of identity is fidelity and pride. Fidelity is the ability to sustain loyalty. False identity is fostered through pride, an overly high opinion of oneself often shown in haughty and arrogant behavior. Healthy pride involves a good self-concept and sense of personal worth. False pride is shown in conceit and hypocrisy and joy in doing harm to others—"I'll show them!" Pride causes isolation and denies one's need for community and others. It makes excessive demands for attention, is self-deceptive, and places oneself at the center of the universe. Spiritually, focus on God and the ego-inflation of pride are incompatible. Obviously, the role of fidelity is crucial for religious commitment as the capacity for duty, truthfulness, genuineness, loyalty, fairness, and devotion marks the person as someone others can trust and count on. Despite the inevitable disillusionment, disappointment, and frustrations which enter all of life, fidelity survives personal crises as it is rooted in a deep sense of self. Religiously, identity is also formed through recognition that one is called by Jesus Christ and an awareness of Jesus' love.[51]

Intimacy versus isolation marks the movement from receiving love to giving love. Intimacy is the capacity to share mutual trust and to regulate cycles of work, recreation, needs, and desires to blend our lives with another. We commit ourselves to concrete affiliations and partnerships, despite the hardships and compromises involved in them.[52] Incorporation into a community is an experience of belonging and intimacy for religious. The tension between bonding and isolation surfaces in the roles this involves. Being sister or brother, minister, family member, friend, and disciple must be balanced and integrated together. When the capacity for intimacy is not present, isolation manifests itself in a mechanical and distant style of relationship which makes community impossible. When the culture of a community isolates a person who is not a member of the dominant culture, the real person is not received. Isolation, however, in this developmental crisis, is more of an individual stance. As the negative pole of this crisis, it is the inability to risk involvement with others, to be oneself. It is often shown in combative and competitive behavior. Suspicion, backbiting, and outbursts of rancor are all faces of competitive and negative spirit of isolation. Protective partnerships which do not move outward toward others feed a sense of isolation. Different from the privacy needed for friendship, these are often dependencies where people still are bolstering their identity—incapable yet of real intimacy.

The virtue-vice polarity of intimacy versus isolation is lust and love. Lust, in its traditional form, shows itself as a drive for unrestrained sexual gratification. However, it also shows itself as lust for power. The shared spirit of both is momentary gratification and power over another. A lustful relationship is opposed to love, even without a sexual component. Disloyalty, cruelty, and unwillingness to assume responsibility for the consequences of one's actions are forms of lust. Lust is not selective of a partner. Lust "burns its bridges" and moves on to another available partner to satisfy its needs. Lust uses

---

[51] Karl Rahner, *The Love of Jesus and the Love of Neighbor* (New York: Crossroad, 1983), 39.
[52] Erikson, *Childhood and Society*, 263.

people and drops them. Love, on the other hand, is the antithesis of lust. Love involves selectivity. A religious selects some friends and decides to invest in some relationships and not in others. A religious is selective in choosing a community; it chooses this congregation and not the other one. Love softens antagonism in close relationships and downgrades and overcomes gender tensions. It supports others through mutual devotion. The mutual devotion of friendship and satisfying intimacy extends to energy for others and for the community outside the relationship. Lust undermines community, even if explicit sexual behavior is not present. It drains a community of energy by expecting the "other" or the group to meet its every need. It knows no end to criticism and blame of others when its expectations are not met. It only plays at intimacy as it refuses to engage the other in mutual giving and receiving. Loving celibate relationships are characterized by mutual respect, equity, reconciliation, compassion, and integrity in sexual language. Celibates can love others deeply yet move on to other relationships or ministries.[53] Religious develop their capacity to love with trusted others and with Jesus. In prayer, Jesus reveals our greatest needs for love along with our potential to be friends, ministers, family members, and intimates who can give and receive love. Because we have received love, we can also give it away. However, this is learned in the ups and downs of learning to love and receive love from people in our lives.

Generativity versus stagnation or the crisis of having concern for establishing the next generation marks middle adulthood. While most people live out their call to be generative through parenting, Erikson holds that monastic communities live their generative call by centering their attention on ultimate concerns. In place of caring for their own children, they make central to their life discerning the care that grounds all existence.[54] Care rather than productivity marks the outcome of the process. Generativity is emotional investment in the next generation or in whatever has been produced or created.

Stagnation is the inability to sustain what has been produced. Instead, stagnation invests in the self as one's own prized progeny. Self-absorption, inability to care for others, loss of interest, respect, or sympathy for those for whom one has responsibility are markers of stagnation. The interpersonal impoverishment of stagnation fosters boredom and self-indulgence. Stagnation distorts thinking as self-preoccupation deforms perceptions of the world and others. In a religious community, this mentality is contagious. Stagnation is more than the end of a ministry or active period of life; it is the death of the spirit.

The virtue-vice tension of generativity versus stagnation is care and acedia. Acedia is the deadly sin of apathy. Acedia is easily confused with sloth, or the unwillingness to work or invest energy. But acedia is more subtle. It is listlessness for the spiritual goods which a religious entered to pursue. In the tradition, acedia is spiritual death (ST. II-II, Q. 35.1). It marks a withdrawal from anything that really matters. One withdraws from everything except the most trivial and surface interests. Other matters are met with

---

[53]Manuel, "Living Chastity", 17.
[54]Donald Capps, *Deadly Sins and Saving Virtues* (Philadelphia, PA: Fortress Press, 1987), 52–3, 191–5.

listlessness and paralysis of the will. In this sense, a religious could be a workaholic yet suffer from the pull of apathy. Deeper desires are suppressed, and the result is care, hope, and the values which they once held no longer guide them. Being detached from their true center of energy, their vocation no longer engages them.

Instead, the person meddles in the lives of others. Ceasing to do their "inner work," they become authorities on what is wrong with others. One author likens apathy to the activity of the Olympian gods, who, lacking any real interest in humankind, toyed with others. They devised conflicts, conspiracies, and deceits to relieve themselves of boredom. Blocking, holding back, and refusal to undertake collaborative work with others—as it is too much effort—are forms of apathy.

Religious community can be destroyed by apathy, and its cure is spiritual regeneration, not a self-improvement program. The spiritual emptiness of apathy is its refusal to desire. It is a spiritual crisis, a crisis of care. Apathy in spiritual tradition is the most serious deadly sin for religious because interest in the spiritual life is anesthetized. On the contrary, religious life is propelled by spiritual desire. The indifference of apathy is offset from within, as no one can do the inner work of another. In the multi-age relationships of communities, there is a great risk that younger people will be drawn into the older members' pathology and take on their cynical and despairing attitude. In this case, the young cannot "rescue"; they need to engage in their own developmental tasks. Destructive and addictive relationships in a community can result from a cycle of enmeshment based on such a "rescue" of others.[55]

Rowan Williams depicts apathy as a response to the inevitable ordinariness and boredom of the Christian life. *Acedia*, or listlessness, is the awareness of the dreariness of one's life, which leads either to breakdown or breakthrough. The breakdown, though perhaps not visible, might be a matter of growing a layer of cynicism, noncommitment, and coping habits which are marked by a "whatever" attitude. All to protect oneself from the real cost of living with dependence on God and others and the uncertainty of life, breakthrough occurs when one can look realistically at suffering, embrace it, and look for sources and remedies to alleviate it.[56]

At this time of great transition in religious life, it is important to recognize the continuing challenge of celibate chastity and the call to care and be constructive in uncertain times. It shows itself in a concern for those who will enter religious life in the future. It desires to leave behind a legacy. Not one of an egotistic need to continue its own contribution, but one that offers a foundation for the future. It takes steps to reduce destructive effects of past choices and tries to bring earlier projects to greater fulfillment. In contrast to earlier struggles with appropriate limits in relationships, the vow challenges the middle-aged and older adult to care at all and to develop a new kind of care. This care is only possible through a deepening of spiritual life, as it is beyond a self-initiated battle of will. Certainly, care as the affective love in the life of senior

---

[55]Ibid., 108.
[56]Rowan Williams, *Passions of the Soul* (London: Bloomsbury/Continuum, 2024), 46–8.

religious fosters daily support of one another in the emotional, physical, and relational losses of later life. Care fuels an attitude toward loss that makes a difference in whether each day contains contentment or complaint.[57] It is care that can bring happiness in diminishment and humor in losses. It is a care that is sustained by knowing God's care for the world. Grounded in God as all care, one offers to the world a new kind of love. Care flows from a healthy dependence on God and a desire for mutuality with others. It is to allow our journey to love through the vow of celibate chastity in religious life to bring us full circle. Then we will know what was meant by T. S. Eliot in commenting on the paradox of a life's journey: "And the end of all our exploring will be to arrive where we started and know the place for the first time."[58] While the desire of our heart at the time of vows was to love God with our whole mind, heart, and soul and our neighbor as ourselves, the journey of this desire takes us through the emotional, developmental, and spiritual challenges of knowing, touching, and sharing this Wholeness which we desire. My becoming requires an openness to the other that is intrinsic to each human soul and their singularity.[59] Only in this do we become ourselves, and the self-fulfillment of love is truly known through the relationships of our lives, the service we offer, and the union with God we have known and begun to taste. It was for this journey that we were created. It would be great if every religious took this path, but most are only on the way in this endeavor. For this reason, the Apostles asked Jesus how many times we need to forgive— we say today, ourselves, others, decisions, events, misunderstandings, past mistakes (Mt. 18:21-22). Jesus said to him, "not seven times, but, I tell you, seventy seven times." There is likely no successful marriage, friendship, or religious commitment that is unaware of the value of Jesus' wisdom, which was likely born of his own human experience.

Celibacy as a Spiritual Capacity and Way of Life

From the beginning, the basic structure of our lives is revealed to us. Our encounters with others surface both a need and a gift. We are born helpless. Physically, we need others to survive. Emotionally, we need their approval and appreciation to thrive and become. C. S. Lewis speaks of love in various human dimensions. He offers a language to describe the way we move from our own singularity to what and who is Other. There

---

[57] Joyce Rupp, *Vessels of Love: Prayers and Poems for the Later Years of Life* (Maryknoll, NY: Orbis Books, 2024).
[58] T. S. Eliot, "Little Gidding," in *Four Quartets: A Poem* (New York: Ecco/ HarperCollins, 2023).
[59] Foley, "Stepping into the River," 32. This notion of singularity applies equally to the heterosexual and homosexual religious: "The universal nature of love and affection should embody both intra-personal relationships and personal relationships. Sexual orientation should not be a source of personal discrimination in the community and mission, by heterosexual or by homosexuals . . . the same criteria that are used to discern the vocation of heterosexuals should also be used in the vocational discernment of homosexuals . . . the call of God, the ability to live the emotions maturely, the ability to live healthy community relations, and the ability to live the mission as an indiscriminate service to all people, beginning with the most needy and excluded." Martinez, "The Virtue of Chastity in Religious Life," 308.

is need-love, not as selfishness, but like the need for food. It is good for us. He remarks, "As soon as we are fully conscious, we discover loneliness. We need others physically, emotionally, intellectually: we need them if we are to know anything, even ourselves."[60] We even bring to God need-love—we do not love God disinterestedly. This is because we are made in God's image.

Paradoxically, our highest spiritual condition is marked by the trust that our otherness to God is our path to nearness, as it is God who fills the gaps and enables us to respond. Our nearness to God because we are created in God's image is Gift. Yet our relationship to God also depends also on whether we approach God in our lives. Nearness to God by likeness and nearness by approach are not identical. Likeness to God is given to us; it can be received with or without thanks and can be used or abused. Approach, on the other hand, is initiated and supported by grace and is something we must do. Our singularity makes the nearness of approach our task, as no one else can do it for us. As Christians, our approach to God is one by imitation of Jesus Christ, as Jesus' human life shows us divine life operating within human conditions.[61] Celibate chastity, therefore, is not taking on a likeness to God by gift, as that has already been given. The desire to vow celibacy is a calling and a gift. But living it out is a path of union with God and others by approach, as it is a directing of our sexual energies and loves according to a particular life pattern.

Lewis argues that while St. John's affirmation that God is love is at the heart of the gospel, it is necessary to make a distinction between love and God. Lewis cautions that when love becomes a god, it becomes a demon, not God. The truth that God is love does not mean its converse, that love is God. Human love, at its height, tends to claim for itself divine authority.[62]

At a human level, it demands of us not to count the cost, override all other commitments, and suggests that any action done for love's sake is correct. However, our human loves, of ideas, of country, of individuals, and of relationships themselves, can draw us into an allegiance we owe only to God. They allure with the clarity which requires total allegiance and mimic a likeness to God. Gift loves, like happiness, strength, freedom, health, and economic and mental capacities, have a likeness to God and can seem like God, but they are not. They are like God only in likeness, as they are reflections of what is good, but not in approach. The likeness has been given to us. It has no necessary connection with that slow and painful approach which must be our own—yet not unaided—task. All the above goods of life can be given a transcendence as ultimate, when they hold only a desired but this-worldly place. Lastly, Lewis adds there is a third type of love, an appreciative love, one not coming from need nor gift. Appreciative love in life recognizes goodness and beauty for its own sake, not because I need it or find it in myself but recognize it in another. It is an attention to beauty which has value, not

---

[60]C. S. Lewis, *The Four Loves* (New York: Harcourt, Brace and World: 1960), 12.
[61]Ibid., 17.
[62]Ibid., 18.

because I say so, but simply because it is. This appreciation can be given to a person, to beauty in the arts, or to nature itself. It seems consistent with the maturation of religious life that appreciative love marks its course. Especially in community life, recognition of the goodness of the other, rather than focus on their weaknesses and irritating qualities, can signal the inwardness of loving God and others that the celibate journey, as well as all mature love, can foster. Need love, gift love, and appreciative love all enter the lifelong challenge of moving from singularity to the other. On this road, it is hoped the religious learn the appreciative love of self, God's world and people, that has its source in God's own gaze.

The Transformational Role of Love

Manuel began his list of practices for living chastity in religious life with, "live close to God and our deepest desires." He ends his list with, "celebrate the holy in the company of Jesus," or find all things in God.[63] For a religious, our own primary relationship is a relationship with God, familiarity with God, and friendship with Christ. Being at home in this world is grounded in the fostering of this primary relationship; everything else flows from it. Relationship with God therefore forms the mirror perspective which impacts one's psychosocial growth as a person. It does not replace the need for friends, companionship, intimacy, and belonging. However, it integrates all the passages of life which engage us in knowing ourselves, loving others, and offering service to the church and to the world.

Contemplative prayer is essential for a life of celibate chastity. A religious life centered in the Eucharist, the sacraments, life of the church, and community and service, and the other vows, fosters a lifestyle in which celibate chastity is possible as an alternative way of loving others deeply. It becomes a way to become sensitive to the inner dictates of the human heart and find a connectiveness with God; more as a matter of fidelity and partnership/espousal than one of law and obedience. The authority of this ongoing religious experience is like an inner connection, not just one of a child to a loving parent, but closer to the love of one to which one has become espoused, as expressed in the Song of Songs. As a particular way of being human, religious life places mystical religion, encounter with God in prayer—available to all—within a carefully selected and nurturing condition of the three vows and community and ministry. The goal is to offer a world of intensity, spirit, and intrinsic meaning.[64] The dynamic of a contemplative life is to foster generosity, the aim of a life of love in any adult lifestyle. It is this generosity which can shape the world and support worldly life to the fullest because it is found by drawing closest to life's center in union with God.

Religious life is a life of touching wholeness, which offers the prospect that human life need not be one which is forever fabricated and fragmented. Hope is sustained, not

---

[63]Manuel, "Living Chastity," 4.
[64]See Walter Capps, *The Monastic Impulse* (New York: Crossroads, 1983), 6–9.

just by problem-solving, yet not without it, but beyond it, in the simplicity of trust in God, which gives rise to reinvestment and commitment. Attention to questions such as, where is God for me today? What are my desires and longings at this point of my life, and where is God in those longings? Do I have some expectations each day about how I will express love? foster openness to touching wholeness.[65] The seeking to live in harmony with all that sustains humankind fundamentally helps one to turn to one's own center in self-discovery. It helps to ground the sharing of God's reality in one's honest search and witness to authenticity. Here, religious life can offer a contribution to cultural transformation, not necessarily in answers to the challenges of marriage, gender, and sexual identity in modern culture, but by its witness to human life in its wholeness. In seeking to recapture what is fundamental in life, it can critique the instrumentalization of others in society, the disregard of the environment, the sole reliance on the technocratic paradigm as the solution to problems, and the false notions held of a successful life. It can speak to the malaise experienced in modern society around our inability to sustain stable relationships and to find societal meaning beyond growth in the gross national product. Is it possible to affirm and not just criticize? Can we collaborate beyond self-defeating competition and power over others?

Religious life has a long tradition in the West of offering an alternative to societal patterns. Today it has the potential to draw on a tradition far older than the anxieties of the post-industrial complex.[66] The contemplative stance is incarnational in that it connects to what is central to the world, to gain perspective on the world. It offers insight into the sustainability of life and care for the world, in an alternative way to giving life as parents, yet sustained by the same hope. All adults care about what matters ultimately in a life course and hold that a life well-lived is marked by what one leaves behind. We leave behind more than a series of acts; we participate in our own way in the mystery that everything is connected. Religious life centered in a contemplative outlook catches a view from "outside" life which offers a perspective. The fostering of the human condition comes from more than our remedies for improvement; rather, it rests on an unconditional basis from which to view human life in its essence. The goal of religious life is to witness to the sacred. From there, one can manage the inequalities of life, its injustices and defeats, as well as celebrate its successes and joys. A life in which one "touches" what one cannot see, over time, becomes the wisdom and light by which one sees life and its purpose. It is this witness to wholeness that religious life seeks to offer as those who live it seek wholeness themselves. Through the following of Jesus Christ, we learn this in every century.

---

[65]Manuel, "Living Chastity," 8, 22.
[66]Merkle, *Sensing the Spirit*, 159.

BIBLIOGRAPHY

Amaladoss, Michael, SJ, "Mission in Asia: Perspectives and Challenges," *SEDOS* 54, no. 7/8 (July-August, 2022): 22–6.
Annett, Anthony, "The Economic Vision of Pope Francis," in *The Theological and Ecological Vision of Laudato Si: Everything is Connected,* ed. Vincent J. Miller, London: Bloomsbury/T&T Clark, 2017, 160–74.
Arresto, Vito, FMS, "On Obedience and Mission," *Review for Religious,* January-February 1989, 65–73.
Aschenbrenner, George, "Prayer, Mission and Obedience," *The Way Supplement* 37 (1980): 50–61.
Augustine of Hippo, *The City of God,* trans. Marcus Dodds, New York: Random House, 1950.
Augustine of Hippo, *Confessions,* trans. Henry Chadwick, Oxford: University of Oxford Press, 2009.
Bauman, Zygmunt, "Morality in an Age of Contingency," in *Detraditionalization: Critical Reflection on Authority and Identity,* ed. Paul Heelas, Cambridge, MA: Blackwell Publishers, 1996, 49–58.
Bellah, Robert et al., *Habits of the Heart: Individualism and Commitment in American Life,* Berkley, CA: University of California Press, 1985.
Bishop, Jeffrey P., Lysaught, M. Therese, and Michel, Andrew, *Biopolitics After Neuroscience: Morality and the Economy of Virtue,* London: Bloomsbury, 2022.
Boeve, Lieven, *God Interrupts History: Theology in a Time of Upheaval,* London: Bloomsbury, 2007.
Brink, Laurie, OP, *The Heavens Are Telling the Glory of God: An Emerging Chapter for Religious Life. Science, Theology and Mission,* Collegeville, MN: Liturgical Press, 2022.
Brown, Peter, *The Body and Society: Men, Women and Sexual Renunciation in Early Christianity,* New York: Columbia University Press, 1988.
Browning, Don S., *Religious Thought and Modern Psychologies,* Philadelphia: Fortress Press, 1978.
Burkhard, John E., OFM Conv., *The Sense of the Faith in History: Its Sources, Reception and Theology,* Collegeville, MN: Liturgical Press, 2022.
Cahill, Edward, SJ, "The Catholic Movement: Historical Aspects," in *Readings in Moral Theology, No. 5 Official Catholic Social Teaching,* New York: Paulist Press, 1986.
Capps, Donald, *Deadly Sins and Saving Virtues,* Philadelphia, PA: Fortress Press, 1987.
Capps, Walter, *The Monastic Impulse,* New York: Crossroads, 1983.
Carmody, Denise, "Christology in Karl Rahner's Evolutionary View," *Religion in Life* 49, no. 2 (1980): 185–210.
Carpentier, Rene, "Evangelical Counsels," in *Sacramentum Mundi,* Vol. 2, ed. Karl Rahner, New York: Herder and Herder, 1968, 276–9.
Carter, Stephen L., *Civility, Manners, Morals and the Etiquette of Democracy,* New York: Harper Collins, 1998.
Casanova, Jose, *Public Religions in the Modern World,* Chicago, IL: The University of Chicago Press, 1994.
Castillo, Daniel, "'To Praise, Reverence, and Serve': The Theological Anthropology of Pope Francis," in *The Theological and Ecological Vision of Laudato Si,* ed. Vincent J. Miller, London: T&T Clark, 2017, 95–108.

Bibliography

Christie, Douglas E., "Becoming Painfully Aware: Spirituality and Solidarity in *Laudato Si*," in *The Theological and Ecological Vision of Laudato Si*, ed. Vincent J. Miller, London: T&T Clark, 2017, 109–26.

Chul-Cho, Hyun, SJ, "Interconnectedness and Intrinsic Value as Ecological Principles: An Appropriation of Karl Rahner's Evolutionary Christology," *Theological Studies* 70 (2009): 622–33.

Cimperman, Maria, RSCJ, *Religious Life for Our World: Creating Communities of Hope*, Maryknoll, NY: Orbis Books, 2020.

Cimperman, Maria, RSCJ and Schroeder, Roger P., SVD, eds., *Engaging Our Diversity: Interculturality and Consecrated Life Today*, Maryknoll, NY: Orbis Books, 2020.

Clifford, Catherine with Lampe, Stephen eds., *Vatican II at 60: Re-energizing the Renewal*, Maryknoll, NY: Orbis Books, 2024.

Coakley, Sara, *The New Asceticism: Sexuality, Gender and the Quest for God*, London: Bloomsbury, 2015.

Code of Canon Law, *Latin English Edition*, Washington, DC: Canon Law Society of America, 1983.

Compendium of Catholic Social Doctrine of the Church, Pontifical Council of Justice and Peace, Continuum International Publisher, 2006.

Cone, James, *Speaking the Truth: Ecumenism, Liberation and Black Theology*, Grand Rapids, MI: Eerdmans, 1986.

Confoy, Maryanne, RSC, *Religious Life and Priesthood: Rediscovering Vatican II*, New York: Paulist, 2008.

Connor, James J., SJ, and the fellows of the Woodstock Theological Center, *The Dynamism of Desire: Bernard J.F. Lonergan, S.J. on the Spiritual Exercises of Saint Ignatius of Loyola*, Saint Louis: The Institute of Jesuit Sources, 2006.

Consecratio et Consecratio per Evangelica Consilia, Proceedings of the International Seminar. Pontifical University Antonianum. Rome, March 1–3, 2018. Congregation for the Institutes of Consecrated Life and the Societies of Apostolic Life, Vatican, City: Libreria Editrice Vaticana, 2019.

Crowe, Fredrick E., *The Lonergan Enterprise*, Cambridge: MA: Cowley Publications, 1980.

Curran, Charles E., *Catholic Moral Theology in the United States: A History*, Washington, DC: Georgetown University Press, 2008.

Czerny, Michael, SJ, "Fratelli Tutti's Message for Contemporary Religious," *Concilium*, no. 2 (March, 2022): 126–30.

D'Almeida, Anil, SJ., "Vocation to Live Religiously Poor in India," *Vidyajyoti Journal of Theological Reflection* 82, no. 9 (September 2018): 16–40.

de Weger, Stephen Edward, "Unchaste Celibates: Clergy Sexual Misconduct against Adults-Expresssions, Definitions and Harms," *Religions* 12, no. 393 (2022): 1–27.

Diriat, Alexandra, CSJ, "Le tiers incommode," *Vies Consacree*, no. 2 (April 2022): 29–38.

Dubois, Gerard, "Evangelical and Monastic Obedience," *Cistercian Studies* 8, no. 2 (1973): 87–106.

Dubois, Heather M., "An Ever-Stitched Wholeness: Multidimensional Relationality in Trauma Theory and Schillebeeckx's Theology of Salvation," in *Salvation in the World: The Crossroads of Public Theology*, ed. Stephen van Erp, Christopher Cimorelli, and Christiane Alpers, London: Bloomsbury, 2017, 229–41.

Duffy, Stephen, *The Graced Horizon*, Collegeville: The Liturgical Press, 1992.

Dumas, Bertrand, "The Sacrament of Marriage in Postmodernity: Struggling with 'Spectacularization,'" *Marriage, Families, and Spirituality* 27, no. 2 (2021): 175–95.

Eliot, T.S., "Little Gidding," in *Four Quartets: A Poem*, New York: Ecco/Harper Collins, 2023.

Erhman, Terrence P., CSC., "Ecology: The Science of Interconnections," in *The Theological and Ecological Vision of Laudato Si*, ed. Vincent J. Miller, London: T&T Clark, 2017, 51–73.

Erikson, Erik H., *Childhood and Society,* 2nd rev. ed., New York: W.W. Norton and Co., 1963 (1950).

Erikson, Erik H., *Insight and Responsibility,* New York: W.W. Norton and Co., 1964.

Farley, Margaret A., RSM, "Celibacy Under the Sign of the Cross," in *Changing Questions: Explorations in Christian Ethics,* ed. and intro Jamie L. Manson, New York: Orbis Books, 2015.

Feder, Julie, "Salvation," in *T and T Clark Reader in Edward Schillebeeckx,* ed. Stephen Van Erp and Daniel Minch, London: T&T Clark, 2023, 155–6.

Fitzgerald, Kathryn ACJ, "By Obedience to the Truth," *Review for Religious* 42, no. 5 (1983): 770–3.

Foley, John B., SJ, "Stepping into the River: Reflections on the Vows," *Studies on the Spirituality of Jesuits* 26, no. 4 (September 1994): 1–31.

Francis, Pope, *On Care for Our Common Home, Laudato Si,* Citta del Vaticana: Libreria Editrice Vaticana, 2015.

Francis, Pope, *On Fraternity and Social Friendship: Fratelli Tutti,* Vatican City: Liberia Editrice Vaticana, 2020.

Francis, Pope, "Pope's Anti-corruption ecree for Vatican Limits Gifts to Forty Euros," *Reuters,* April 29, 2021.

Francis, Pope, "Pope to Business Leaders: Use Gifts to Promote the Common Good," *Vatican News,* October 21, 2022.

Francis, Pope, "Clericalism Defiles the Face of the Church," *L'Osservatore Romano,* October 27, 2023.

Frohlich, Mary, RSCJ., *Breathed into Wholeness: Catholicity and Life in the Spirit,* New York: Orbis Books, 2019.

Fuchs, Josef, "Chastity as Vow in the Jesuit Life Project," *The Way Supplement* 19 (Summer, 1973): 96–104.

Geffre, Claude, OP, "The Tension between Desacralization and Spirituality," *Concilium* 9, no. 2 (1966): 57–66.

Genovesi, Vincent, SJ, *In Pursuit of Love: Catholic Morality and Human Sexuality,* Wilmington, DE: Michael Glazier, 1987.

Genovesi, Vincent, SJ, "Sexuality," in *The New Dictionary of Theology,* ed. Jospeh Komonchak et al., Wilmington, DE: Michael Glazier, 1989, 947–54.

Godzieba, Anthony J., *A Theology of the Presence and Absence of God,* Collegeville, MN: Liturgical Press, 2018.

Gorski, Philip S. and Perry, Samuel L., *The Flag and the Cross: White Christian Nationalism and the Threat to American Democracy,* Oxford: Oxford University Press, 2022.

Guindon, Andre, OMI, "A Theory of Sexual Ethics for Concerned Christians," in *Readings in Moral Theology, No. 8. Dialogue About Catholic Sexual Teaching,* eds. Charles E. Curran and Richard A. McCormick, Mahwah, NJ: Paulist Press, 1993, 22–46.

Haight, Roger, SJ, *Christian Spirituality for Seekers: Reflections on the Spiritual Exercises of Ignatius Loyola,* New York: Orbis Books, 2012.

Hales, E.E.E., *Pope John and His Revolution,* New York: Image Books, 1966.

Haughey, John, SJ, "Charisms: An Ecclesiological Exploration," in *Retrieving Charisms for the 21st Century,* ed. Doris Donnelly, Collegeville, MN: The Liturgical Press, 1999.

Hebblethwaite, Peter and Margaret, John, *XXIII, Pope of the Century,* New York: Continuum, 2001.

Hemmerle, Klaus, "Power," in *Encyclopedia of Theology: The Concise Sacramentum Mundi,* ed. Karl Rahner, New York: Crossroad, 1982, 1263–6.

Highfield, Ron, "Freedom to Say No? Karl Rahner's Doctrine of Sin," *Theological Studies* 56 (1985): 485–505.

Hinze, Christine Firer, "What is Enough? Catholic Social Thought, Consumption and Material Sufficiency," in *Having: Property and Possession in Religious and Social Life,* ed. William Schweiker and Charles Mathewes, Grand Rapids, MI: Eerdmans, 2004, 162–88.

Bibliography

James, William, *The Varieties of Religious Experience,* New York: Penguin, 1982.

Jedin, Hubert, "Pope Benedict XV, Pius XI, and Pius XII," in *History of the Church in the Modern Age,* ed. Hubert Jedin, London: Burns and Oates, 1981.

Joas, Hans, *Do We Need Religion?* trans. Alex Skinner, London: Paradigm, 2008.

Joas, Hans, *Faith as an Option: Possible Futures for Christianity,* trans. Alex Skinner, Stanford, CA: Stanford University Press, 2014.

Johnson, Mary, SNDdeN, Gautier, Mary, and Wittberg, Patricia SC, Do, Thu, LHC, *Migration for Mission: International Catholic Sisters in the United States,* New York: Oxford University Press, 2019.

King, Jason and Rubio, Julie Hanlon, eds., *Catholic Perspectives on Sex, Love and Families,* Collegeville, MN: The Liturgical Press, 2020.

Kulak, Avron, "Between Singularity and Plurality: Kierkegaard and the Paradox of Absolute Difference," *Journal of Kierkegaard Studies Yearbook* 26, no. 1 (January 2021): 223–39.

Langan, John P., SJ, "The Good of Obedience in a Culture of Autonomy," *Studies in the Spirituality of the Jesuits* 32, no. 1 (January 2000): 1–32.

Lasch, Christopher, *The True and Only Heaven: Progress and Its Critics,* New York: Norton, 1991.

Lasnoski, Kent, "Marriage and Householding in Christ," in *Catholic Perspectives: Sex, Love and Families,* ed. Jason King and Julie Hanlon Rubio, Collegeville, MN: The Liturgical Press, 2020, 59–67.

Lederach, J.P., *The Moral Imagination: The Art and Soul of Building Peace,* New York: Oxford University Press, 2005.

Lee, Bernard J., SM, "The Social Matrix of Religious Obedience," *Review for Religious* 67, no. 3 (2008): 290–303.

Lewis, C.S., *The Four Loves,* New York: Harcourt, Brace and World, 1960.

Lobo, Joseph, "Synodality in the Public Square: Synodality, Post Consciousness, Majoritatism and Public Rationality," *Third Millenium: Indian Journal of Evangelization* XXV, no. 1 (2022): 6–19.

Lohfink, Gerard, *The Forty Parables of Jesus,* trans. Linda M. Mahoney, Collegeville, MN: The Liturgical Press, 2021.

Lonergan, Bernard, SJ, *Insight,* San Francisco: Harper and Row, 1978.

Lonergan, Bernard, SJ, "The Ongoing Genesis of Methods," in *A Third Collections: Papers by Bernard J. F. Lonergan, S.J.,* ed. Frederick E. Crowe, New York: Paulist Press, 1985.

Lonergan, Bernard, SJ, *Method in Theology,* Toronto: University of Toronto Press, 1990.

Lonergan, Bernard, SJ, "The Mediation of Christ in Prayer," in *Philosophical and Theological Papers, 1958-1964,* Vol. 6, ed. Robert C. Croken, Frederick E. Crowe, and Robert M. Doran, Toronto: University of Toronto Press, 1996, 160–82.

Lonergan, Bernard, SJ, "Healing and Creating in History," in *The Lonergan Reader,* ed. Mark D. Morelli and Elizabeth A. Morelli [Murray], Toronto: University of Toronto Press, 1997, 136–8.

Lucinai, Rafael, *Synodality: A New Way of Proceeding in the Church,* trans. Joseph Owens, SJ, Mahwah, NJ: Paulist Press, 2022.

Mansford, Emmanuel, CFR, "Love Does Silly Things: The Prophetic Power of the Vow of Poverty," *Religious Life Review* 53, no. 286 (2014): 133–45.

Manuel, Gerdenio Sonny, SJ, "Living Chastity: Psychosexual Well-Being in Jesuit Life," *Studies in the Spirituality of Jesuits* 41, no. 2 (2009): 1–36.

Markus, Robert A., *Christianity and the Secular,* Notre Dame, IN: University of Notre Dame Press, 2006.

Martinez, Felicisimo OP, "The Virtue of Chastity in Religious Life," *Religious Life* 54, no. 294 (2015): 301–8.

Mathewes, Charles, "On Using the World," in *Having: Property and Possession in Religious and Social Life,* ed. William Schweiker and Charles Mathewes, Grand Rapids, MI: Eerdmans, 2004, 189–221.

May, William F., "Sin," in *The New Dictionary of Theology,* Collegeville, MN: The Liturgical Press, 1990, 954–67.
McManus, Kathleen Anne, OP, *Unbroken Communion: The Place and Meaning of Suffering in the Theology of Edward Schillebeeckx,* Washington, DC: Rowman and Littlefield, 2003.
Menninger, Karl, *Whatever Became of Sin?* New York: Bantam Books, 1978.
Merkle, Judith A., SNDdeN, *Committed by Choice,* Collegeville, MN: The Liturgical Press, 1993.
Merkle, Judith A., SNDdeN, *A Different Touch: A Study of the Vows in Religious Life,* Collegeville, MN: The Liturgical Press, 1998.
Merkle, Judith A., SNDdeN, *From the Heart of the Church: The Catholic Social Tradition,* Collegeville, MN: The Liturgical Press, 2004.
Merkle, Judith A., SNDdeN, *Being Faithful: Christian Commitment in Modern Society,* London: T&T Clark, 2010.
Merkle, Judith A., SNDdeN, *Beyond Our Lights and Shadows: Charism and Institution in the Church,* London: T&T Clark, 2016.
Merkle, Judith A., SNDdeN, *Discipleship, Secularity and the Modern Self: Dancing to Silent Music,* London: T&T Clark, 2020.
Merkle, Judith A., SNDdeN, *Sensing the Spirit: Toward the Future of Religious Life,* London: T&T Clark, 2023.
Mescher, Marcus, *The Study Guide to the Encyclical Letter of Pope Francis: Fratelli Tutti: On Fraternity and Social Friendship,* Mahwah, NJ: Paulist Press, 2021.
Metz, Johann Baptist, *Faith in History and Society,* New York: Seabury Press, 1980.
Miller, Vincent, *Consuming Religion: Christian Faith and Practice in a Consumer Culture,* New York: Continuum, 2004.
Miller, Vincent, ed., *The Theological and Ecological Vision of Laudato Si: Everything is Connected,* London: Bloomsbury, 2017.
Molinski, Waldemar, "Vow," in *Sacramentum Mundi,* Vol. 6, New York: Herder and Herder, 1970.
Molinski, Waldemar, "Marriage," in *Encyclopedia of Theology: The Concise Sacramentum Mundi,* ed. Karl Rahner, New York: Crossroads, 1982, 905–31.
Neiman, Susan, *Evil in the Modern World: An Alternative History of Philosophy,* Princeton: Oxford University Press, 2002.
Nocetti, Sera, *Reforming the Church: A Synodal Way of Proceeding*, Mahwah, NJ: Paulist Press, 2023.
Oliver, Mary, "The Summer Day," in *New and Selected Poems,* Boston: Beacon Press, 1992.
Olkowich, Nicholas, "Complicating the Reception of Lonergan on Sacralization and Secularization," *Irish Theological Quarterly* 86, no. 2 (2021): 164–83.
Palmer, Helen, *The Enneagram in Love and Work,* San Francisco, CA: Harper and Row, 1993.
Peck, Scott, *People of the Lie: The Hope for Healing Human Evil,* Greenwich, CT: Touchstone Books, 1998.
Peters, Danielle, "Charism and the Consecrated Life in the Twentieth and Twenty-First Centuries," *Marian Library Studies* 31 (2013): 47–72. https://ecommons.udayton.edu/ml_studies/vol31/iss1/19.
The Pope Speaks 14, no. 2 (1969) 95.
Radcliff, Timothy, OP, "Synod Retreat Meditation: Conversation on the way to Emmaus," *Vatican News*, October 2, 2023.
Rahner, Karl, SJ, *The Charismatic Element in the Church,* New York: Herder and Herder, 1961.
Rahner, Karl, SJ, *Christian in the Marketplace,* New York: Sheed and Ward, 1966.
Rahner, Karl, SJ, "Christology in an Evolutionary View," in *Theological Investigations*, vol. 5, trans. Karl-H Kruger, London: Darton, Longman and Todd/Seabury Press, 1966.
Rahner, Karl, SJ, "Grace and Freedom," in *Sacramentum Mundi,* Vol. 2, ed. Karl Rahner, New York: Herder and Herder, 1968, 424–7.

Bibliography

Rahner, Karl, SJ, "Christian Living Formerly and Today," in *Theological Investigations VII*, trans. David Bourke, New York: The Seabury Press, 1971.

Rahner, Karl, SJ, "On the Evangelical Counsels," in *Theological Investigations,* VIII, trans. David Bourke, New York: Herder and Herder, 1971.

Rahner, Karl, SJ, *The Shape of the Church to Come,* trans. Edward Quinn, New York: The Seabury Press, 1971.

Rahner, Karl, SJ, "On the Theology of the Incarnation," in *A Rahner Reader,* ed. Gerald A. McCool, New York: Crossroad, 1975, 145–53.

Rahner, Karl, SJ, "Relationship between Nature and Grace: The Supernatural Existential," in *A Rahner Reader,* ed. Gerald A. McCool, New York: Crossroad, 1975, 185–90.

Rahner, Karl, SJ, *Foundations of the Christian Faith: An Introduction to the Idea of Christianity,* New York: Herder and Herder, 1978.

Rahner, Karl, SJ, "Justified and Sinner at the Same Time," in *Theological Investigations* VI, trans. Karl-H. Kruger, New York, Crossroad, 1982.

Rahner, Karl, SJ, "Reflections on a Theology of Renunciation," in *Theological Investigations,* Vol. III, trans. Karl-H. and Boniface Kruger, New York: Crossroads, 1982.

Rahner, Karl, SJ, "Hope," in *The Practice of Faith: A Handbook of Contemporary Spirituality,* New York: Crossroad, 1983.

Rahner, Karl, SJ, "The Certainty of Faith," in *The Practice of Faith: A Handbook of Contemporary Spirituality,* New York: Crossroad, 1983.

Rahner, Karl, SJ, *The Love of Jesus and the Love of Neighbor,* New York: Crossroad, 1983.

Rahner, Karl, SJ, "The One Christ and the Universality of Salvation," in *Theological Investigations,* vol. 16, trans. David Moreland, OSB, New York: Crossroad, 1983.

Rahner, Karl, SJ, "The Situation of Faith Today," in *The Practice of Faith: A Handbook of Contemporary Spirituality,* New York: Crossroad, 1983.

Rahner, Karl, SJ, "The Christian Understanding of Redemption," in *Theological Investigations,* Vol. 21, trans. Hugh M. Riley, New York: Crossroad, 1988.

Rahner, Karl, SJ, "The Dignity and Freedom of Man," in *Theological Investigations* II, trans. Karl-H. Kruger, New York: Crossroad, 1990.

Rosa, Hartmut, *Resonance: A Sociology of Our Relationship to the World,* trans. James C. Wagner, Cambridge: Polity Press, 2019.

Rossi, Philip, SJ, "Faith, Autonomy, and the Limits of Agency in a Secular Age," in *At the Limits of the Secular: Catholic Reflections on Faith and Public Life*, ed. William Barbieri, Grand Rapids, MI: Wm B. Eerdmans, 2014, 226–49.

Rossi, Philip, SJ, "Seekers, Dwellers, and the Plural Contingencies of Grace: Hospitality, Otherness and the Enactment of Human Wholeness," in *Seekers and Dwellers in a Time of Secularity,* ed. Philip J. Rossi, Washington, DC: Council for Research in Values and Philosophy, 2016, 285–300.

Rubio, Julie Hanlan and Schutz, Paul J., *Beyond Bad Apples: Understanding Clergy Perpetuated Sexual Abuse as a Structural Problem and Cultivating Strategies for Change.* Ignatian Center for Jesuit Education, Santa Clara University, 2024. @ www.scu.edu.

Rupp, Joyce, *Vessels of Love: Prayers and Poems for the Later Years of Life,* Maryknoll, NY: Orbis Books, 2024.

Ryan, Robin, CP, *God and the Mystery of Human Suffering: A Theological Conversation Across the Ages,* Mahwah, NJ: Paulist Press, 2011.

Ryan, Robin, CP, *Jesus and Salvation: Soundings in the Christian Tradition and Contemporary Theology,* Collegeville, MN: Liturgical Press, 2015.

Sasongko, Nindyo, "A Caravan of Solidarity: An Asian Constructive Theology for a Triune Economy of Gift," *Exchange* 44 (2015): 381–402.

Schillebeeckx, Edward, *Jesus: An Experiment in Christology,* New York: Crossroad, 1981.

Schillebeeckx, Edward, *Christ: The Experience of Jesus as Lord,* New York: Herder and Herder, 1984.
Schillebeeckx, Edward, *The Schillebeeckx Reader,* ed. Robert J. Schreiter, New York: Crossroad, 1984.
Schillebeeckx, Edward, *Church and the Human Story of God,* New York: Crossroad, 1990.
Schneiders, Sandra M., IHM, *Finding the Treasure: Locating Religious Life in a New Ecclesial and Cultural Context,* Mahwah, NJ: Paulist Press, 2000.
Schneiders, Sandra M., IHM, *Selling All: Commitment, Consecrated Celibacy, and Community in Catholic Religious Life,* Mahwah, NJ: Paulist Press, 2001.
Schneiders, Sandra M., IHM, *Buying the Field: Catholic Religious Life in Mission to the World,* Mahwah, NJ: Paulist Press, 2013.
Schweiker, William, "Reconsidering Greed," in *Having: Property and Possession in Religious and Social Life,* ed. William Schweiker and Charles Matthews, Grand Rapids, MI: Eerdmans, 2004, 249–71.
Scialabba, George, "What Were We Thinking: The Intolerable Inequalities We Take for Granted," *Commonweal,* January 2023, 20–5.
Scott, Margaret, "Greening the Vows: *Laudato Si* and Religious Life," *The Way* 54, no. 4 (October 2015), 83–93.
Sedmak, Clemens and Hickey, Kelli Reagan, *Counting the Cost: Financial Decision-Making, Discipleship and Christian Living,* Collegeville, MN: The Liturgical Press, 2023.
Segundo, Juan Luis, *Faith and Ideologies,* trans. John Drury, New York: Orbis, 1984.
Shorter, Edward, *The Making of the Modern Family,* New York: Basic Books, 1977.
Soelle, Dorothee, *The Silent Cry: Mysticism and Resistance,* trans. Barbara and Martin Rumscheidt, Minneapolis, MN: Fortress Press, 2001.
Steck, Christopher, SJ, *The Ethical Thought of Hans Urs Von Balthasar,* New York: Crossroads, 2001.
Tanner, Kathryn, *Theories of Culture: A New Agenda for Theology,* Minneapolis, MN: Fortress Press, 1997.
Taylor, Charles, *Sources of Self: Making of Modern Identity,* Cambridge, MA: Harvard University Press, 1989.
Taylor, Charles, *Multiculturalism and the Politics of Recognition.* The University Center for Human Values, Princeton, NJ: Princeton University Press, 1994.
Taylor, Charles, *A Secular Age,* Cambridge, MA: The Belknap Press of Harvard University Press, 2007.
Taylor, Charles, "A Catholic Modernity," in *Dilemmas and Connections: Selected Essays,* Cambridge, MA: The Belknap Press of Harvard University, 2011, 167–87.
Taylor, Charles, *Cosmic Connections: Poetry in the Age of Disenchantment,* Cambridge, MA: The Belknap Press of Harvard University Press, 2024.
Ulanov, Ann and Barry, *Primary Speech: A Psychology of Prayer,* Louisville, KY: Westminster John Knox Press, 1982.
Ulanov, Ann and Barry, *Cinderella and Her Sisters,* Philadelphia, PA: The Westminster Press, 1983.
Ulanov, Ann and Barry, *The Witch and the Clown: Two Archetypes of Human Sexuality,* Ashville, NC: Chiron Publications, 2018.
Van Erp, Stephen, Cimorelli, Christopher, and Alpers, Christiane, eds., *Salvation in the World: The Crossroads of Public Theology,* London: T&T Clark, 2017.
Van Erp, Stephen and Minch, Daniel, eds., *T&T Clark Reader in Edward Schillebeeckx,* London: T&T Clark, 2023.
Vanhoye, Albert, SJ, "The Biblical Question of '*Charisms*' after Vatican II," in *Vatican II: Assessment and Perspectives: Twenty-Five Years After (1962-1987),* Vol. 1, ed. Rene Latourelle, Mahwah, NJ: Paulist Press, 1988.

Bibliography

Weber, Max, *Economy and Society,* Vol. I, ed. Guenther Roth and Claus Wittich, Berkeley, CA: University of California Press, 1978.

Williams, Rowan, *Passions of the Soul,* London: Bloomsbury Continuum, 2024.

Williamson, Enid, "The Notion of Charism in Religious Life," *Studia Canonica* 19, no. 1 (1985): 99–116.

Wittberg, Patricia, SC, "Dyads and Triads: The Sociological Implications of Small-Group Living Arrangements," *Review for Religious,* January-February 1990, 43–51.

Wittberg, Patricia, SC, *Pathways to Re-Creating Religious Communities,* Mahwah, NJ: Paulist Press, 1996.

Wittberg, Patricia, SC, *From Piety to Professionalism and Back? Transformations of Organized Religious Virtuosity,* Lanham, MD: Lexington Books, 2006.

Wittberg, Patricia SC, Gautier, Mary, Simmons, Gemma CJ, and Becquart, Natalie XMCJ, *God's Call is Everywhere: A Global Analysis of Contemporary Religious Vocations for Women,* Collegeville, MN: Liturgical Press, 2023.

Wolf, Friedrich, "Dogmatic Constitution on the Church, Chapter VI: Religious," trans. Richard Strachan, *Commentary on the Documents of Vatican II,* 5 vols., ed. Herbert Vorgrimler, New York: Herder and Herder, 1967-1969, I, 273–81.

Wolfe Wentzel, Regina, "CEO Perspectives on Morality and Business," in *Business Ethics and Catholic Social Thought,* ed. Daniel Finn, Washington, DC: Georgetown University Press, 2021, 9–24.

INDEX

agency   111–12, 114, 128
Amaladoss, Michael   8
Annett, Anthony   59, 127
Alpers, Christiane   23, 56
Aquinas, Thomas   39, 45, 89, 126, 148
asceticism   122–3
Aschenbrenner, George   107
Augustine of Hippo   22, 35, 90
authenticity   82, 91, 105, 132, 153
   two paths of development   40–3, 81
autonomy   81–2, 89, 91, 99, 100, 114, 116–17

Bauman, Zygmunt   17–18
Bellah, Robert   59, 114
Benedict XVI   55
bias   44
Biopolitics after Neuroscience   31
Boeve, Lieven   20
Bonhoeffer, Dietrich   61
Brink, Laurie   21
Brown, Peter   72
Browning, Don   93
Burkhard, John   15

Capps, Donald   96, 116, 118, 119, 148, 149
Capps, Walter   152
Carmody, Denise   51, 55
Carpentier, Rene   69–72, 79, 106
Carter, Stephen   18
Casanova, Jose   80
Cassian   117
Castillo, Daniel   44
Catholic Action   73
celibacy, celibate chastity
   affective   65, 144
   creation   135, 150
   definition   131
   gender identity   139
   genital   65, 138, 144–5
   human challenge   137–40
      generativity-stagnation, care-acedia   148–50
      identity-identity confusion, fidelity-pride   146–7
      intimacy-isolation, lust-love   147–9
   intimacy   138–45
   lived reality   140–9
   loneliness   139, 144
   love   151–2

   marital love   131, 137, 140, 143–5
   prayer/transformation   152–3
   primary   143
   religiously motivated   131, 134, 141–2
   sexual integration   137–9, 143, 144
   sexuality   65, 143–6
   sexual orientation   150
   singularity-other   64–7, 132–5, 137–8, 141
   societal attitudes   132, 139–40
   spiritual capacity   150–3
   theology of sexuality   131, 139–40
   wholeness   132, 135–8, 150
Christie, Douglas   55
Chul-Cho, Hyun   33
church
   baptismal call   76
   charismatic/institutional   74
   culture   140
   Synod   76, 135
   Vatican II   38–9, 74, 76–7, 127, 142
Cimorelli, Christopher   23, 56
Cimperman, Maria   31
Clifford, Catherine   38
Coakley, Sara   132
community   47, 56–7, 111, 127
Compendium of Catholic Social Doctrine   125
Confoy, Maryanne   29
Connor, James and Woodstock Fellows   43
Consecratio et Consecratio   57
contemplative stance   153
contingency   15–17, 61, 80, 102, 111, 113, 115, 117
Crowe, Frederick   42
Curran, Charles   131

D'Almeida, Anil   84, 121
desacralization   38
Descartes, René   33
de Weger, Stephen   140
dialectical thinking   92, 126
Diriat, Alexandra   76
Do, Thu   31
Dubois, Gerard   76, 92, 98, 104
Dubois, Heather   22, 23
Duffy, Stephen   51
Dumas, Bertrand   70

Ehrman, Terrence   50
Eliot, T. S.   150

Index

Erikson, Erik   93–5, 133, 147
eschatology   55
exclusive humanism   12, 29, 113, 122
expressive individualism   13, 39

faith
   human   133
   religious   137
Farley, Margaret   67, 134, 140
Feder, Julie   56, 57
Fitzgerald, Kathryn   103
Foley, John   137, 138, 146, 150
Francis of Assisi   115
Francis (Pope)   17, 111, 112, 124, 140, 146
Frankl, Victor   25
Fratelli Tutti   7, 60, 76, 99, 123
freedom   53, 59, 66, 67, 112, 114, 115
Frohlich, Mary   57, 133
Fuchs, Josef   132

Gautier, Mary   31
Geffre, Claude   38
Genovesi, Vincent   65
Gittens, Anthony   128
Gorski, Phillip   136
grace   29, 39, 45–7, 51, 55, 62, 63, 70, 74, 83, 97, 106, 114–16, 124, 128, 141, 151
Great Chain of Being   32
Guindon, Andre   144

Haight, Roger   19
Haughey, John   45, 78
Hebblethwaite, Margaret   34
Hebblethwaite, Peter   34
Hemmerle, Klaus   100
Hickey, Kelli Reagan   121, 124
Highfield, Ron   53
Hinze, Christine Firer   121, 124, 127

identity   62, 64, 146
Ignatius of Loyola   91
immanent frame   13, 59, 61–3, 84, 124
indifference   124–6
integral ecology   63, 121
interiority   50–2, 80
   capacity   42–3
   definition   40
Irenaeus   97

James, William   84
Jedin, Hubert   74
Jesus Christ
   evolutionary framework   50–3, 55
   paschal mystery   67–8, 84, 107
   union with   97, 104, 107, 128

Joas, Hans   15, 16, 80, 83
John Paul II   46, 111, 127
Johnson, Mary   31
justification   53–5

Kierkegaard, Soren   133–7
King, Jason   66
Kulak, Avron   133–6

Langan, John   89, 91, 98, 101, 104
Lasch, Christopher   59, 125
Lasnoski, Kent   70
Laudato Si   7, 50, 54, 59, 63, 67, 75, 120, 123, 126
law of the cross   67–8, 104–7
Lee, Bernard   103
Levo, Lynn   138, 139
Lewis, C. S.   151
liberation theology   121
Lobo, Joseph   14
Lohfink, Gerhard   110
Lonergan, Bernard   40–3, 47–9, 67, 81, 82, 106, 107, 139
Luciani, Rafael   15, 30, 39

Mansford, Emmanuel   111, 115, 124
Manuel, Gerdenio Sonny   140–2, 144, 146, 148, 149, 152, 153
Markus, Robert   35
marriage   70–2, 77–8, 80, 81, 84
Martinez, Felicisimo   107, 138, 150, 151
Massaro, Thomas   7
Mathewes, Charles   121, 122
McManus, Kathleen   27
mediation   49
   definition   43
   mutual self-mediation   44–8, 67–7, 80, 107, 151
   self   44
Menninger, Karl   54
Merkle, Judith   8, 11, 18, 31, 32, 33, 37, 46, 62, 66, 70, 72, 77, 78, 79, 89, 93, 94, 95, 102, 107, 111, 113, 115, 116, 122, 126, 127, 133, 134, 139, 141, 43, 146, 153
Mescher, Marcus   99
Metz, Johann Baptist   84
Miller, Vincent   13, 59
Minch, Daniel   56
mission   63, 95–6, 121–3, 128–9, 135, 136
Molinski, Waldemar   72
monasticism   72, 78

Newtonian worldview   33
Neiman, Susan   24, 115
Nocetti, Sera   61, 78, 100–2

164

Index

Obedience (gospel)   105–8
   autonomy-plurality   58–61, 103
   collaboration   100, 102
   consultation   101
   finitude   99, 105
   human challenge   93–7
      industry-inferiority, competence-envy   96–7
      initiative-guilt, purpose-greed   95–6
      trust-mistrust, gluttony-hope   94–5
   lived reality   98–103
   mutuality   102–3
   power   99
   prayer   105
   secular culture   90–2
   spiritual capacity   103–8
   transformational obedience   101–3
Oliver, Mary   92
Olkowich, Nicholas   36
ordinary mysticism   80

Palmer, Helen   116
Paul VI   76
Peck, Scott   54
Perry, Samuel   136
Peters, Danielle   74, 77, 78
poverty
   agency-finitude   61–4
   budget   120–1
      transformational   124
   community   124
   economy   110–11, 121
   finitude   111–16, 128
   greed   112
   human challenge   116–19
      autonomy-shame/doubt, will-anger   116–17
      integrity-despair, wisdom-melancholy   118–19
   lived reality   119–28
   mammon   109–10, 122, 124, 128
   maximal demand   124–6
   order of mutual benefit   124, 126
   spiritual capacity   128–9
   transformational poverty   121–2, 126

Radcliff, Timothy   135
Rahner, Karl   24, 26, 27, 31, 47, 50, 52–4, 74, 80, 92, 93, 95, 114, 119, 120, 134, 147
religion
   Christendom   35, 38
   nature   112, 114, 115, 126
   questioning of   12–18, 112–13, 125, 126
   religious life   14–15, 31, 36–8, 49, 58

religious life
   assumptions/interpretation   29–30, 80, 83, 109–16
   charism   44–8, 77–9, 103, 127
   constitutions   79
   culture   37, 121
   singularity-other   132–3
   theological shifts   30–2, 139
   web of relationships   30, 116, 152–3
   world   31, 77, 80
renewal   19, 120
Rossi, Phillip   19, 20, 61, 63, 66, 80, 99, 114, 115
Rubio, Julie Hanlan   66, 140, 145
Rupp, Joyce   150
Ryan, John   125

sacralization   35, 38
Sasongko, Nindyo   111
Schillebeeckx, Edward   23–7, 56, 63, 113, 136
Schneiders, Sandra   30, 79, 101, 131, 134, 141, 142
Schultz, Paul   140, 145
Schweiker, William   112, 121
Scialabba, George   110
Scott, Margaret   44
secular age   11
secularization   11, 23
Sedmak, Clemens   121, 124
Segundo, Juan Luis   133, 136
Shorter, Edward   132
signs of the times   38–9, 77
singularity   133
Socrates   133
Soelle, Dorothee   59, 60
spirituality
   contradiction/suffering   49, 53, 67–8, 84, 107, 136–7, 149
   contrast experience   23–6
   finitude   63, 111–16
   hope   63, 83, 128, 152
   real presence   18
   religious experience   83–4, 106
   renunciation   119–23
   sacred-secular   34–9, 46, 57, 61, 75, 80
   seekers-dwellers   19–20
   spiders   22–3, 32
   tourist-vagabond   17–18
Steck, Christopher   39

Tanner, Kathryn   37
technocratic paradigm   63, 123

Ulanov, Ann and Barry   84, 97, 143

Van Erp, Stephen   23, 56
Vanhoye, Albert   45

Index

vows 83, 84, 134
   church 72–7, 135
   counsels 69–77
   definition 81
   ecclesiastical law 76, 79
   eschatological dimension 55, 125
   exclusivity 82
   gestalt 46, 57, 65, 67, 93, 106, 132, 138, 141–2, 145, 153
   history 73–5, 141–2
   Holy Spirit 98, 103, 105
   human condition 56, 61–2
   human development 81–2
   postmodern 84
   profession 79, 81
   public 83
   purpose 77, 126, 141–2
   vita apostolica 71, 74, 75, 92
   wholeness 39, 56–7, 61, 67, 79–81, 85, 115, 150, 152

Weber, Max 77, 122
Wentzel, Regina Wolfe 111
wholeness 8–10, 20–2, 61, 84, 104, 112, 119, 122, 125, 126, 128
   community 57–8, 83, 118
   contingency 27–8, 111
   paschal mystery 26–7, 106–8
Williams, Rowan 95–7, 117, 149
Williamson, Enid 74
Wittberg, Patricia 7, 18, 19, 31, 35, 56, 73, 139
Wolf, Friedrich 78